Image Comics presents

hawaiian dick ™

THE LAST RESORT

WWW.IMAGECOMICS.COM

FOR IMAGE COMICS

ERIK LARSEN • Publisher

TODD MCFARLANE • President

MARC SILVESTRI • CEO

JIM VALENTINO • Vice-President

ERIC STEPHENSON • Executive Director

JIM DEMONAKOS • PR & Marketing Coordinator

MIA MACHATTON • Accounts Manager

TRACI HUI • Administrative Assistant

JOE KEATINGE • Traffic Manager

ALLEN HUI • Production Manager

JONATHAN CHAN • Production Artist

DREW GILL • Production Artist

CHRIS GIARRUSSO • Production Artist

HAWAIIAN DICK VOL. 2: THE LAST RESORT.
OCTOBER 2006. FIRST PRINTING

Published by Image Comics, Inc.
Office of publication:
1942 University Avenue, Suite 305
Berkeley, California 94704.

hawaiian dick™

 WRITTEN BY B. Clay Moore

DRAWN BY Steven Griffin
Nick Derington

COLOR, book production
and design BY Steven Griffin

Dialogue fonts by blambot.com

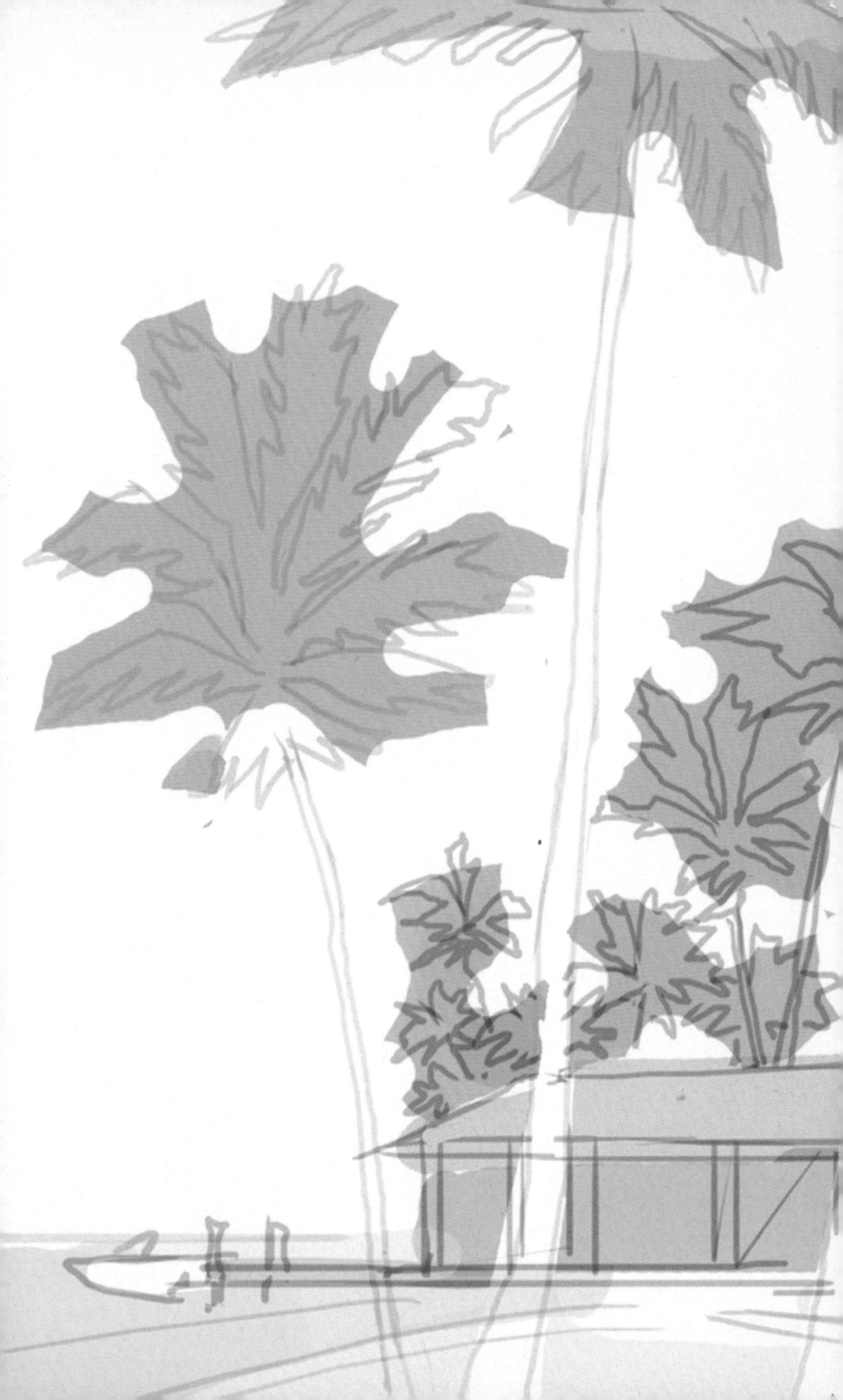

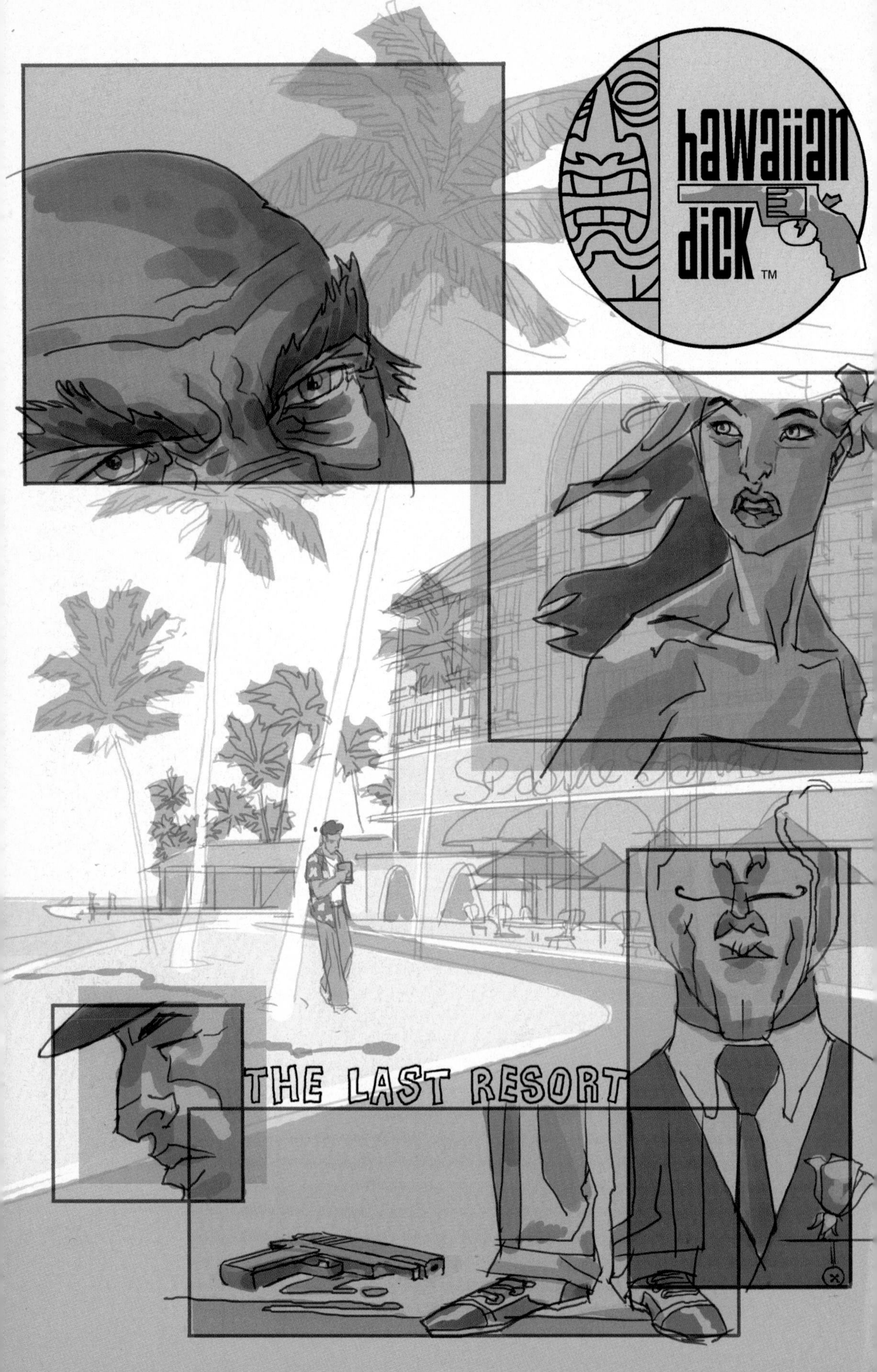

hawaiian dick
TM
THE LAST RESORT

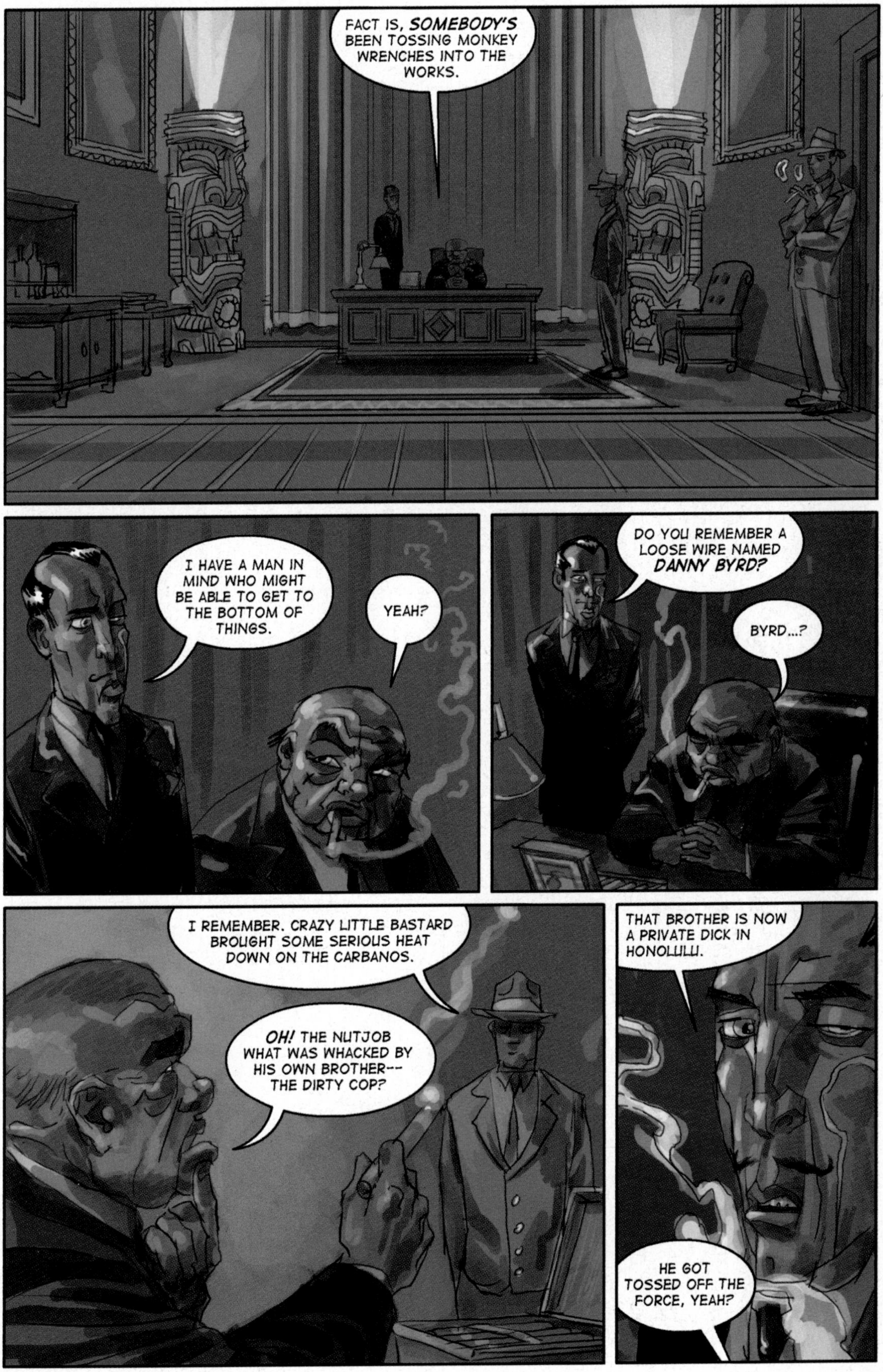
FACT IS, SOMEBODY'S BEEN TOSSING MONKEY WRENCHES INTO THE WORKS.
I HAVE A MAN IN MIND WHO MIGHT BE ABLE TO GET TO THE BOTTOM OF THINGS.
YEAH?
DO YOU REMEMBER A LOOSE WIRE NAMED DANNY BYRD?
BYRD...?
I REMEMBER. CRAZY LITTLE BASTARD BROUGHT SOME SERIOUS HEAT DOWN ON THE CARBANOS.
OH! THE NUTJOB WHAT WAS WHACKED BY HIS OWN BROTHER--- THE DIRTY COP?
THAT BROTHER IS NOW A PRIVATE DICK IN HONOLULU.
HE GOT TOSSED OFF THE FORCE, YEAH?

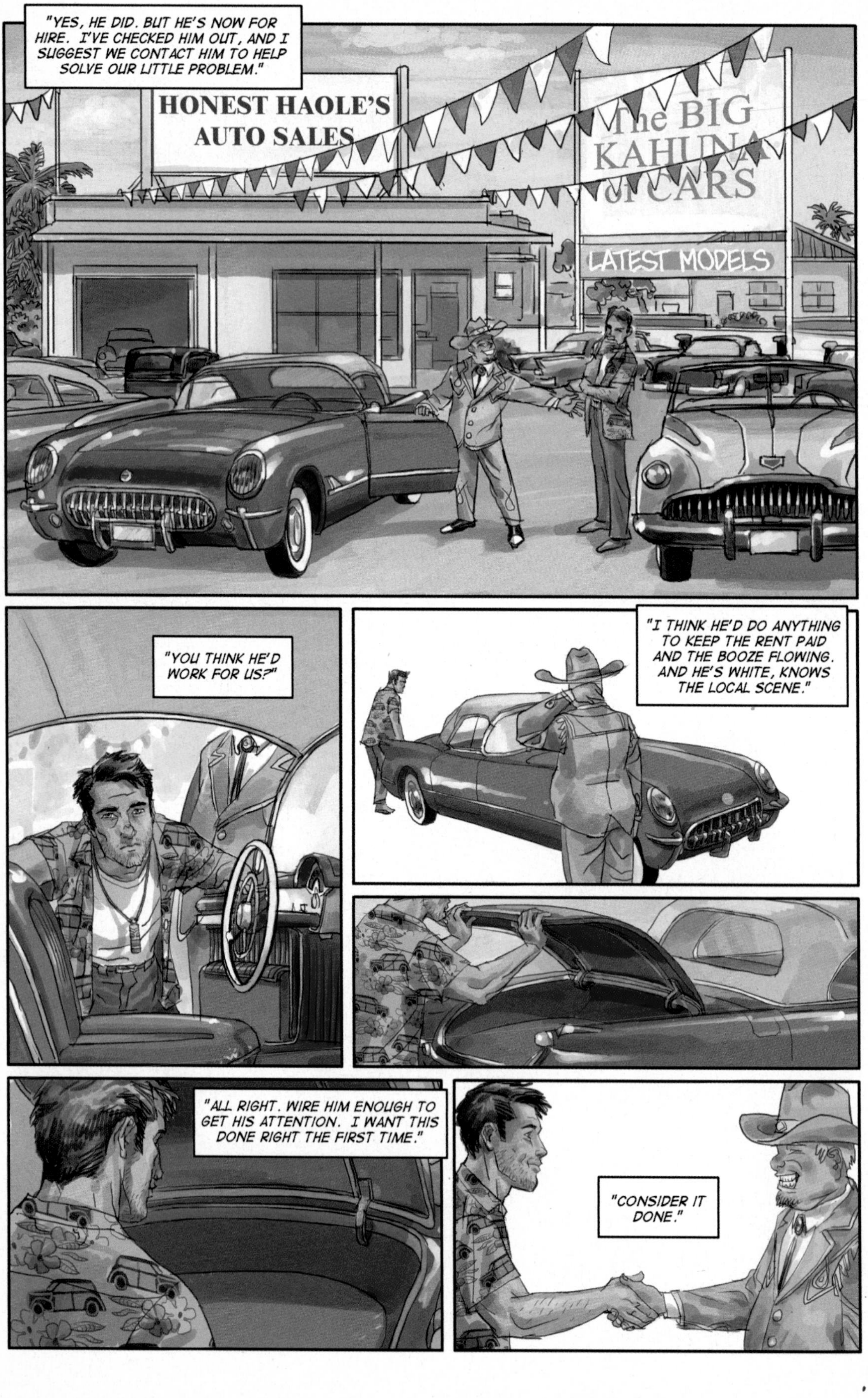
"YES, HE DID. BUT HE'S NOW FOR HIRE. I'VE CHECKED HIM OUT, AND I SUGGEST WE CONTACT HIM TO HELP SOLVE OUR LITTLE PROBLEM."
HONEST HAOLE'S AUTO SALES
The BIG KAHUNA of CARS
LATEST MODELS
"YOU THINK HE'D WORK FOR US?"
"I THINK HE'D DO ANYTHING TO KEEP THE RENT PAID AND THE BOOZE FLOWING. AND HE'S WHITE, KNOWS THE LOCAL SCENE."
"ALL RIGHT. WIRE HIM ENOUGH TO GET HIS ATTENTION. I WANT THIS DONE RIGHT THE FIRST TIME."
"CONSIDER IT DONE."

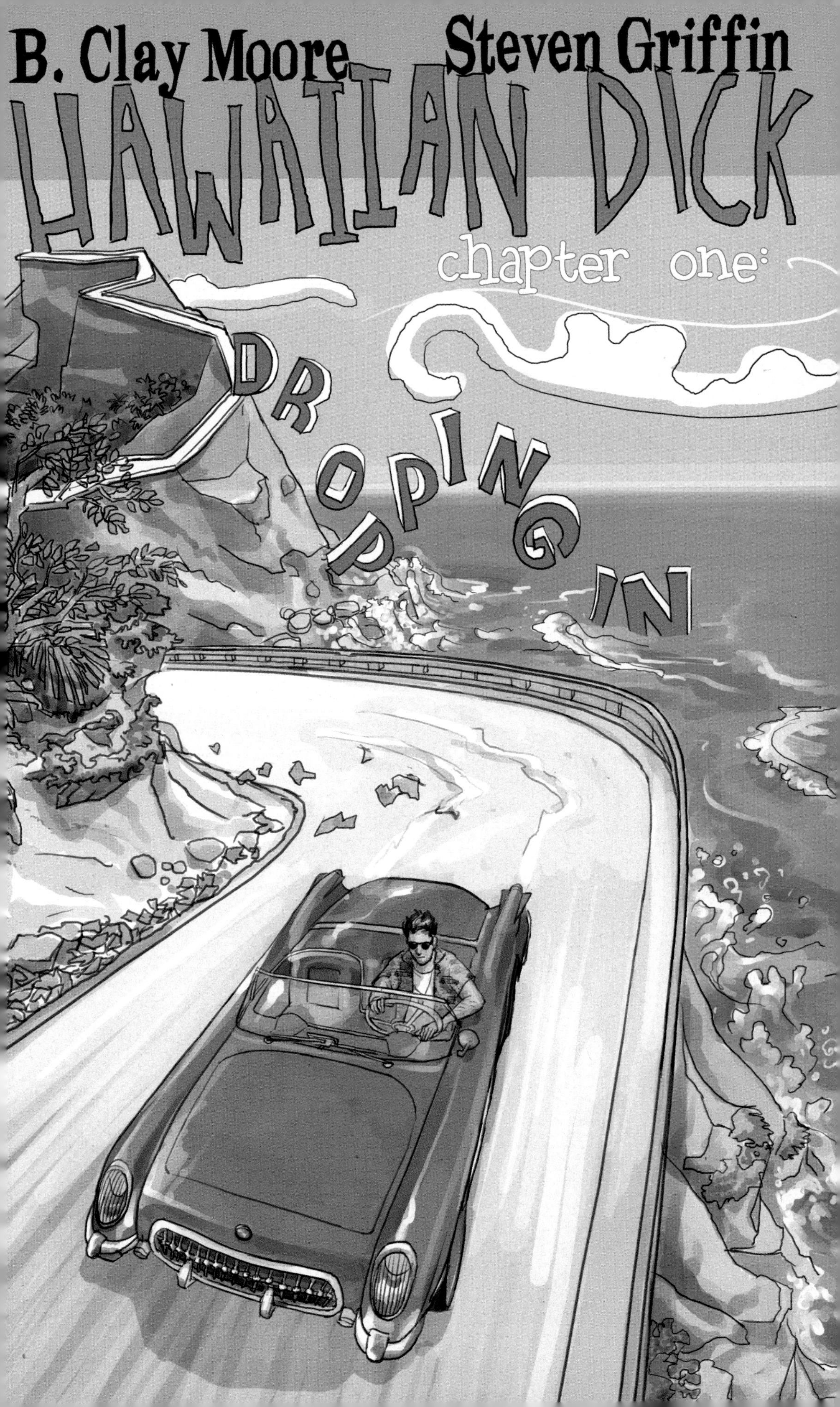

B. Clay Moore
Steven Griffin
HAWAIIAN DICK
chapter one:
DROPPING IN

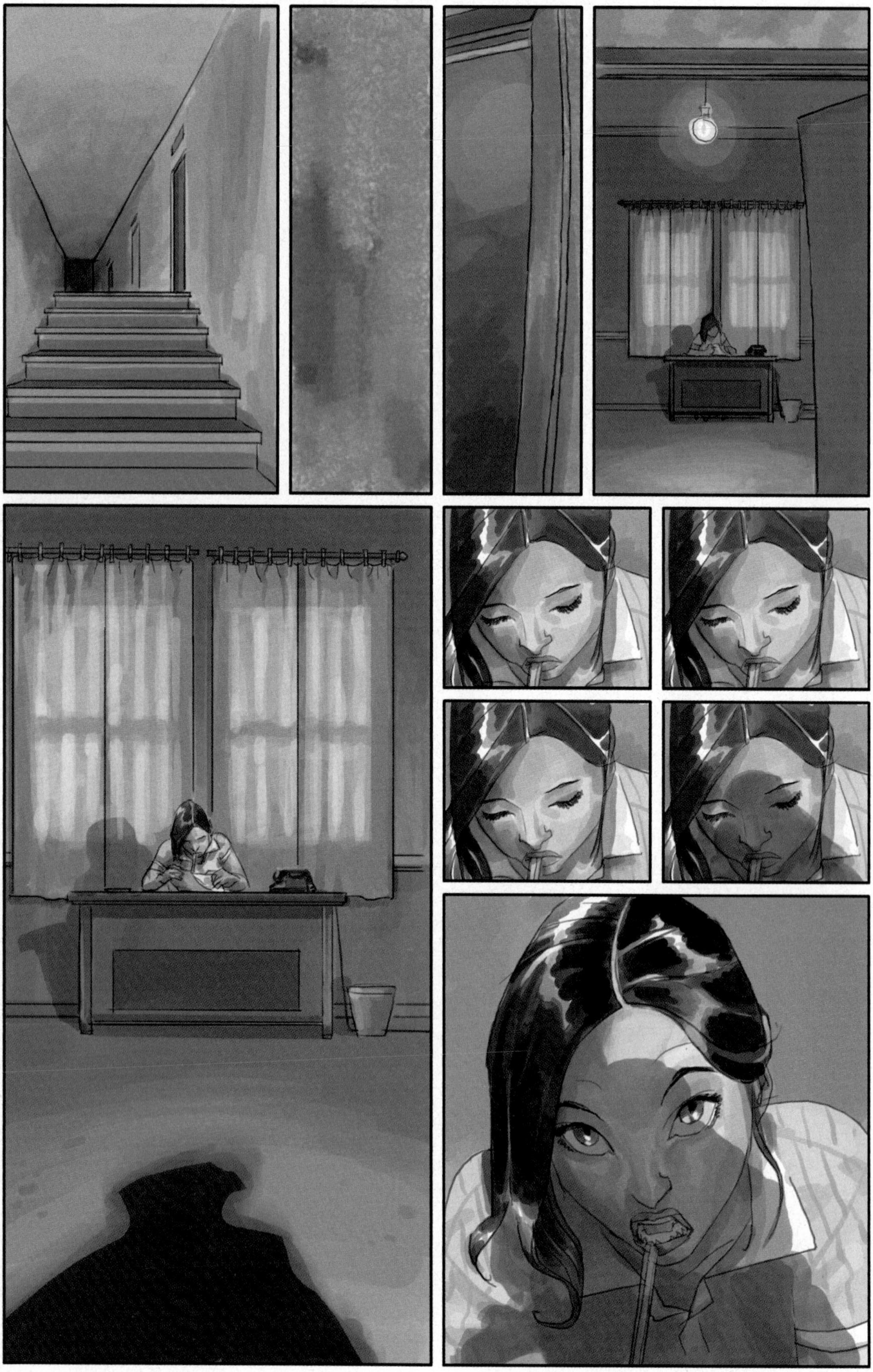

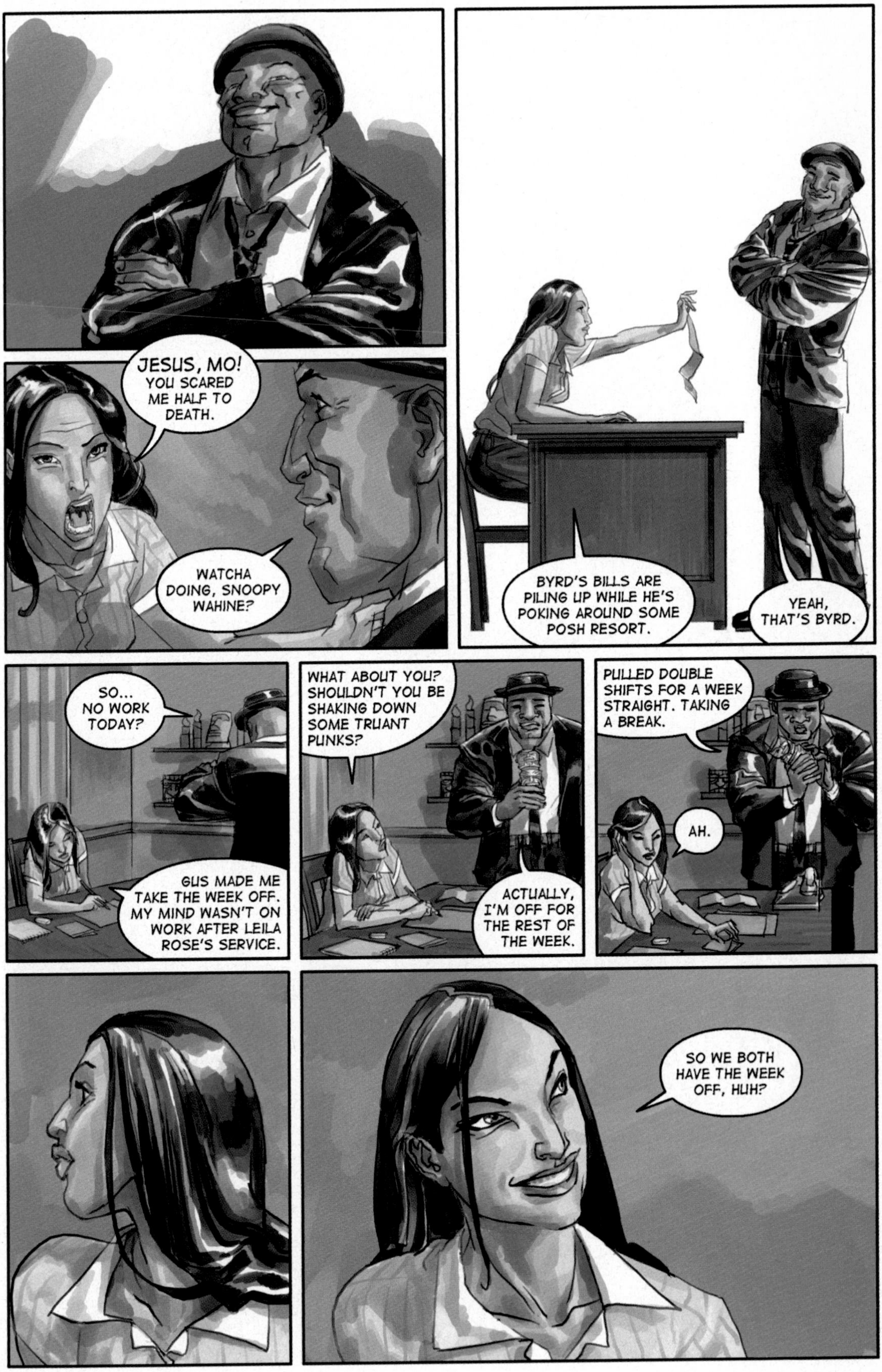
JESUS, MO! YOU SCARED ME HALF TO DEATH.
WATCHA DOING, SNOOPY WAHINE?
BYRD'S BILLS ARE PILING UP WHILE HE'S POKING AROUND SOME POSH RESORT.
YEAH, THAT'S BYRD.
SO... NO WORK TODAY?
GUS MADE ME TAKE THE WEEK OFF. MY MIND WASN'T ON WORK AFTER LEILA ROSE'S SERVICE.
WHAT ABOUT YOU? SHOULDN'T YOU BE SHAKING DOWN SOME TRUANT PUNKS?
ACTUALLY, I'M OFF FOR THE REST OF THE WEEK.
PULLED DOUBLE SHIFTS FOR A WEEK STRAIGHT. TAKING A BREAK.
AH.
SO WE BOTH HAVE THE WEEK OFF, HUH?

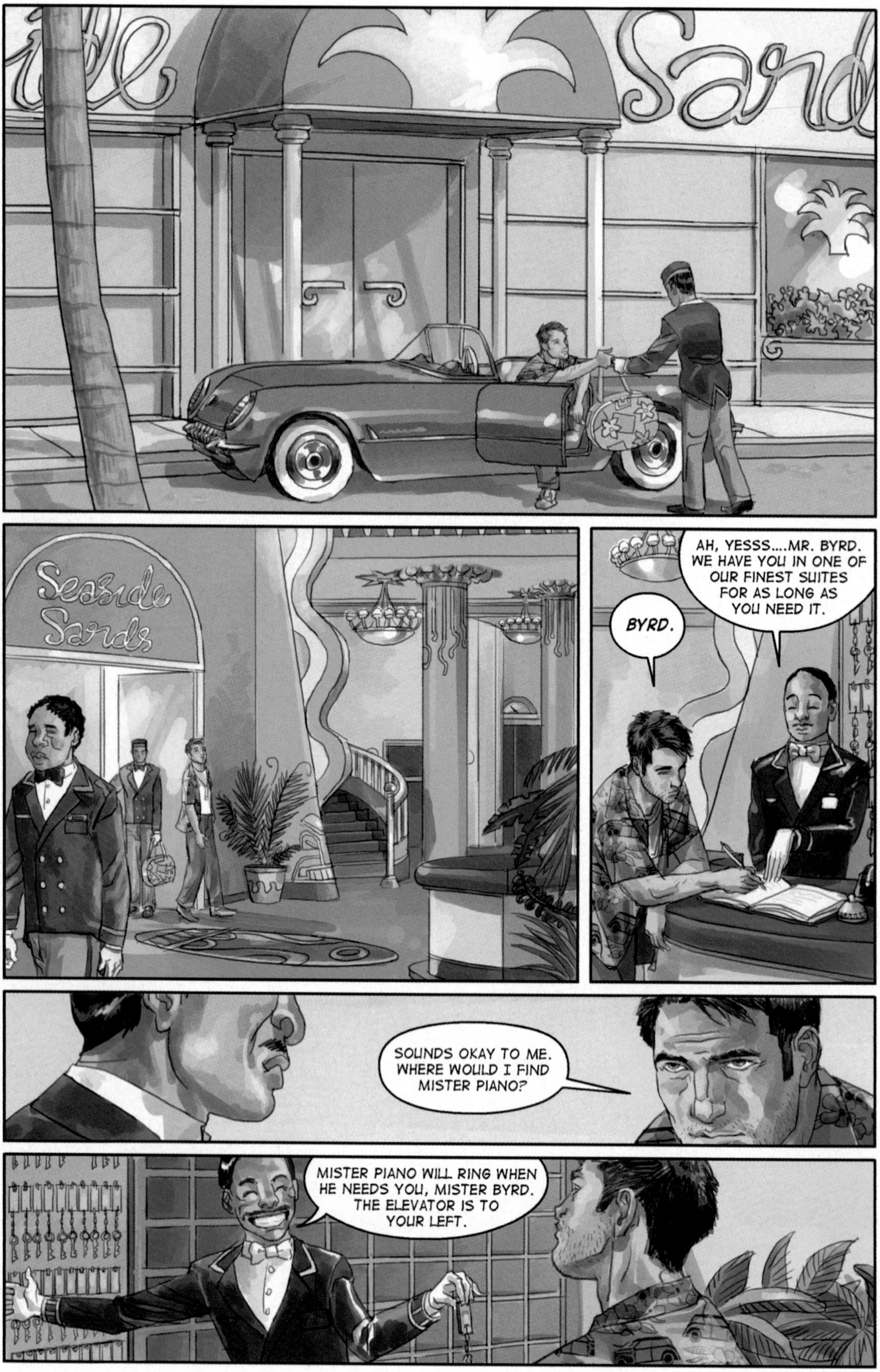
Seaside Sands
BYRD.
AH, YESSS....MR. BYRD. WE HAVE YOU IN ONE OF OUR FINEST SUITES FOR AS LONG AS YOU NEED IT.
SOUNDS OKAY TO ME. WHERE WOULD I FIND MISTER PIANO?
MISTER PIANO WILL RING WHEN HE NEEDS YOU, MISTER BYRD. THE ELEVATOR IS TO YOUR LEFT.

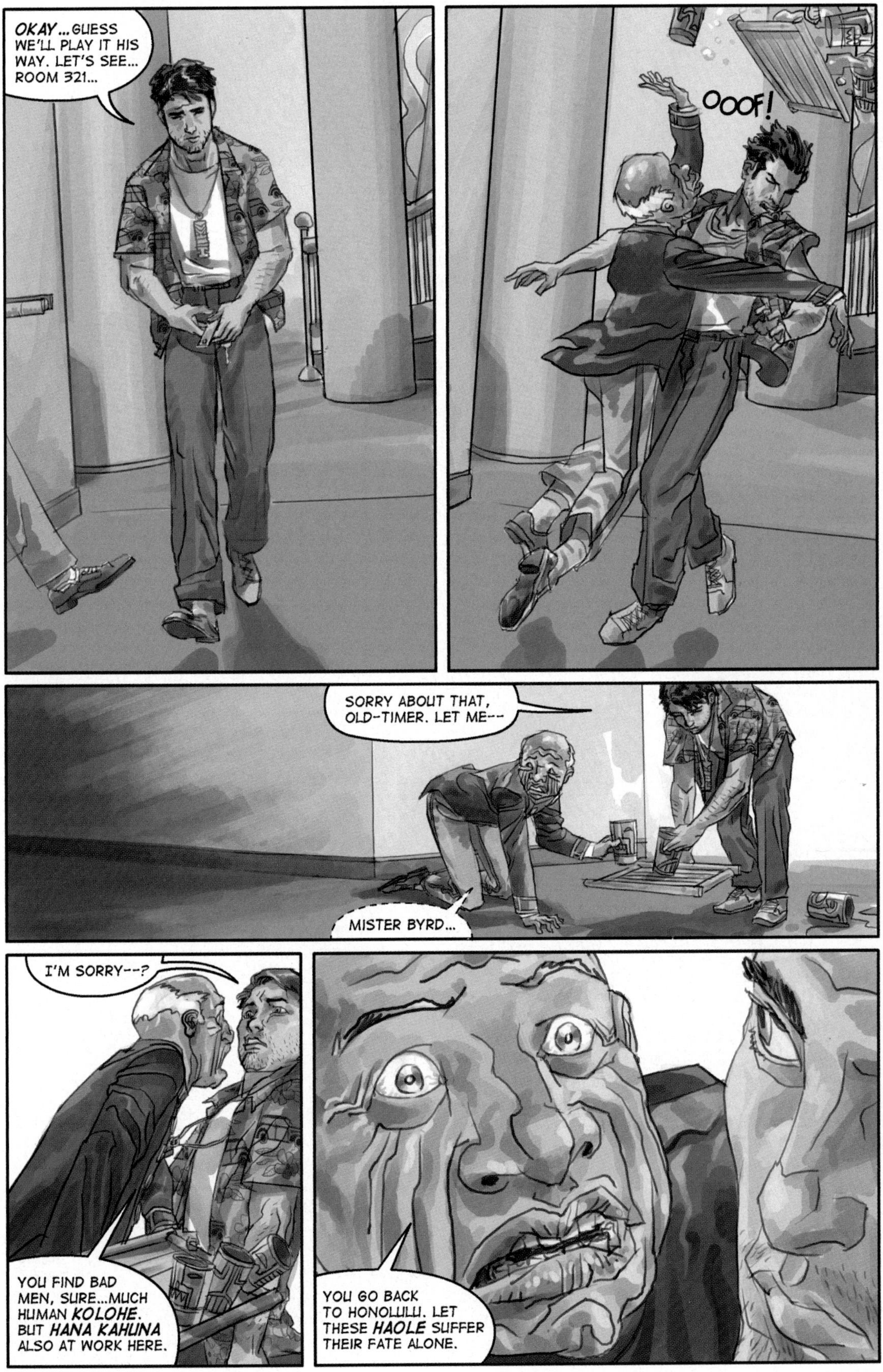
OKAY... GUESS WE'LL PLAY IT HIS WAY. LET'S SEE... ROOM 321...
OOOF!
SORRY ABOUT THAT, OLD-TIMER. LET ME--
MISTER BYRD...
I'M SORRY--?
YOU FIND BAD MEN, SURE...MUCH HUMAN KOLOHE. BUT HANA KAHUNA ALSO AT WORK HERE.
YOU GO BACK TO HONOLULU. LET THESE HAOLE SUFFER THEIR FATE ALONE.

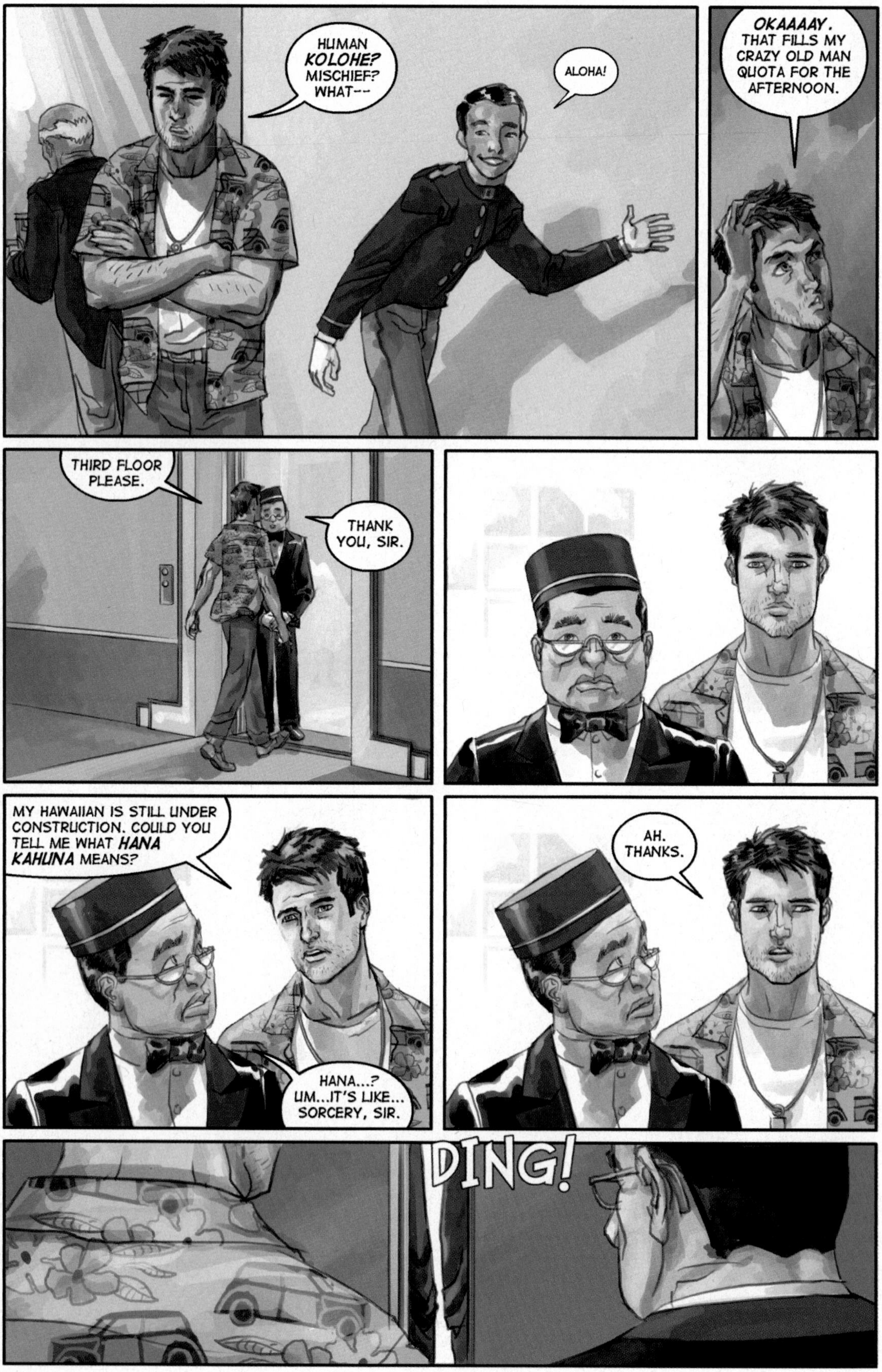
HUMAN KOLOHE? MISCHIEF? WHAT--
ALOHA!
OKAAAAY. THAT FILLS MY CRAZY OLD MAN QUOTA FOR THE AFTERNOON.
THIRD FLOOR PLEASE.
THANK YOU, SIR.
MY HAWAIIAN IS STILL UNDER CONSTRUCTION. COULD YOU TELL ME WHAT HANA KAHUNA MEANS?
HANA...? UM...IT'S LIKE... SORCERY, SIR.
AH. THANKS.
DING!

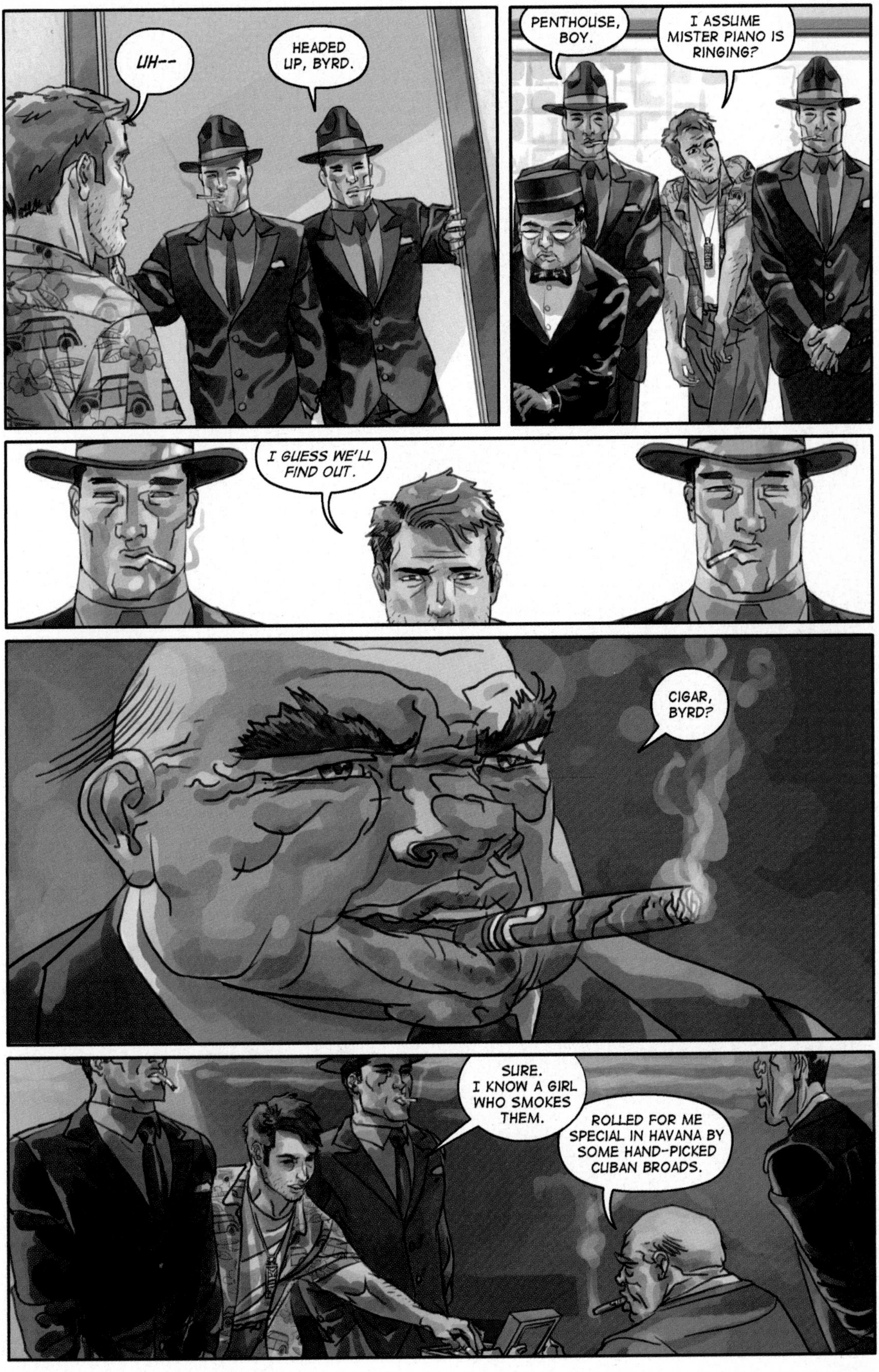
UH--
HEADED UP, BYRD.
PENTHOUSE, BOY.
I ASSUME MISTER PIANO IS RINGING?
I GUESS WE'LL FIND OUT.
CIGAR, BYRD?
SURE. I KNOW A GIRL WHO SMOKES THEM.
ROLLED FOR ME SPECIAL IN HAVANA BY SOME HAND-PICKED CUBAN BROADS.

BOYS, GIVE THE MAN SOME AIR. *JESUS!*

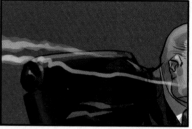

IT'S THE COP THING, BYRD. EVEN THOUGH YOU LOST THE BADGE, THEY STILL SMELL IT ON YA. DON'T LET 'EM GET YOUR GOAT.

MR. PIANO...

I KNOW, I KNOW. SHUT YER YAP, PIANO. TELL ME WHY I'M HERE, RIGHT?

HEH HEH.

SO I'M TELLIN', I'M TELLIN'.

YOU KNOW WHAT THAT IS, BYRD?

UM—

IT'S COMPETITION, MR. BYRD. AND I GOT NOTHING AGAINST IT, UNDER NORMAL CIRCUMSTANCES.

BUT—

EXACTLY! YOU'RE A SHARP KNIFE, BYRD. IT AIN'T NORMAL. 'CAUSE IT'S A GANG OF POTATO FARMIN' MICKS TRYIN' TO KNOCK ME OUT WHILE THEY BUILD THEIR SHRINE TO CABBAGE AND WHISKEY.

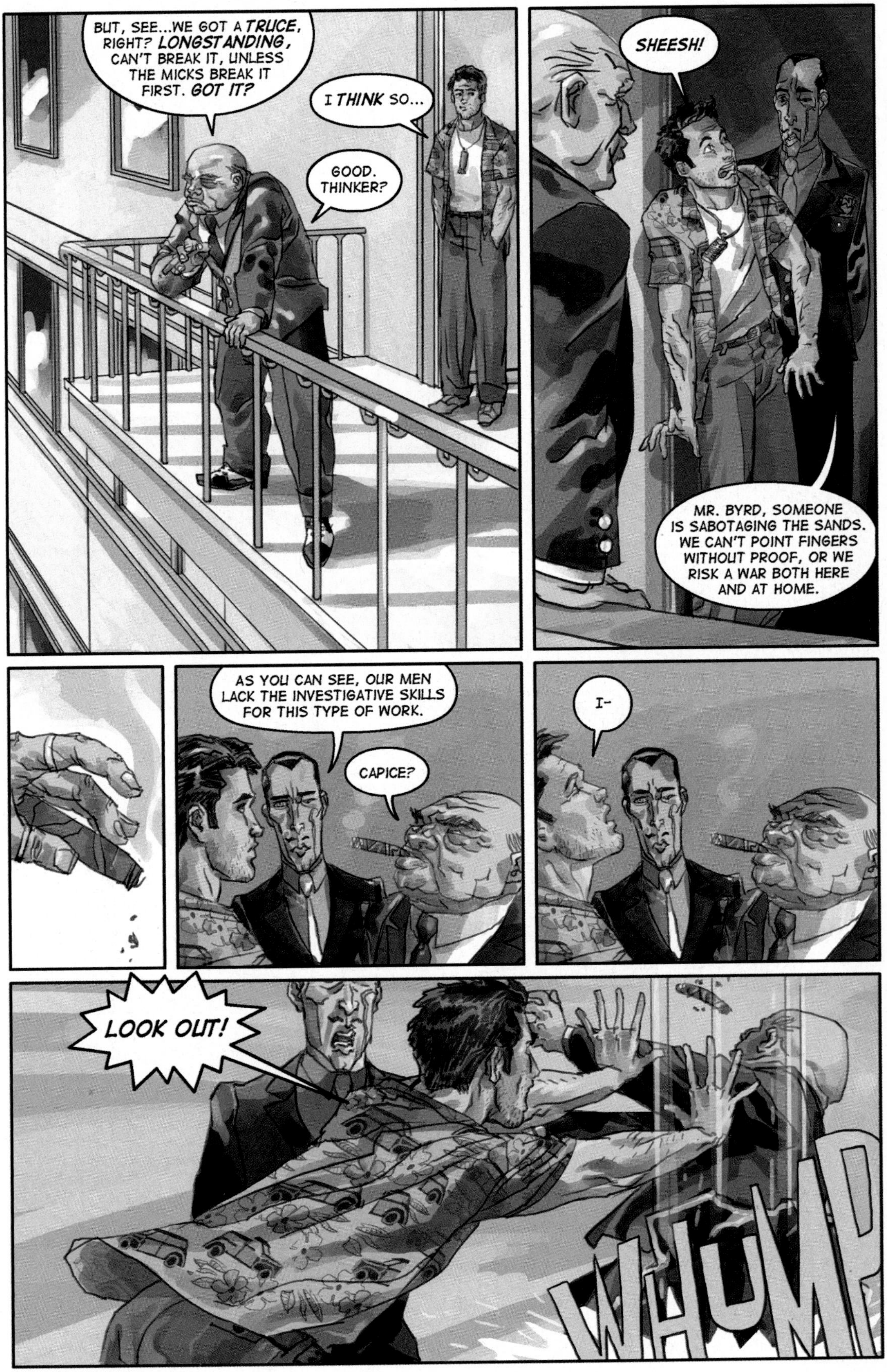
BUT, SEE...WE GOT A TRUCE, RIGHT? LONGSTANDING, CAN'T BREAK IT, UNLESS THE MICKS BREAK IT FIRST. GOT IT?
I THINK SO...
GOOD. THINKER?
SHEESH!
MR. BYRD, SOMEONE IS SABOTAGING THE SANDS. WE CAN'T POINT FINGERS WITHOUT PROOF, OR WE RISK A WAR BOTH HERE AND AT HOME.
AS YOU CAN SEE, OUR MEN LACK THE INVESTIGATIVE SKILLS FOR THIS TYPE OF WORK.
CAPICE?
I--
LOOK OUT!
WHUMP

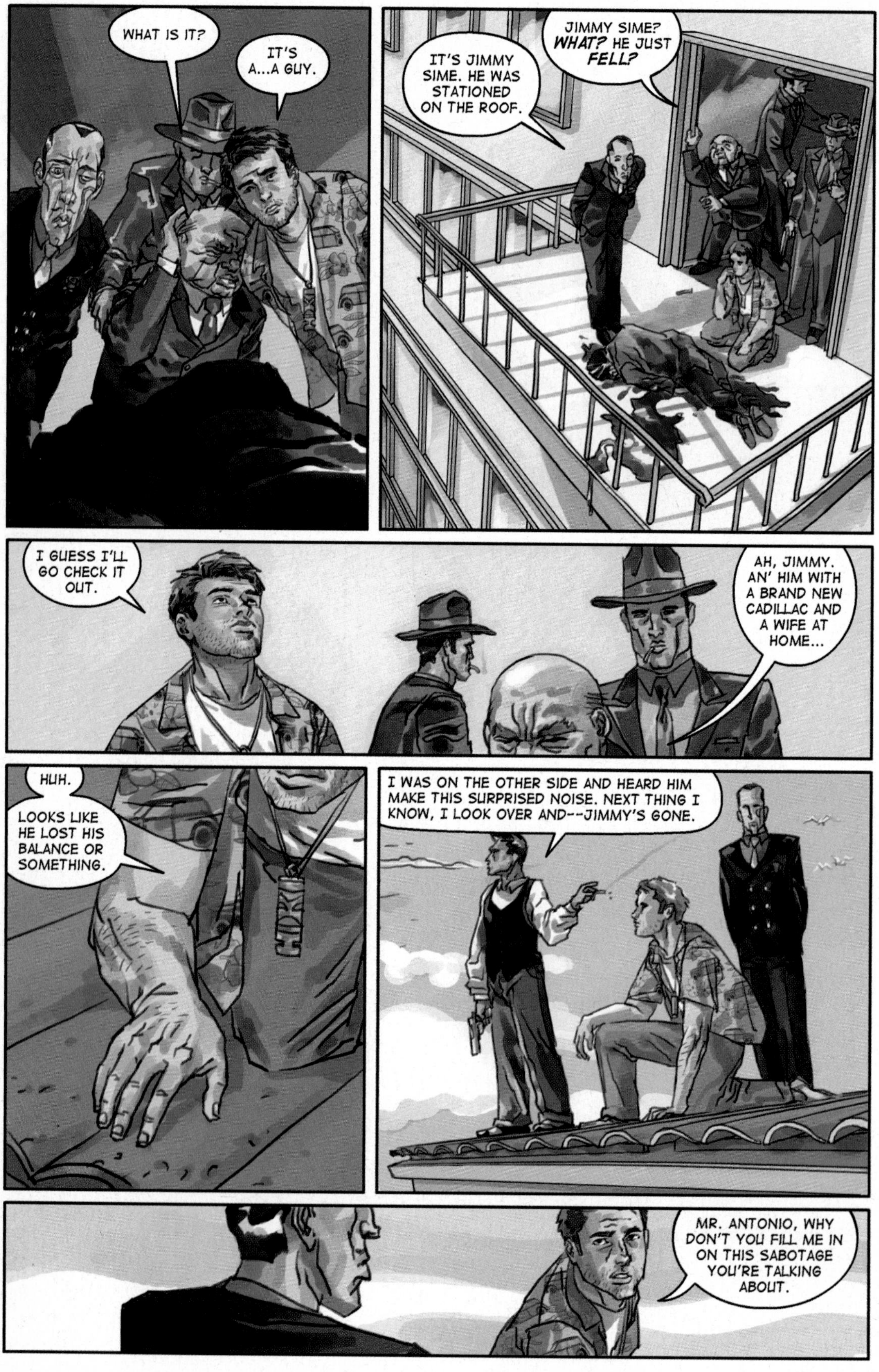
WHAT IS IT?
IT'S A...A GUY.
IT'S JIMMY SIME. HE WAS STATIONED ON THE ROOF.
JIMMY SIME? WHAT? HE JUST FELL?
I GUESS I'LL GO CHECK IT OUT.
AH, JIMMY. AN' HIM WITH A BRAND NEW CADILLAC AND A WIFE AT HOME...
HUH.
LOOKS LIKE HE LOST HIS BALANCE OR SOMETHING.
I WAS ON THE OTHER SIDE AND HEARD HIM MAKE THIS SURPRISED NOISE. NEXT THING I KNOW, I LOOK OVER AND--JIMMY'S GONE.
MR. ANTONIO, WHY DON'T YOU FILL ME IN ON THIS SABOTAGE YOU'RE TALKING ABOUT.

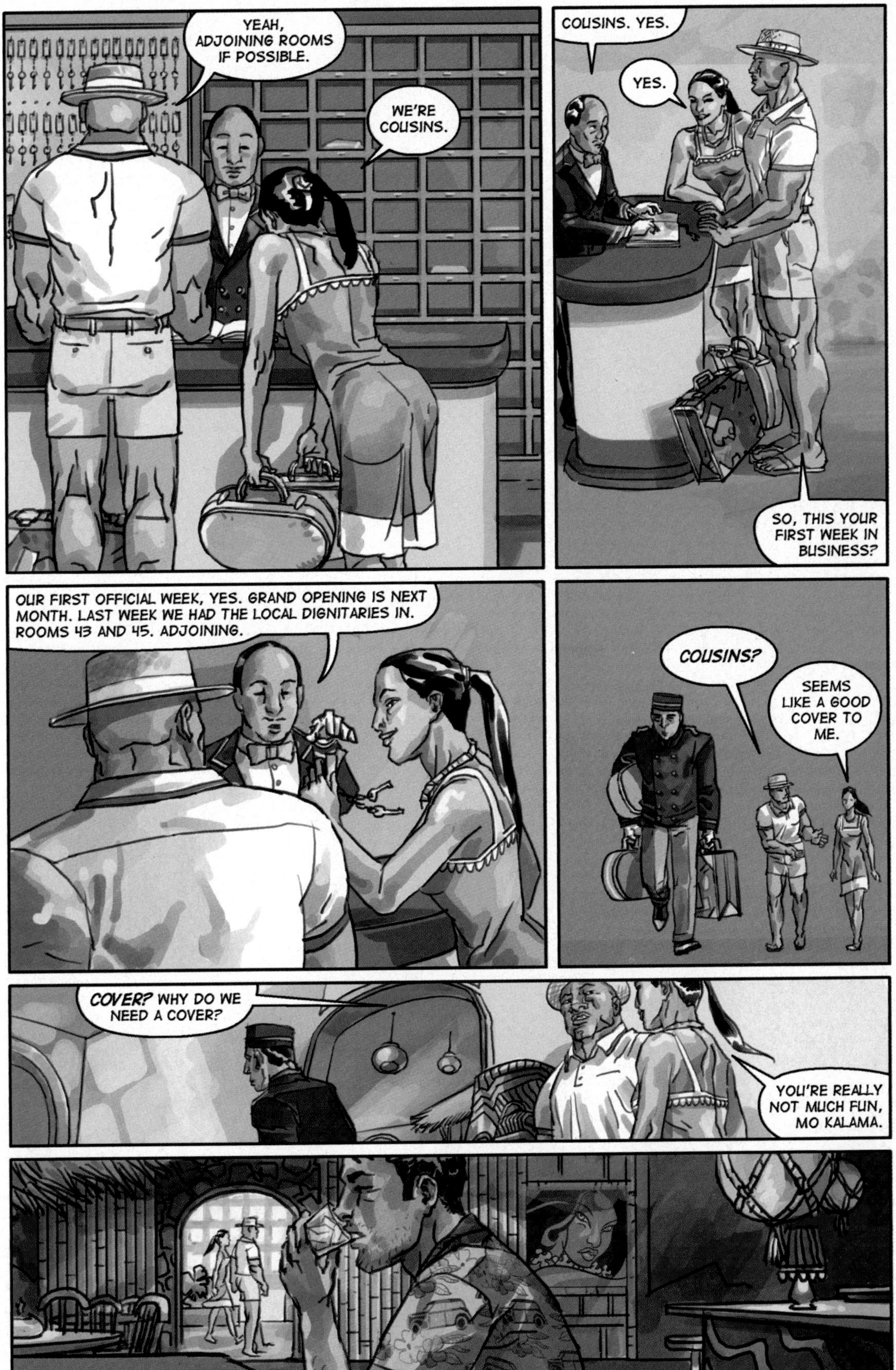
YEAH, ADJOINING ROOMS IF POSSIBLE.
WE'RE COUSINS.
COUSINS. YES.
YES.
SO, THIS YOUR FIRST WEEK IN BUSINESS?
OUR FIRST OFFICIAL WEEK, YES. GRAND OPENING IS NEXT MONTH. LAST WEEK WE HAD THE LOCAL DIGNITARIES IN. ROOMS 43 AND 45. ADJOINING.
COUSINS?
SEEMS LIKE A GOOD COVER TO ME.
COVER? WHY DO WE NEED A COVER?
YOU'RE REALLY NOT MUCH FUN, MO KALAMA.

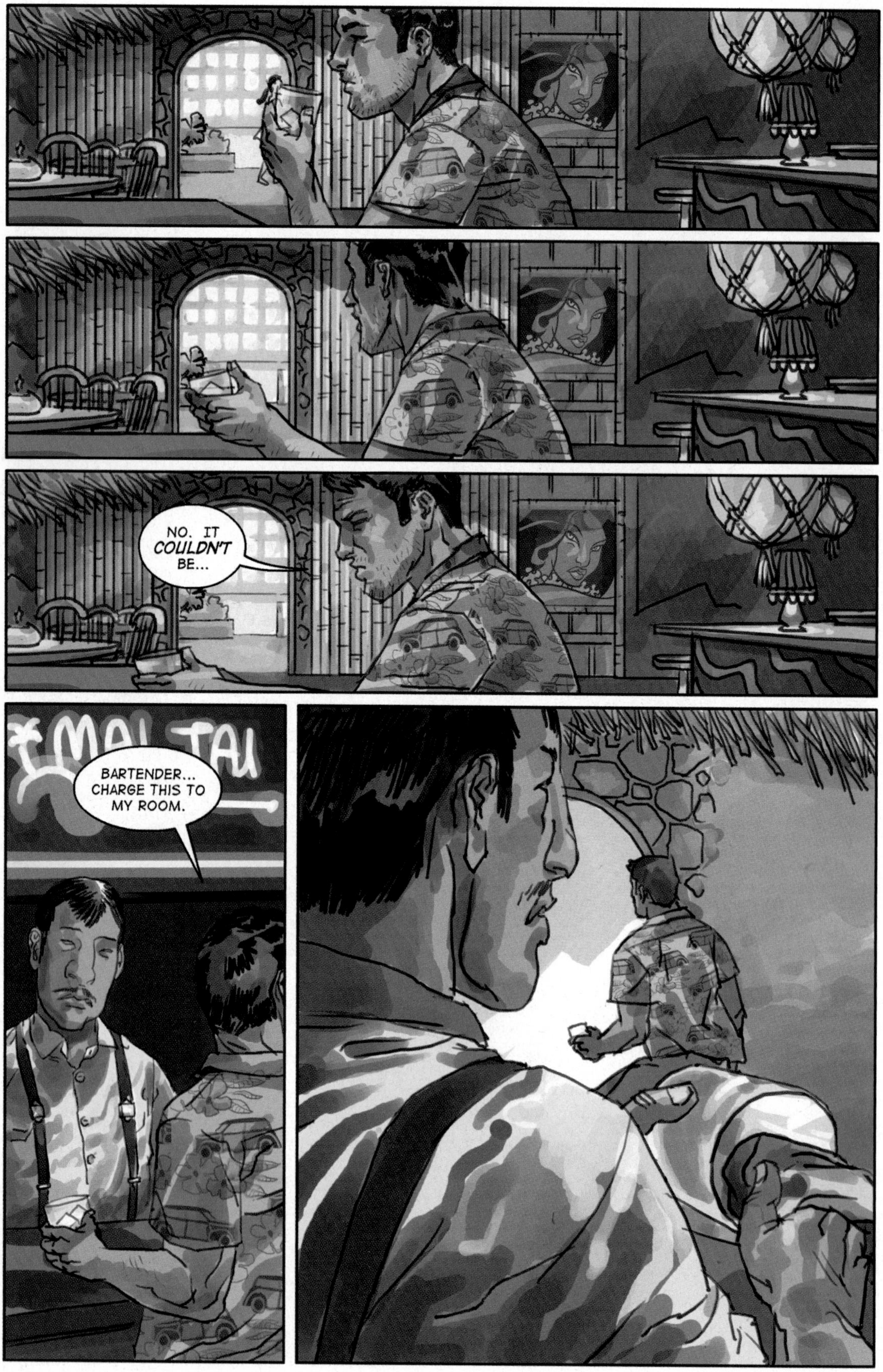
NO. IT COULDN'T BE...
I MAI TAI
BARTENDER... CHARGE THIS TO MY ROOM.

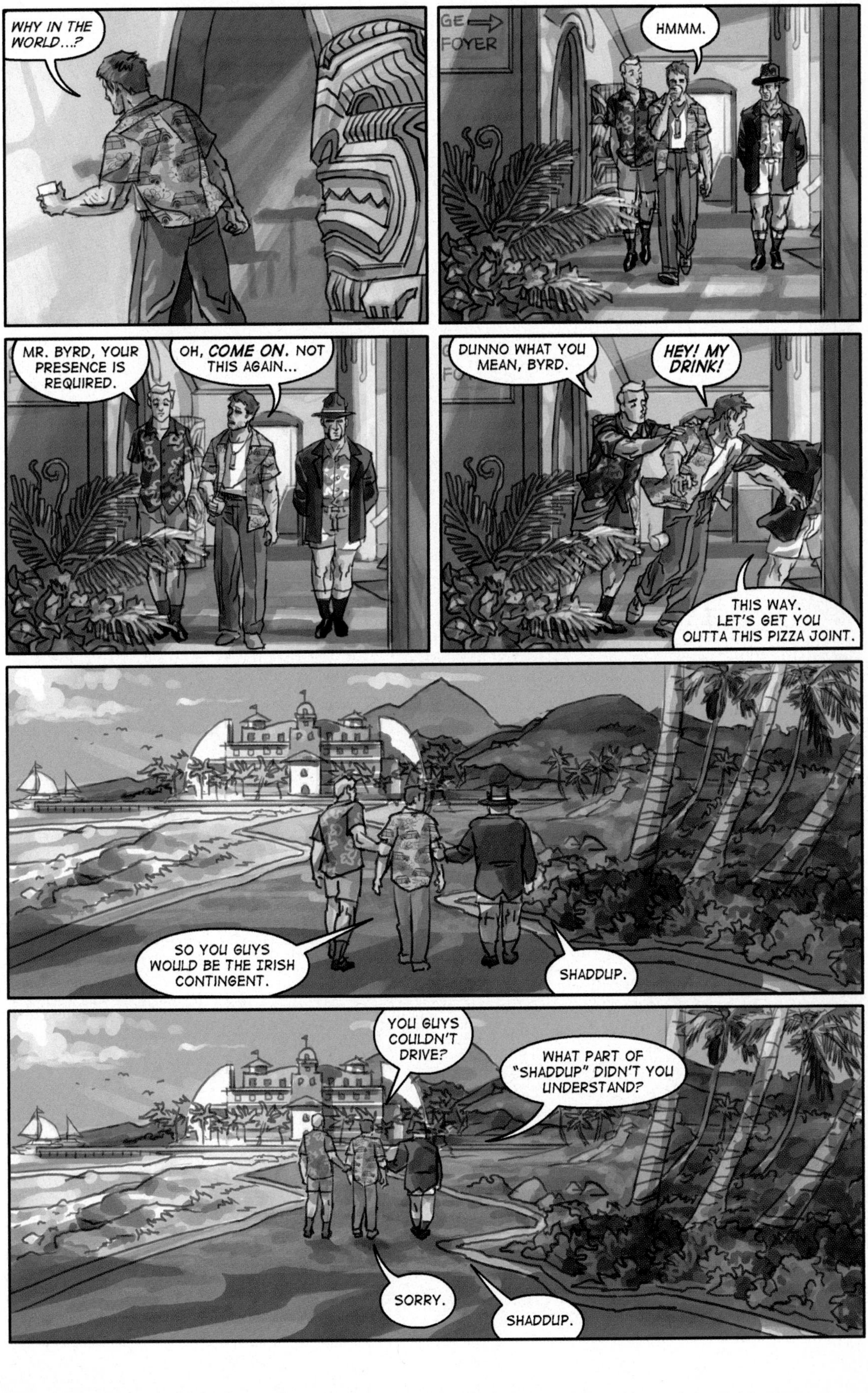
WHY IN THE WORLD...?
GE
FOYER
HMMM.
MR. BYRD, YOUR PRESENCE IS REQUIRED.
OH, COME ON. NOT THIS AGAIN...
DUNNO WHAT YOU MEAN, BYRD.
HEY! MY DRINK!
THIS WAY. LET'S GET YOU OUTTA THIS PIZZA JOINT.
SO YOU GUYS WOULD BE THE IRISH CONTINGENT.
SHADDUP.
YOU GUYS COULDN'T DRIVE?
WHAT PART OF "SHADDUP" DIDN'T YOU UNDERSTAND?
SORRY.
SHADDUP.

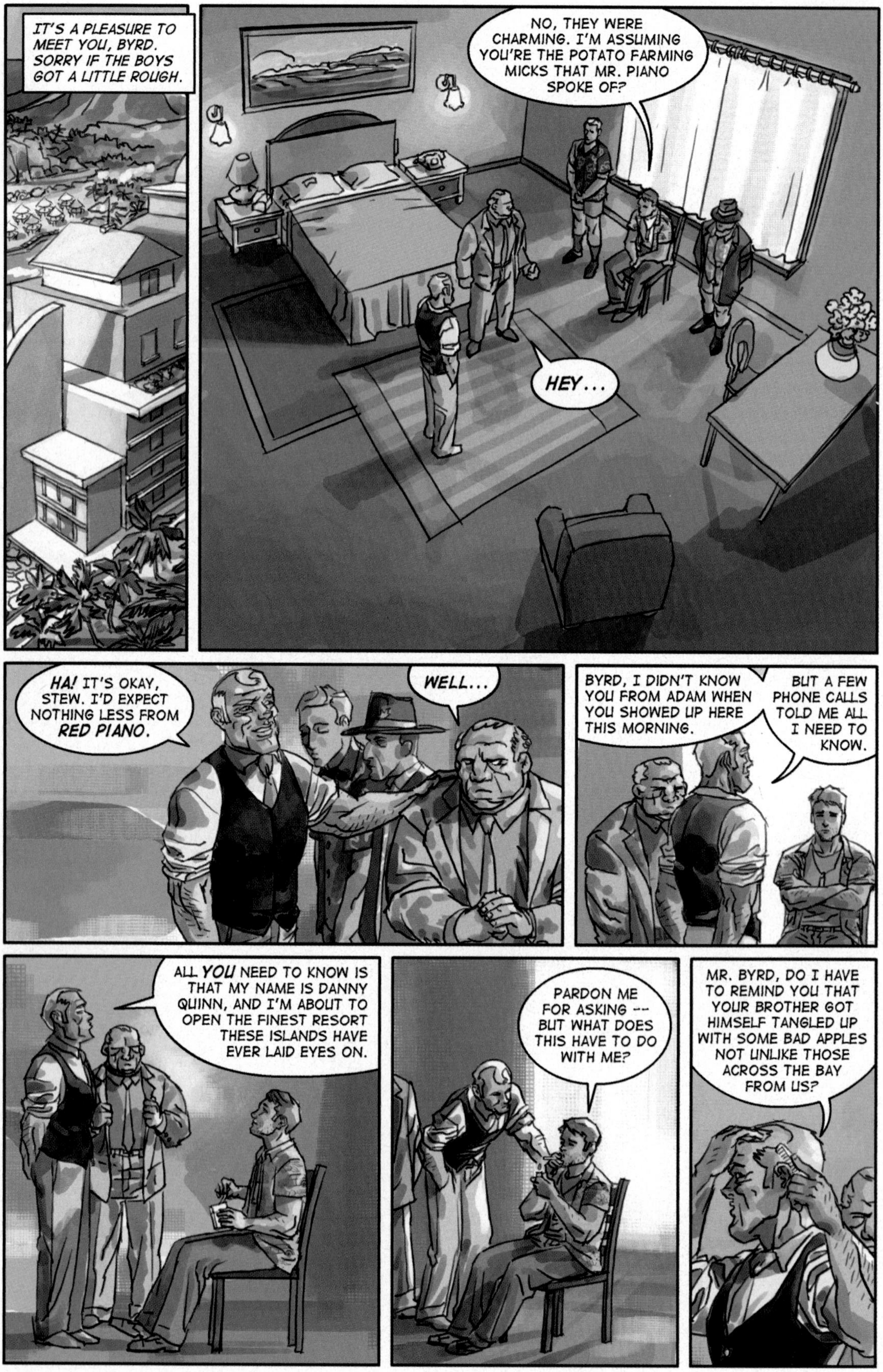
IT'S A PLEASURE TO MEET YOU, BYRD. SORRY IF THE BOYS GOT A LITTLE ROUGH.
NO, THEY WERE CHARMING. I'M ASSUMING YOU'RE THE POTATO FARMING MICKS THAT MR. PIANO SPOKE OF?
HEY...
HA! IT'S OKAY, STEW. I'D EXPECT NOTHING LESS FROM RED PIANO.
WELL...
BYRD, I DIDN'T KNOW YOU FROM ADAM WHEN YOU SHOWED UP HERE THIS MORNING.
BUT A FEW PHONE CALLS TOLD ME ALL I NEED TO KNOW.
ALL YOU NEED TO KNOW IS THAT MY NAME IS DANNY QUINN, AND I'M ABOUT TO OPEN THE FINEST RESORT THESE ISLANDS HAVE EVER LAID EYES ON.
PARDON ME FOR ASKING -- BUT WHAT DOES THIS HAVE TO DO WITH ME?
MR. BYRD, DO I HAVE TO REMIND YOU THAT YOUR BROTHER GOT HIMSELF TANGLED UP WITH SOME BAD APPLES NOT UNLIKE THOSE ACROSS THE BAY FROM US?

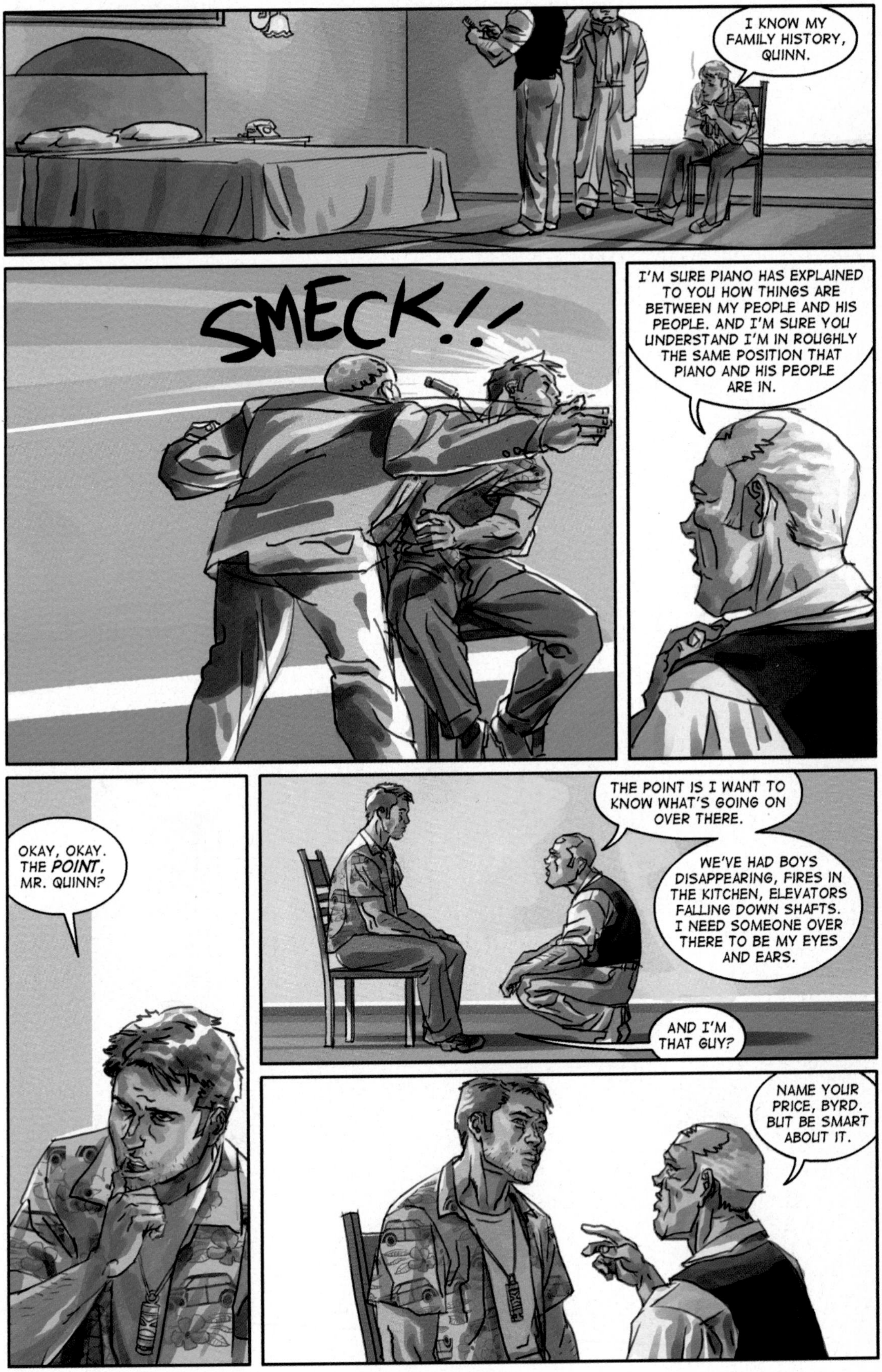
I KNOW MY FAMILY HISTORY, QUINN.
SMECK!!!
I'M SURE PIANO HAS EXPLAINED TO YOU HOW THINGS ARE BETWEEN MY PEOPLE AND HIS PEOPLE. AND I'M SURE YOU UNDERSTAND I'M IN ROUGHLY THE SAME POSITION THAT PIANO AND HIS PEOPLE ARE IN.
OKAY, OKAY. THE *POINT*, MR. QUINN?
THE POINT IS I WANT TO KNOW WHAT'S GOING ON OVER THERE.
WE'VE HAD BOYS DISAPPEARING, FIRES IN THE KITCHEN, ELEVATORS FALLING DOWN SHAFTS. I NEED SOMEONE OVER THERE TO BE MY EYES AND EARS.
AND I'M THAT GUY?
NAME YOUR PRICE, BYRD. BUT BE SMART ABOUT IT.

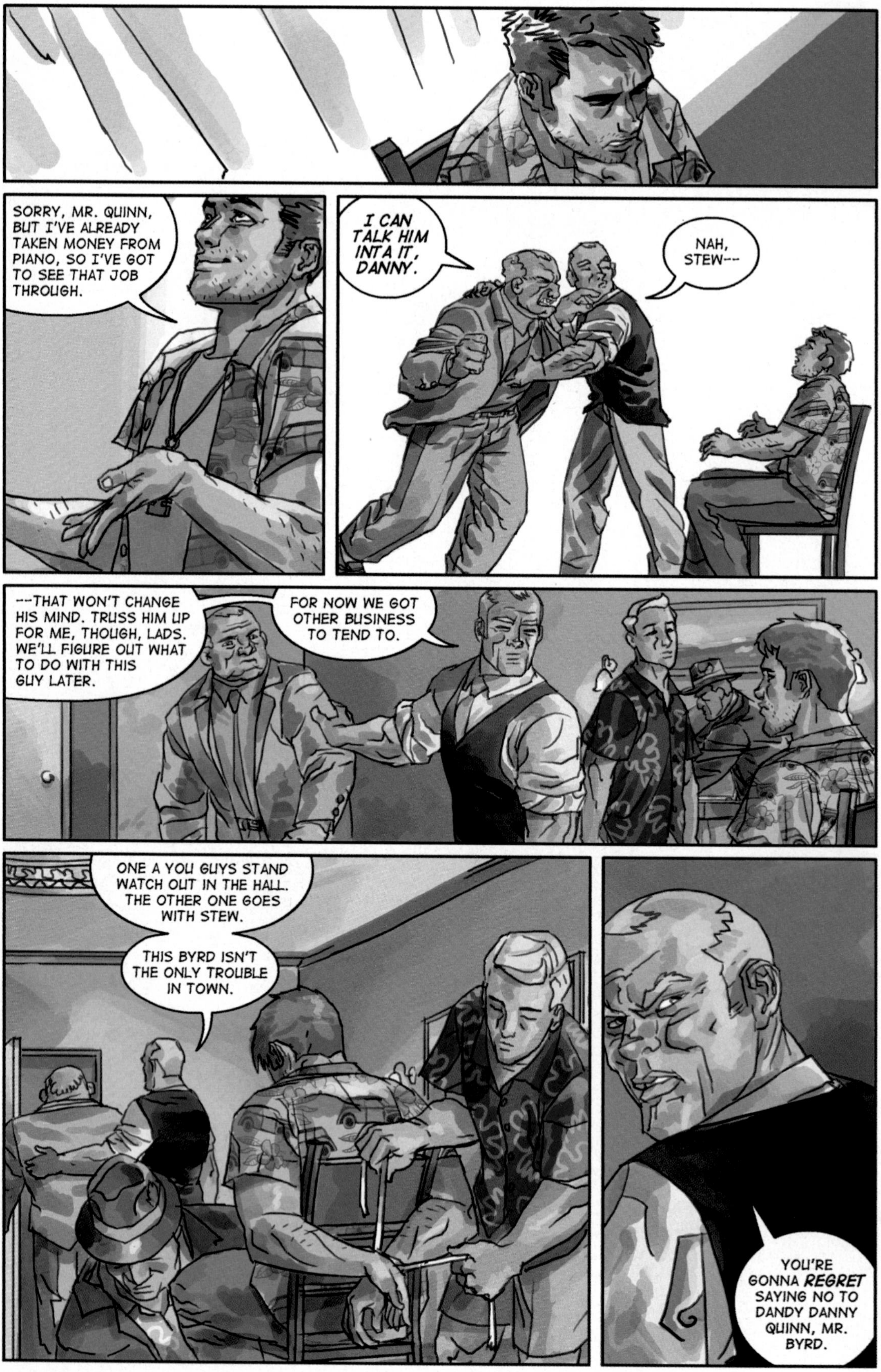
SORRY, MR. QUINN, BUT I'VE ALREADY TAKEN MONEY FROM PIANO, SO I'VE GOT TO SEE THAT JOB THROUGH.
I CAN TALK HIM INTA IT, DANNY.
NAH, STEW--
--THAT WON'T CHANGE HIS MIND. TRUSS HIM UP FOR ME, THOUGH, LADS. WE'LL FIGURE OUT WHAT TO DO WITH THIS GUY LATER.
FOR NOW WE GOT OTHER BUSINESS TO TEND TO.
ONE A YOU GUYS STAND WATCH OUT IN THE HALL. THE OTHER ONE GOES WITH STEW.
THIS BYRD ISN'T THE ONLY TROUBLE IN TOWN.
YOU'RE GONNA REGRET SAYING NO TO DANDY DANNY QUINN, MR. BYRD.

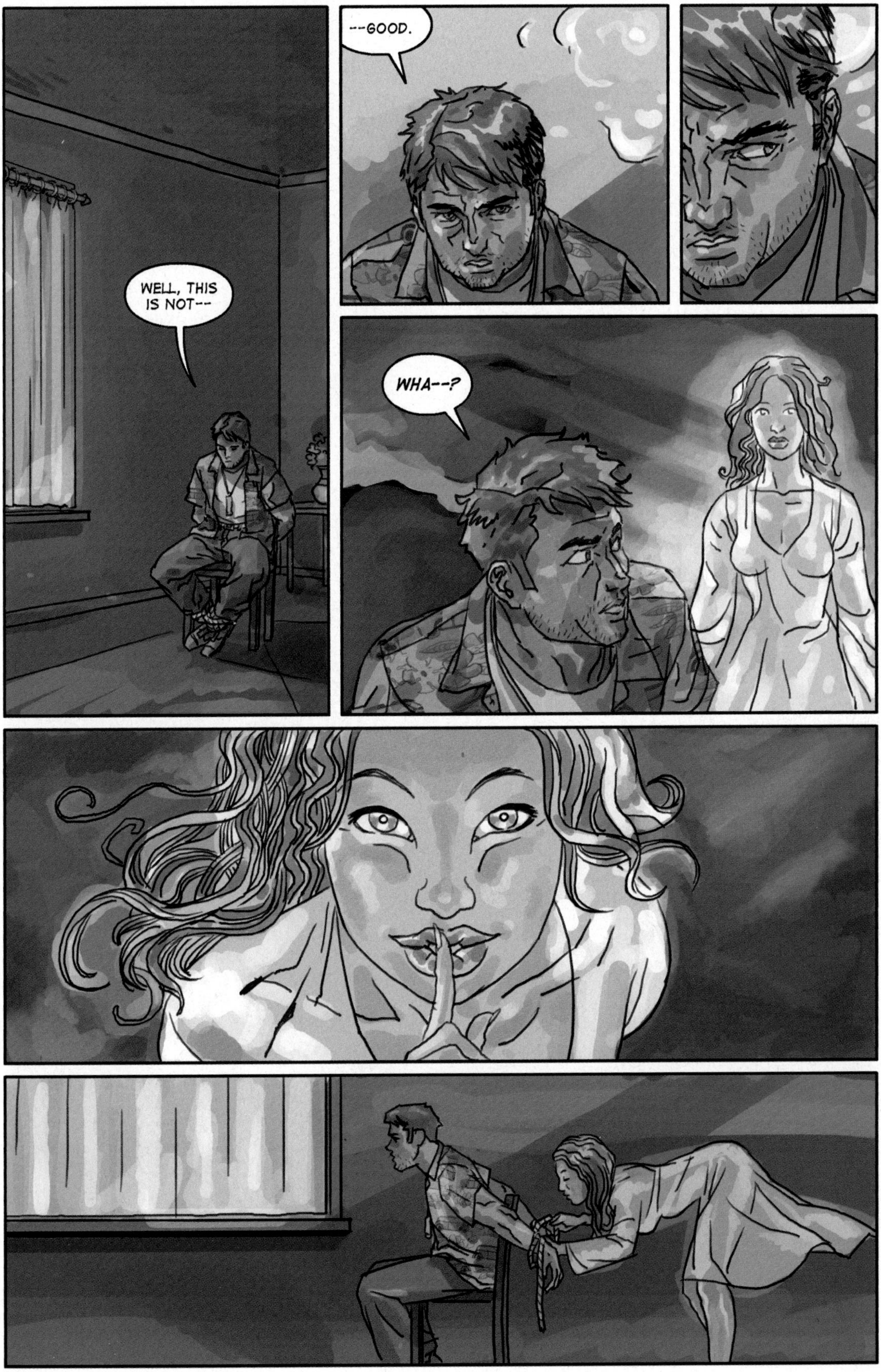
WELL, THIS IS NOT--
--GOOD.
WHA--?

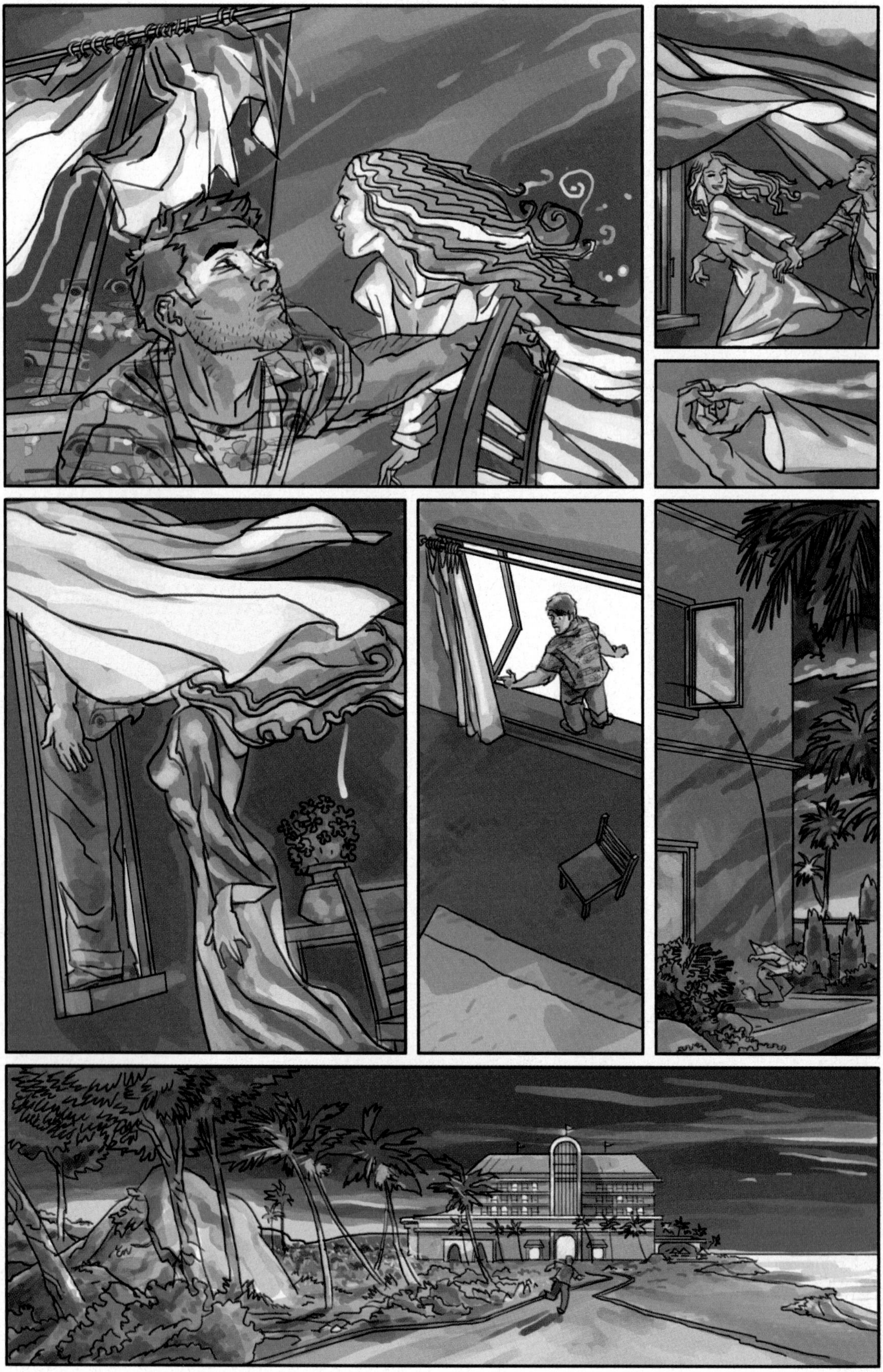

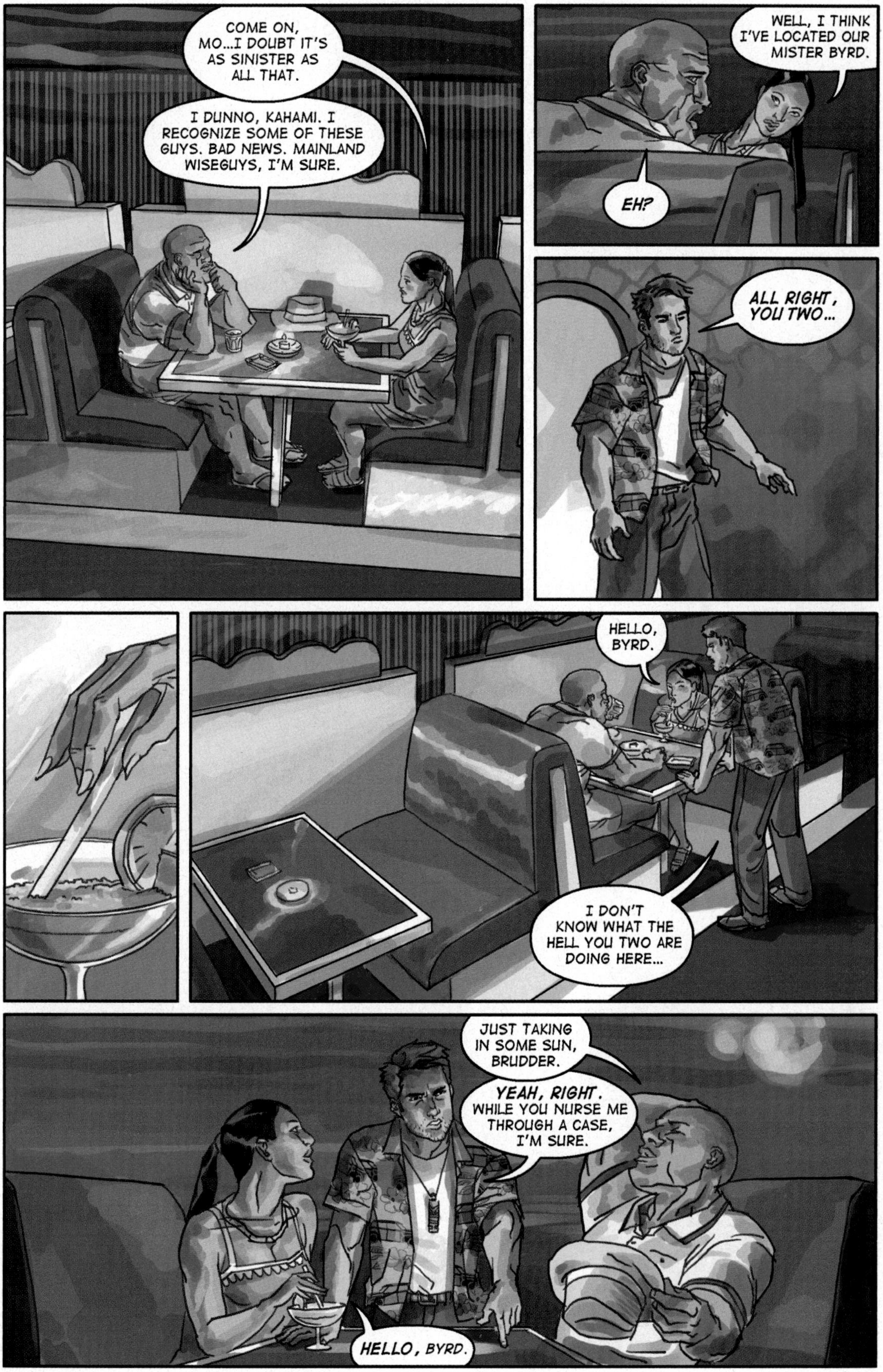
COME ON, MO...I DOUBT IT'S AS SINISTER AS ALL THAT.
I DUNNO, KAHAMI. I RECOGNIZE SOME OF THESE GUYS. BAD NEWS. MAINLAND WISEGUYS, I'M SURE.
WELL, I THINK I'VE LOCATED OUR MISTER BYRD.
EH?
ALL RIGHT, YOU TWO...
HELLO, BYRD.
I DON'T KNOW WHAT THE HELL YOU TWO ARE DOING HERE...
JUST TAKING IN SOME SUN, BRUDDER.
YEAH, RIGHT. WHILE YOU NURSE ME THROUGH A CASE, I'M SURE.
HELLO, BYRD.

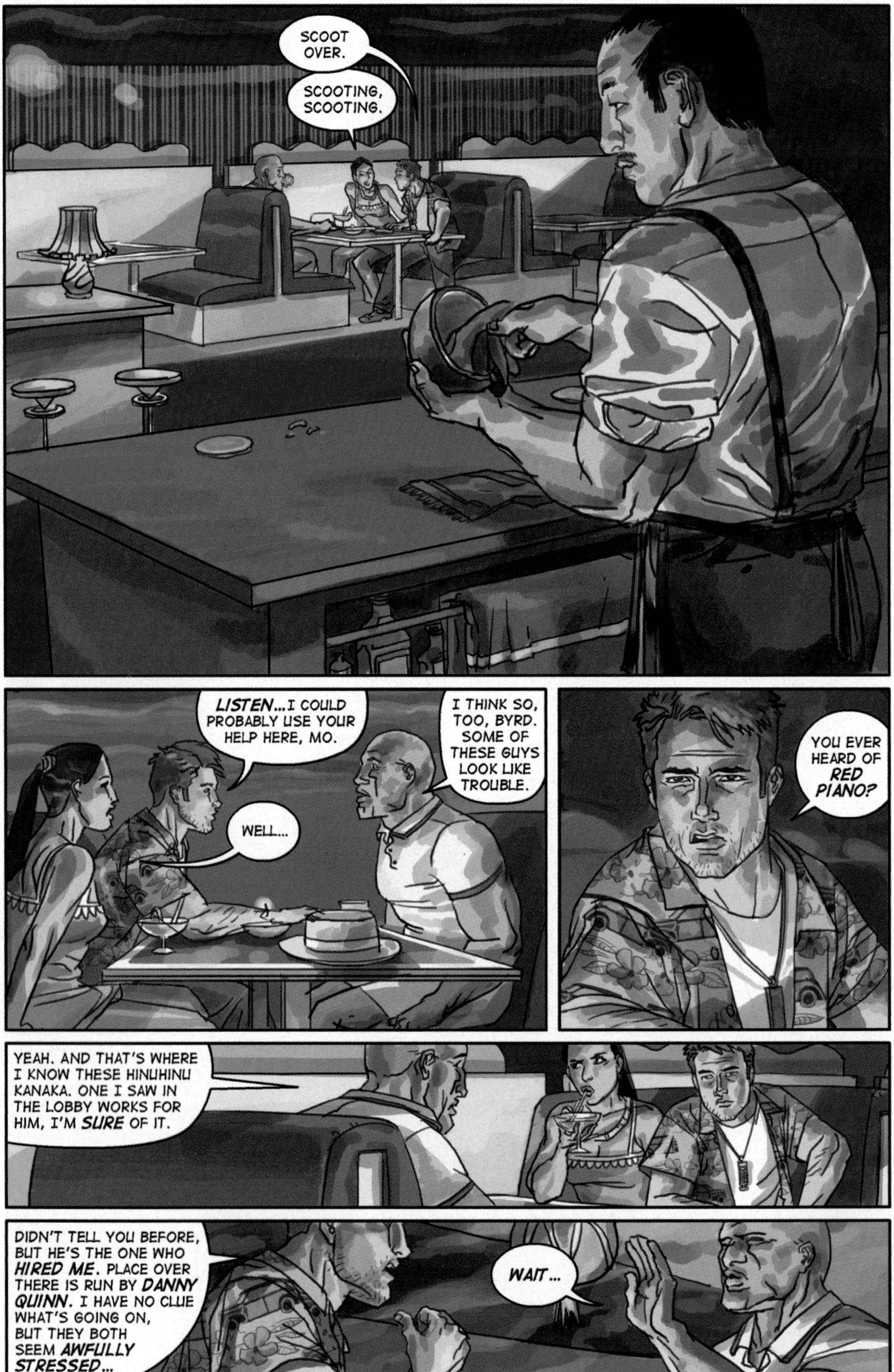

SCOOT OVER.
SCOOTING, SCOOTING.
LISTEN... I COULD PROBABLY USE YOUR HELP HERE, MO.
WELL...
I THINK SO, TOO, BYRD. SOME OF THESE GUYS LOOK LIKE TROUBLE.
YOU EVER HEARD OF RED PIANO?
YEAH. AND THAT'S WHERE I KNOW THESE HINUHINU KANAKA. ONE I SAW IN THE LOBBY WORKS FOR HIM, I'M SURE OF IT.
DIDN'T TELL YOU BEFORE, BUT HE'S THE ONE WHO HIRED ME. PLACE OVER THERE IS RUN BY DANNY QUINN. I HAVE NO CLUE WHAT'S GOING ON, BUT THEY BOTH SEEM AWFULLY STRESSED...
WAIT...

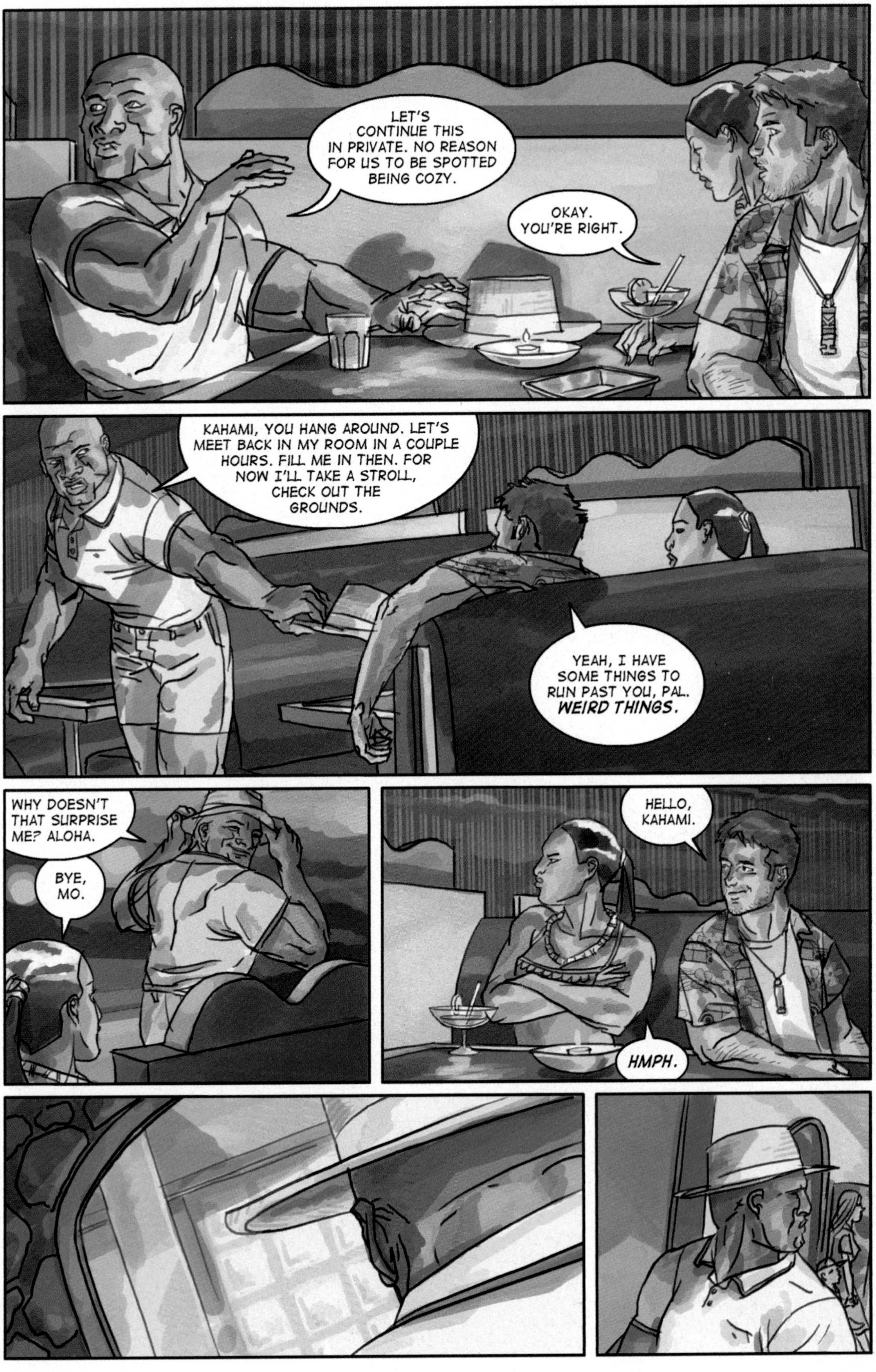
LET'S CONTINUE THIS IN PRIVATE. NO REASON FOR US TO BE SPOTTED BEING COZY.
OKAY. YOU'RE RIGHT.
KAHAMI, YOU HANG AROUND. LET'S MEET BACK IN MY ROOM IN A COUPLE HOURS. FILL ME IN THEN. FOR NOW I'LL TAKE A STROLL, CHECK OUT THE GROUNDS.
YEAH, I HAVE SOME THINGS TO RUN PAST YOU, PAL. *WEIRD THINGS.*
WHY DOESN'T THAT SURPRISE ME? ALOHA.
BYE, MO.
HELLO, KAHAMI.
HMPH.

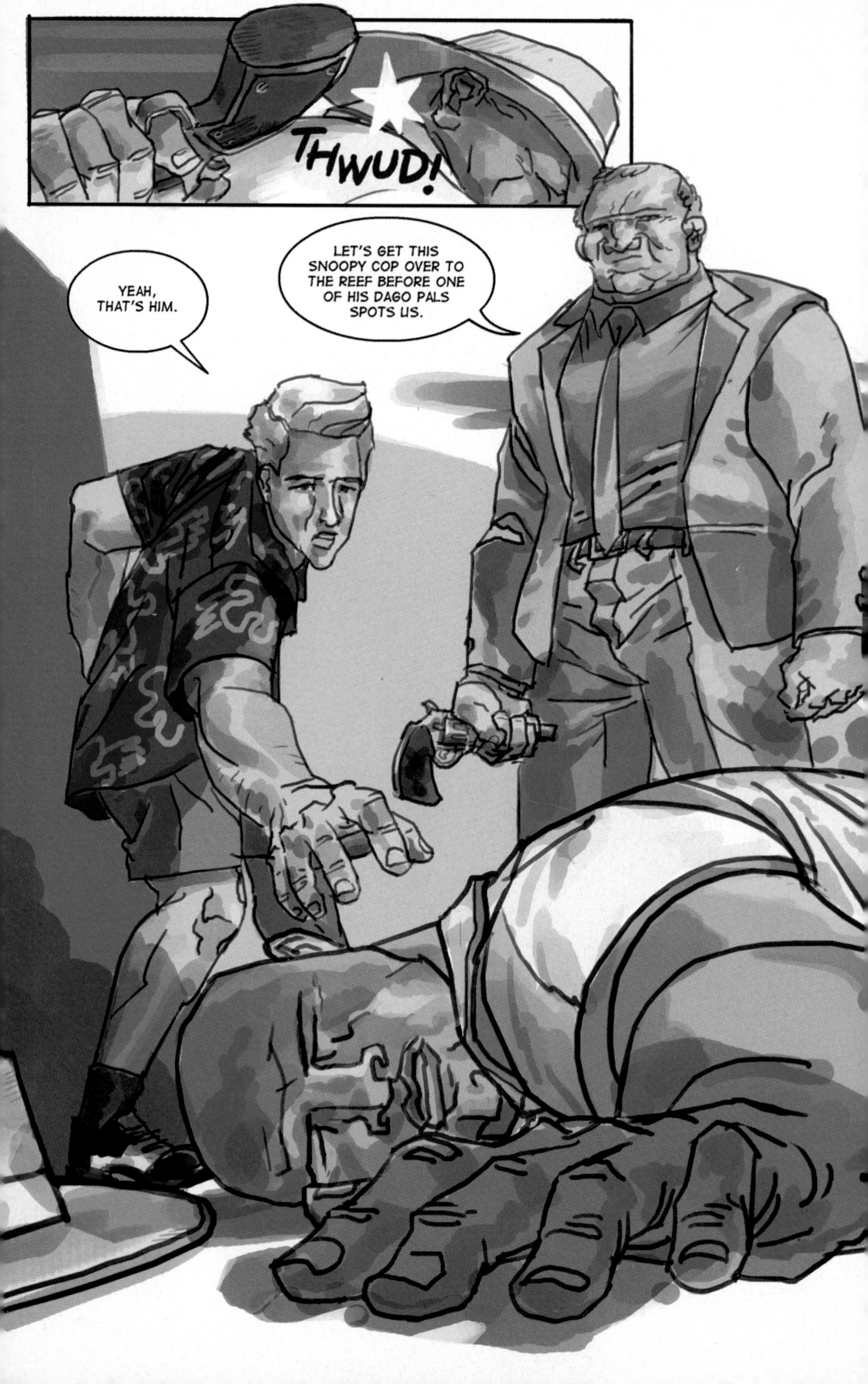
THWUD!
YEAH, THAT'S HIM.
LET'S GET THIS SNOOPY COP OVER TO THE REEF BEFORE ONE OF HIS DAGO PALS SPOTS US.

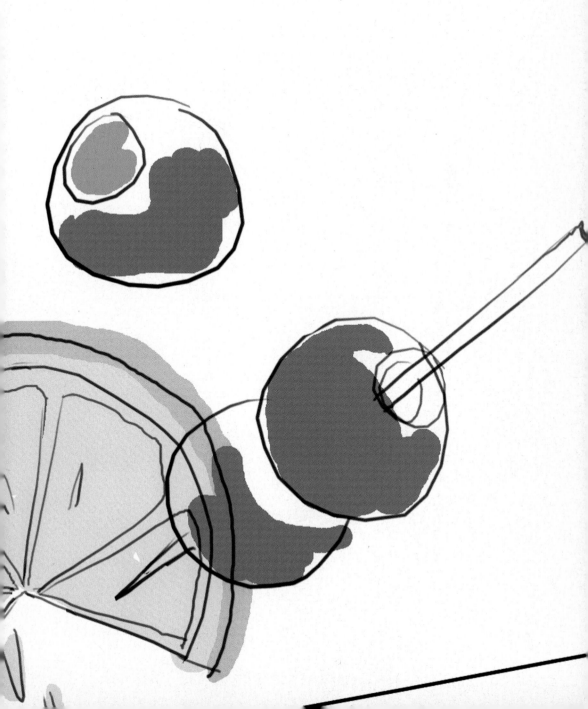

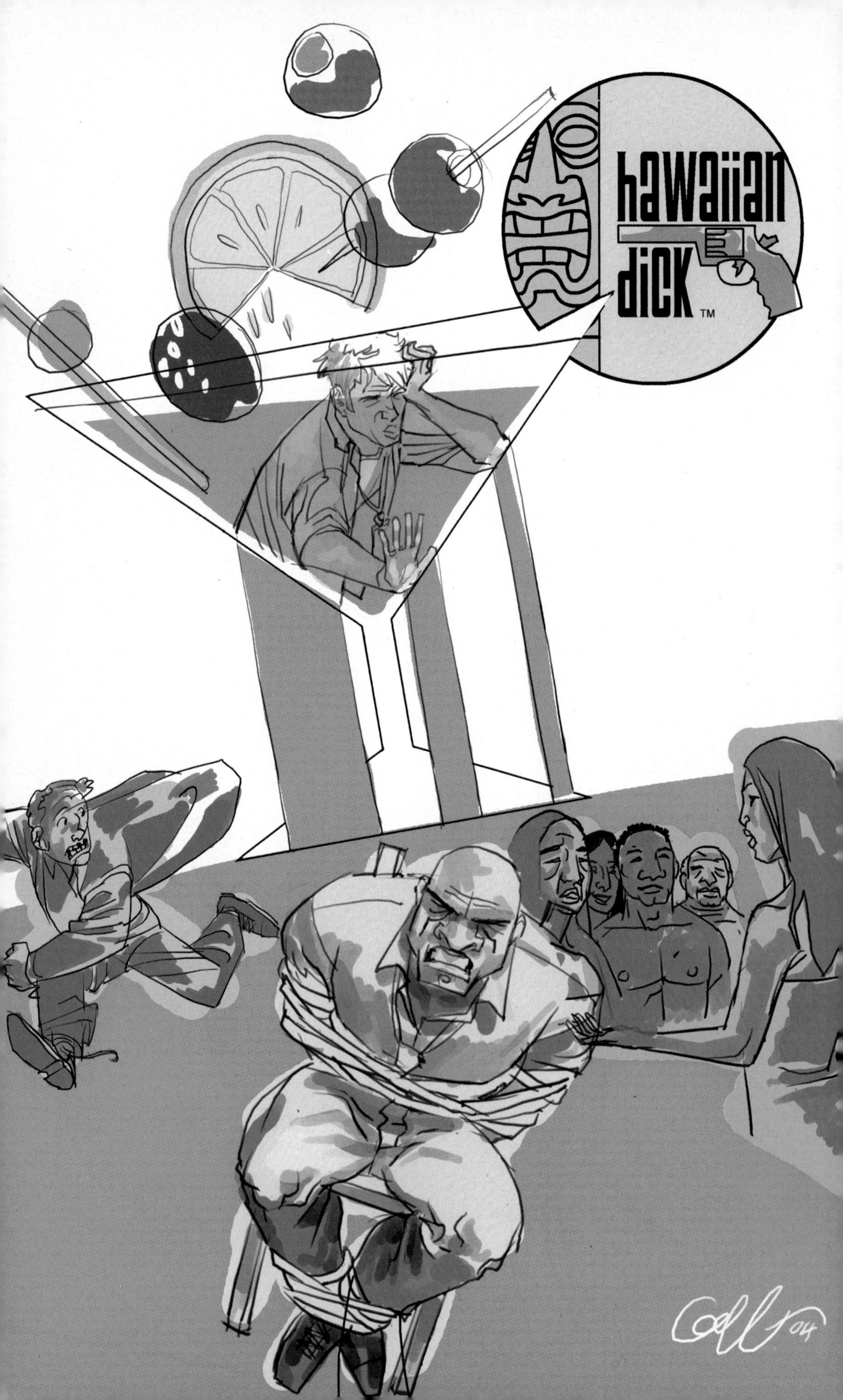
hawaiian
dick
TM

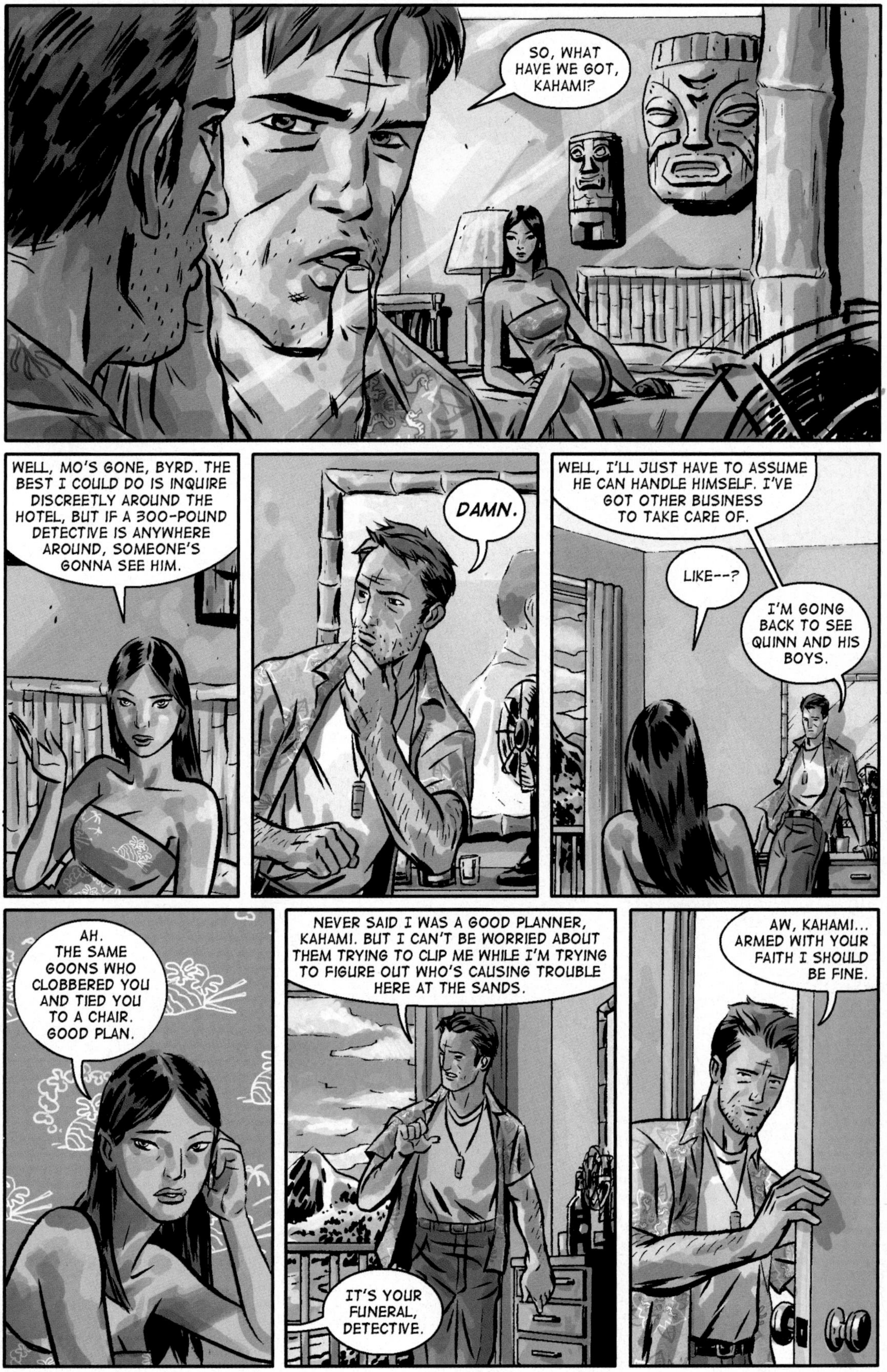
SO, WHAT HAVE WE GOT, KAHAMI?
WELL, MO'S GONE, BYRD. THE BEST I COULD DO IS INQUIRE DISCREETLY AROUND THE HOTEL, BUT IF A 300-POUND DETECTIVE IS ANYWHERE AROUND, SOMEONE'S GONNA SEE HIM.
DAMN.
WELL, I'LL JUST HAVE TO ASSUME HE CAN HANDLE HIMSELF. I'VE GOT OTHER BUSINESS TO TAKE CARE OF.
LIKE--?
I'M GOING BACK TO SEE QUINN AND HIS BOYS.
AH. THE SAME GOONS WHO CLOBBERED YOU AND TIED YOU TO A CHAIR. GOOD PLAN.
NEVER SAID I WAS A GOOD PLANNER, KAHAMI. BUT I CAN'T BE WORRIED ABOUT THEM TRYING TO CLIP ME WHILE I'M TRYING TO FIGURE OUT WHO'S CAUSING TROUBLE HERE AT THE SANDS.
IT'S YOUR FUNERAL, DETECTIVE.
AW, KAHAMI... ARMED WITH YOUR FAITH I SHOULD BE FINE.

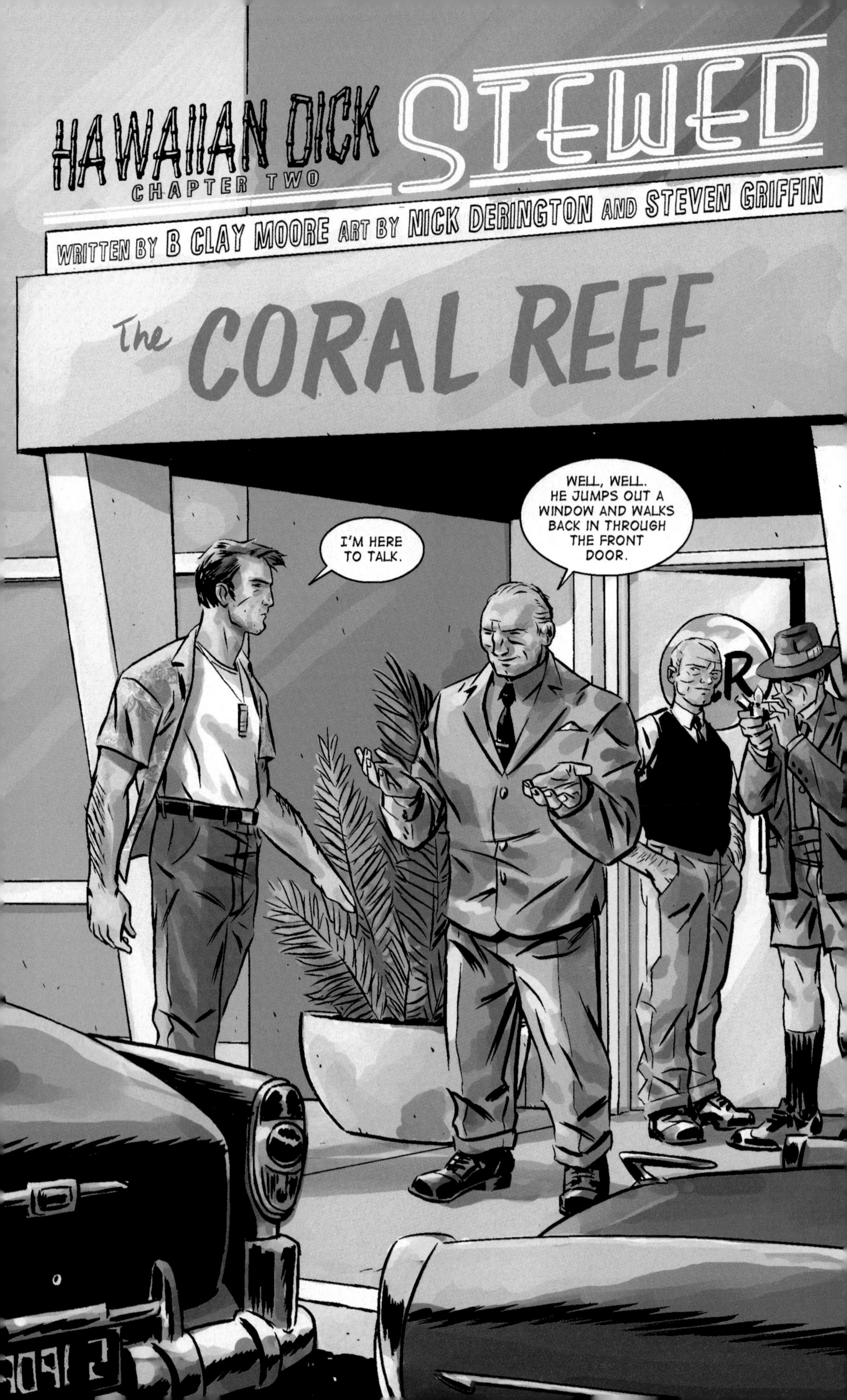
HAWAIIAN DICK
CHAPTER TWO
STEWED
WRITTEN BY B CLAY MOORE ART BY NICK DERINGTON AND STEVEN GRIFFIN
The CORAL REEF
I'M HERE TO TALK.
WELL, WELL. HE JUMPS OUT A WINDOW AND WALKS BACK IN THROUGH THE FRONT DOOR.

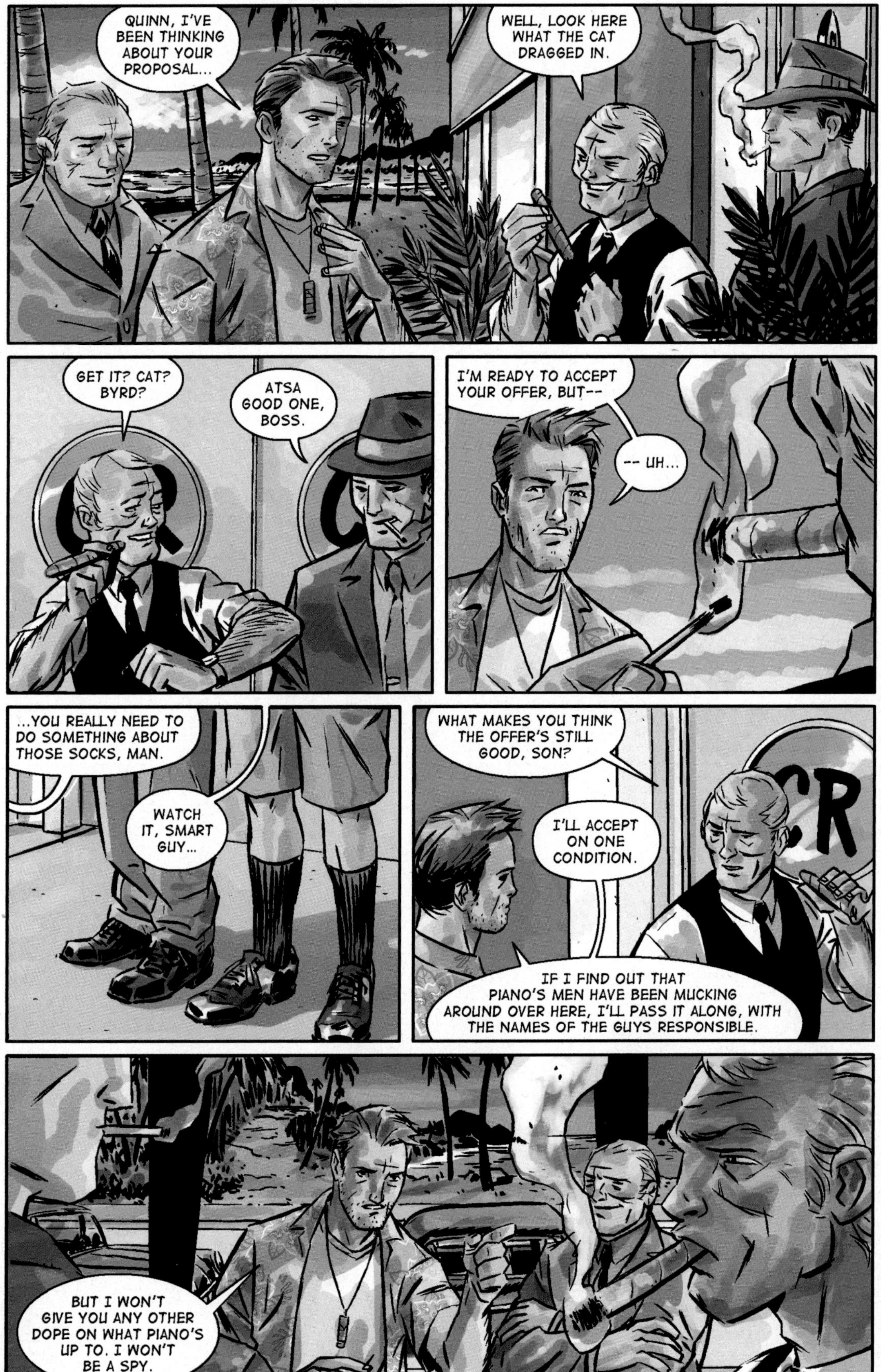
QUINN, I'VE BEEN THINKING ABOUT YOUR PROPOSAL...
WELL, LOOK HERE WHAT THE CAT DRAGGED IN.
GET IT? CAT? BYRD?
ATSA GOOD ONE, BOSS.
I'M READY TO ACCEPT YOUR OFFER, BUT--
-- UH...
...YOU REALLY NEED TO DO SOMETHING ABOUT THOSE SOCKS, MAN.
WATCH IT, SMART GUY...
WHAT MAKES YOU THINK THE OFFER'S STILL GOOD, SON?
I'LL ACCEPT ON ONE CONDITION.
IF I FIND OUT THAT PIANO'S MEN HAVE BEEN MUCKING AROUND OVER HERE, I'LL PASS IT ALONG, WITH THE NAMES OF THE GUYS RESPONSIBLE.
BUT I WON'T GIVE YOU ANY OTHER DOPE ON WHAT PIANO'S UP TO. I WON'T BE A SPY.

HMM.

AH, THAT'S FAIR ENOUGH. PART O' ME ADMIRES YOUR LOYALTY TO AN EMPLOYER, BYRD.

YEAH. I'LL BE IN TOUCH.

OH, I KNOW YOU WILL, LAD.

WELL....THAT WAS A WISE DECISION.

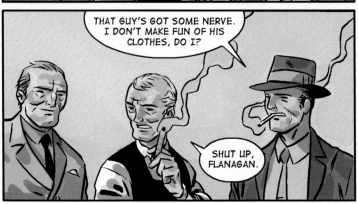

THAT GUY'S GOT SOME NERVE. I DON'T MAKE FUN OF HIS CLOTHES, DO I?

SHUT UP, FLANAGAN.

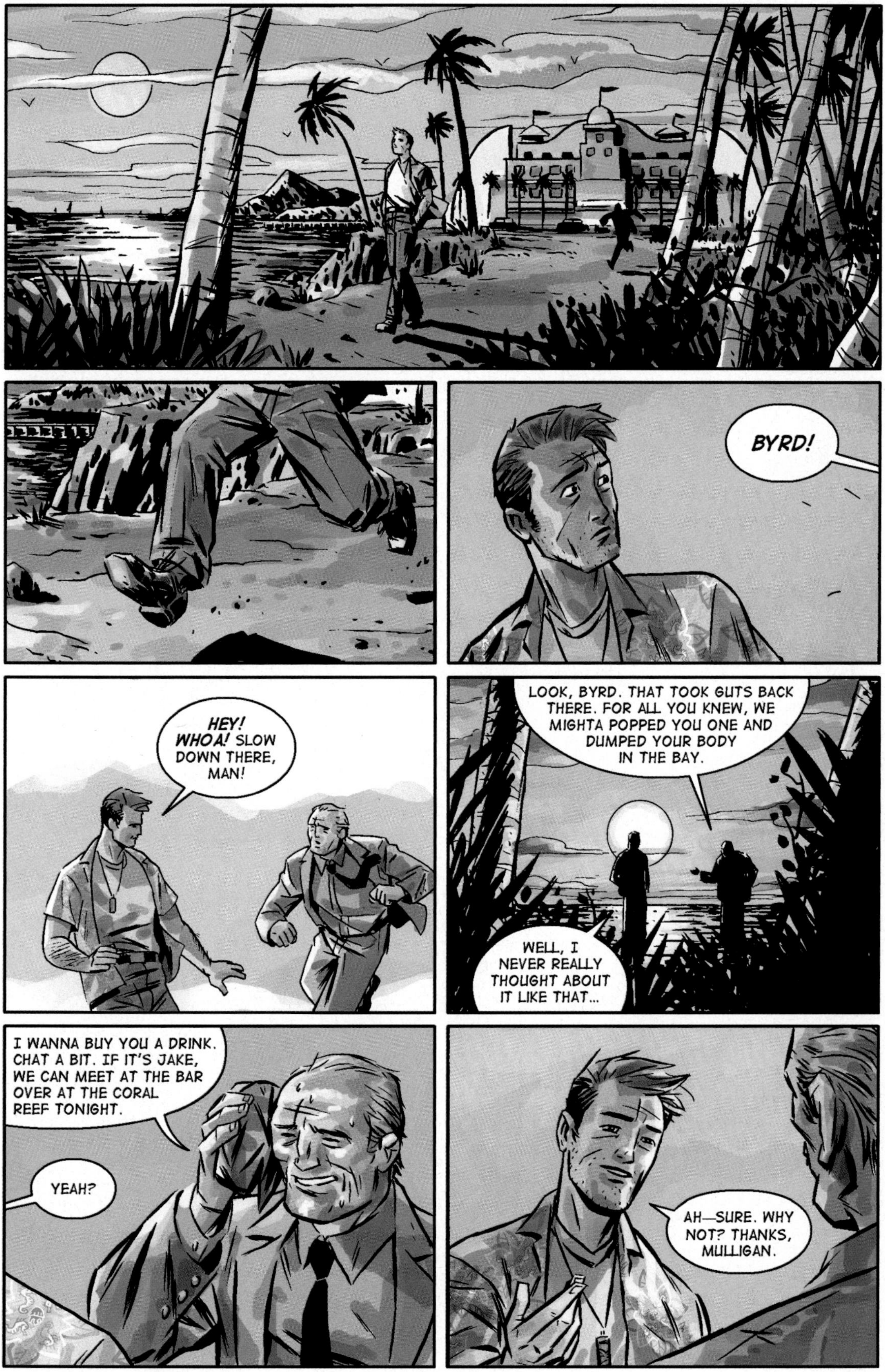
BYRD!
HEY! WHOA! SLOW DOWN THERE, MAN!
LOOK, BYRD. THAT TOOK GUTS BACK THERE. FOR ALL YOU KNEW, WE MIGHTA POPPED YOU ONE AND DUMPED YOUR BODY IN THE BAY.
WELL, I NEVER REALLY THOUGHT ABOUT IT LIKE THAT...
I WANNA BUY YOU A DRINK. CHAT A BIT. IF IT'S JAKE, WE CAN MEET AT THE BAR OVER AT THE CORAL REEF TONIGHT.
YEAH?
AH—SURE. WHY NOT? THANKS, MULLIGAN.

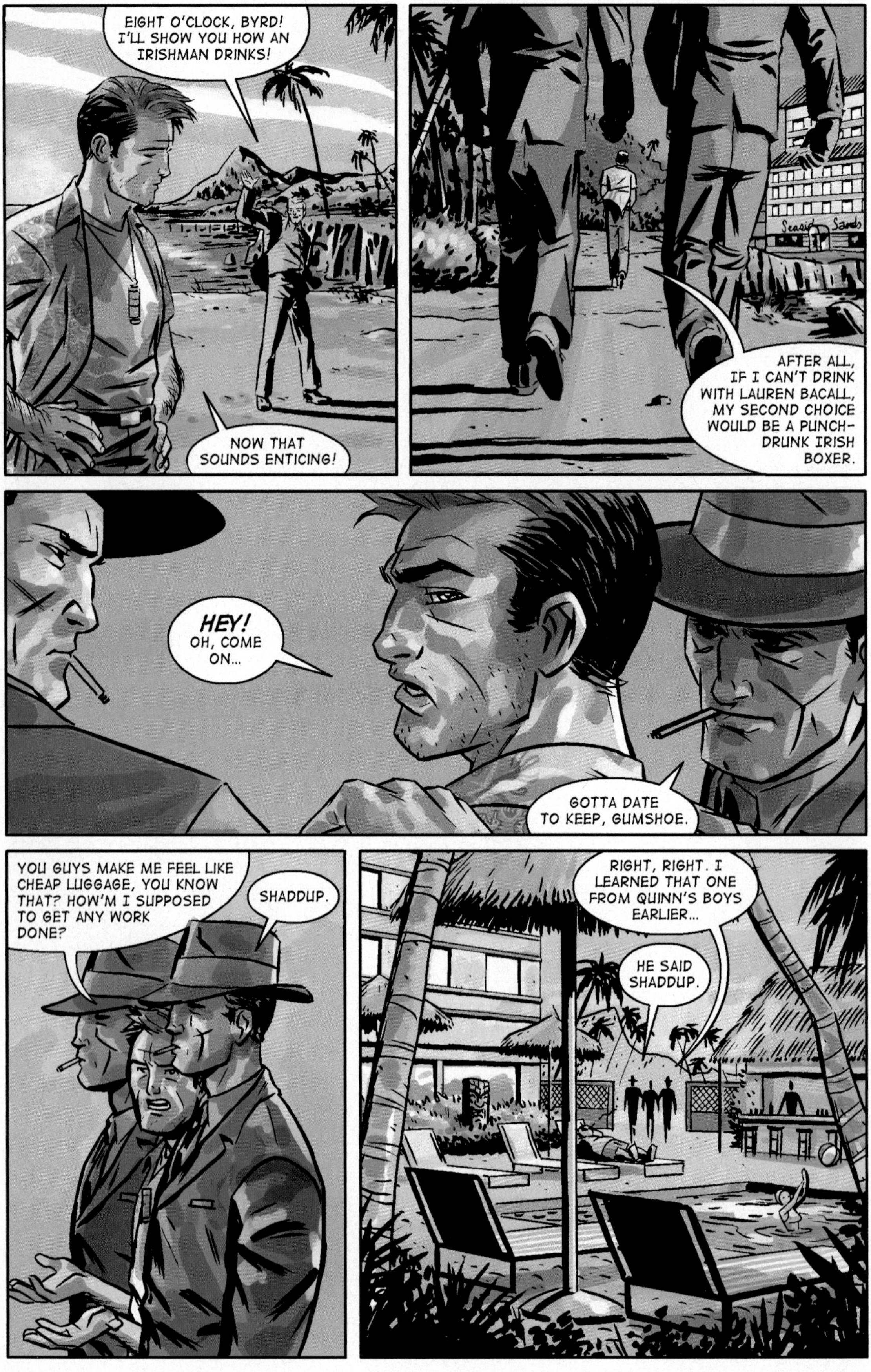
EIGHT O'CLOCK, BYRD! I'LL SHOW YOU HOW AN IRISHMAN DRINKS!
NOW THAT SOUNDS ENTICING!
Seaside Sands
AFTER ALL, IF I CAN'T DRINK WITH LAUREN BACALL, MY SECOND CHOICE WOULD BE A PUNCH-DRUNK IRISH BOXER.
HEY! OH, COME ON...
GOTTA DATE TO KEEP, GUMSHOE.
YOU GUYS MAKE ME FEEL LIKE CHEAP LUGGAGE, YOU KNOW THAT? HOW'M I SUPPOSED TO GET ANY WORK DONE?
SHADDUP.
RIGHT, RIGHT. I LEARNED THAT ONE FROM QUINN'S BOYS EARLIER...
HE SAID SHADDUP.

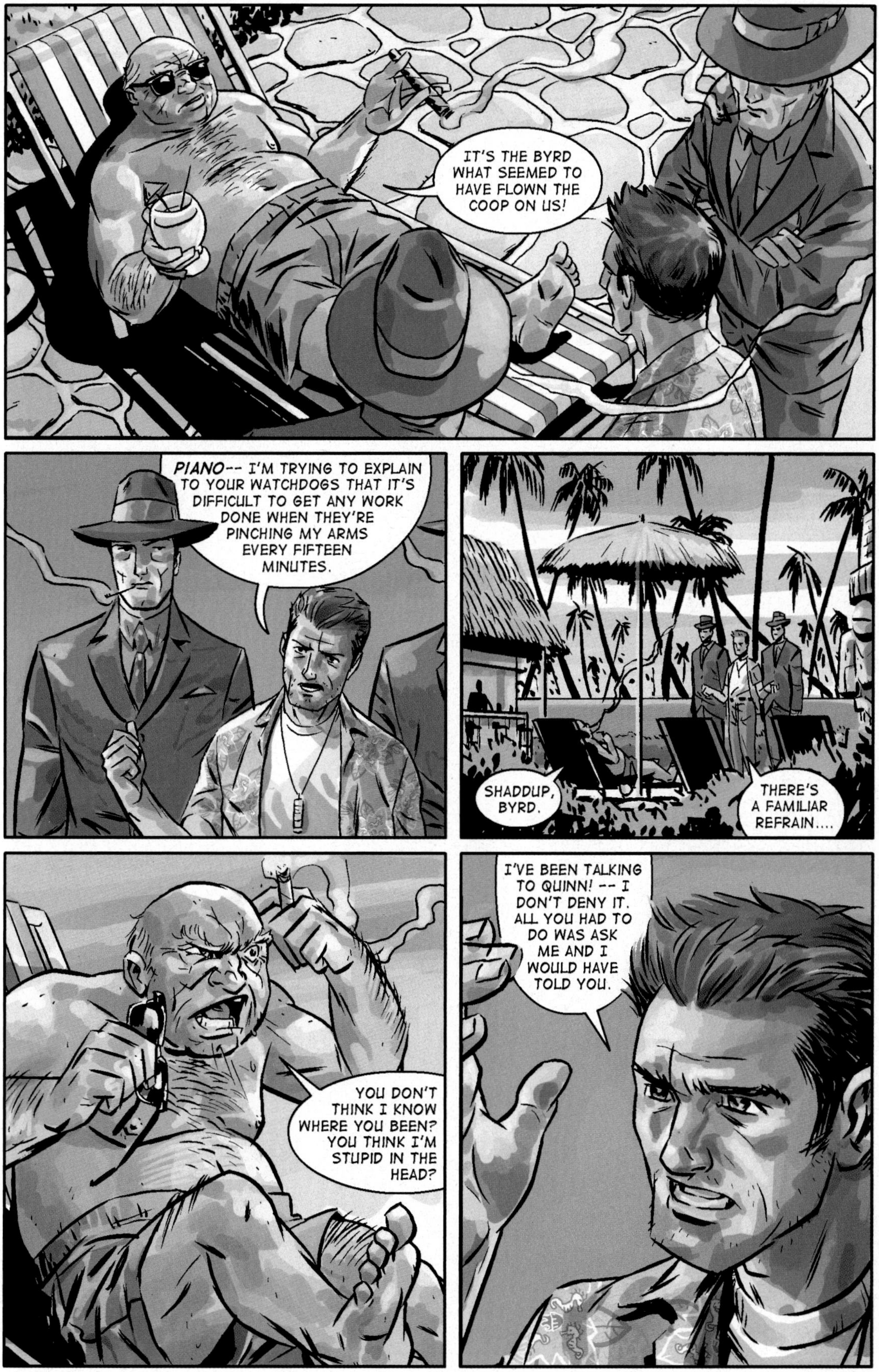
IT'S THE BYRD WHAT SEEMED TO HAVE FLOWN THE COOP ON US!
PIANO-- I'M TRYING TO EXPLAIN TO YOUR WATCHDOGS THAT IT'S DIFFICULT TO GET ANY WORK DONE WHEN THEY'RE PINCHING MY ARMS EVERY FIFTEEN MINUTES.
SHADDUP, BYRD.
THERE'S A FAMILIAR REFRAIN....
YOU DON'T THINK I KNOW WHERE YOU BEEN? YOU THINK I'M STUPID IN THE HEAD?
I'VE BEEN TALKING TO QUINN! -- I DON'T DENY IT. ALL YOU HAD TO DO WAS ASK ME AND I WOULD HAVE TOLD YOU.

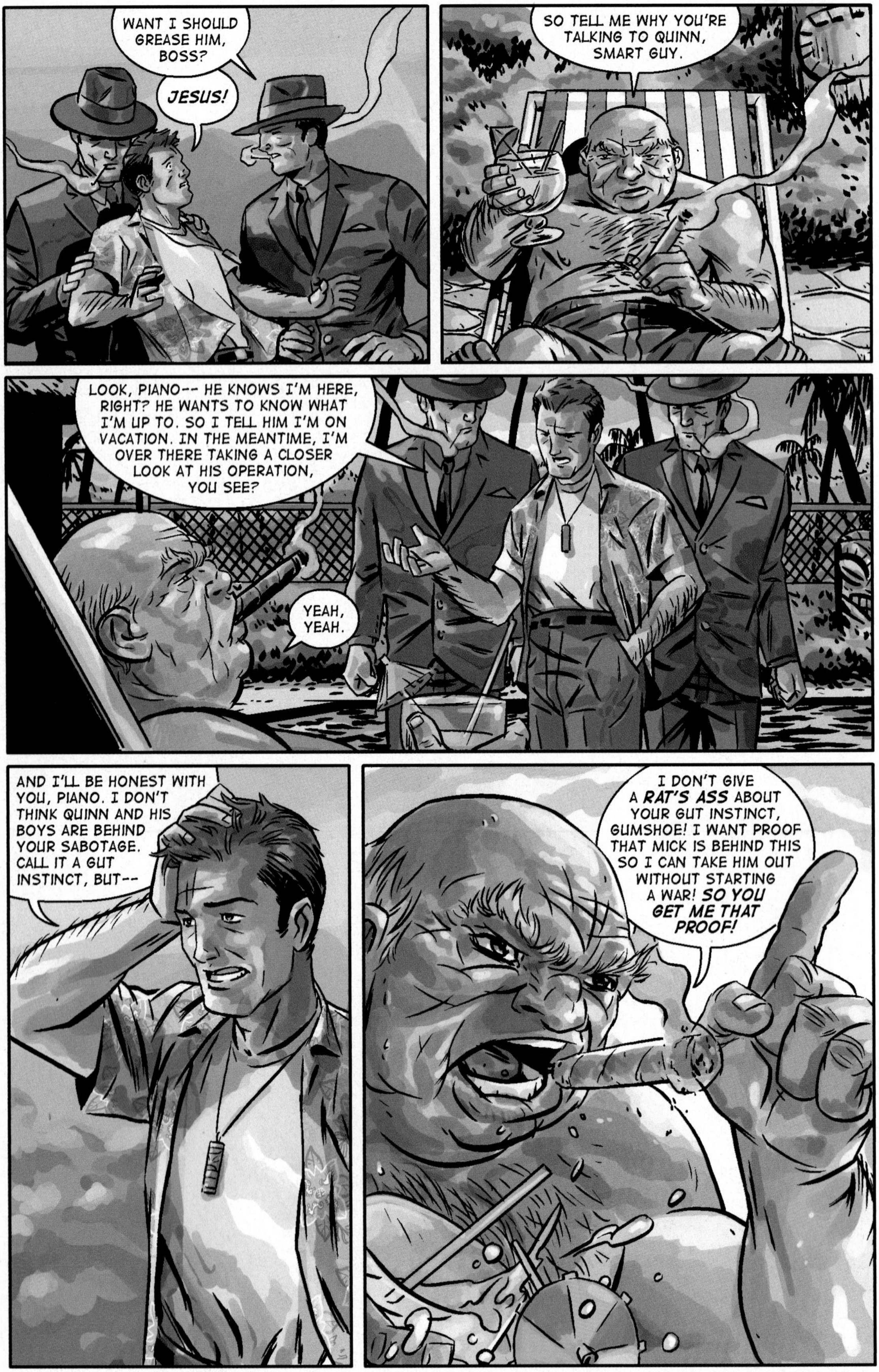
WANT I SHOULD GREASE HIM, BOSS?
JESUS!
SO TELL ME WHY YOU'RE TALKING TO QUINN, SMART GUY.
LOOK, PIANO-- HE KNOWS I'M HERE, RIGHT? HE WANTS TO KNOW WHAT I'M UP TO. SO I TELL HIM I'M ON VACATION. IN THE MEANTIME, I'M OVER THERE TAKING A CLOSER LOOK AT HIS OPERATION, YOU SEE?
YEAH, YEAH.
AND I'LL BE HONEST WITH YOU, PIANO. I DON'T THINK QUINN AND HIS BOYS ARE BEHIND YOUR SABOTAGE. CALL IT A GUT INSTINCT, BUT--
I DON'T GIVE A RAT'S ASS ABOUT YOUR GUT INSTINCT, GUMSHOE! I WANT PROOF THAT MICK IS BEHIND THIS SO I CAN TAKE HIM OUT WITHOUT STARTING A WAR! SO YOU GET ME THAT PROOF!

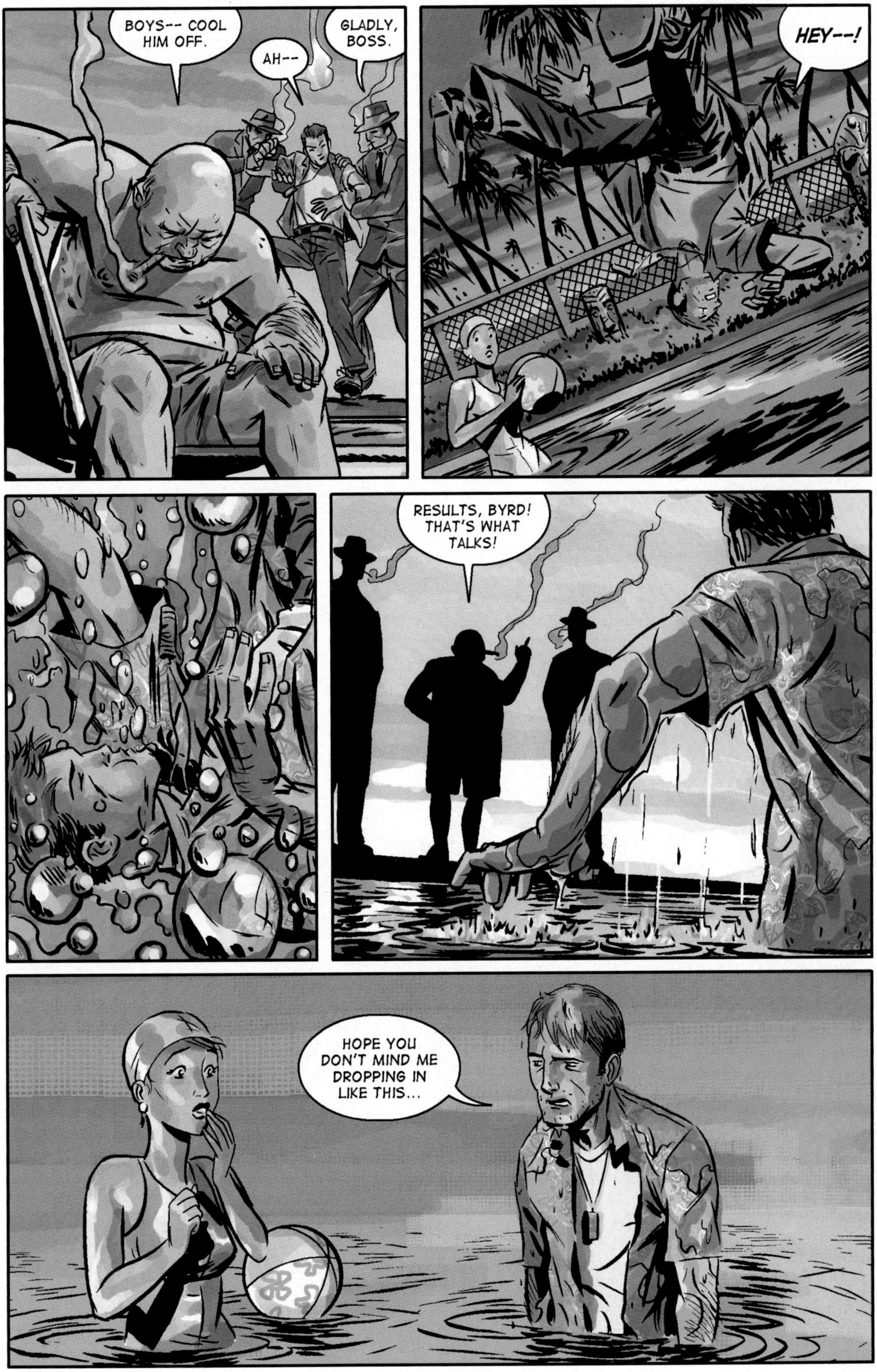
BOYS-- COOL HIM OFF.
AH--
GLADLY, BOSS.
HEY--!
RESULTS, BYRD! THAT'S WHAT TALKS!
HOPE YOU DON'T MIND ME DROPPING IN LIKE THIS...

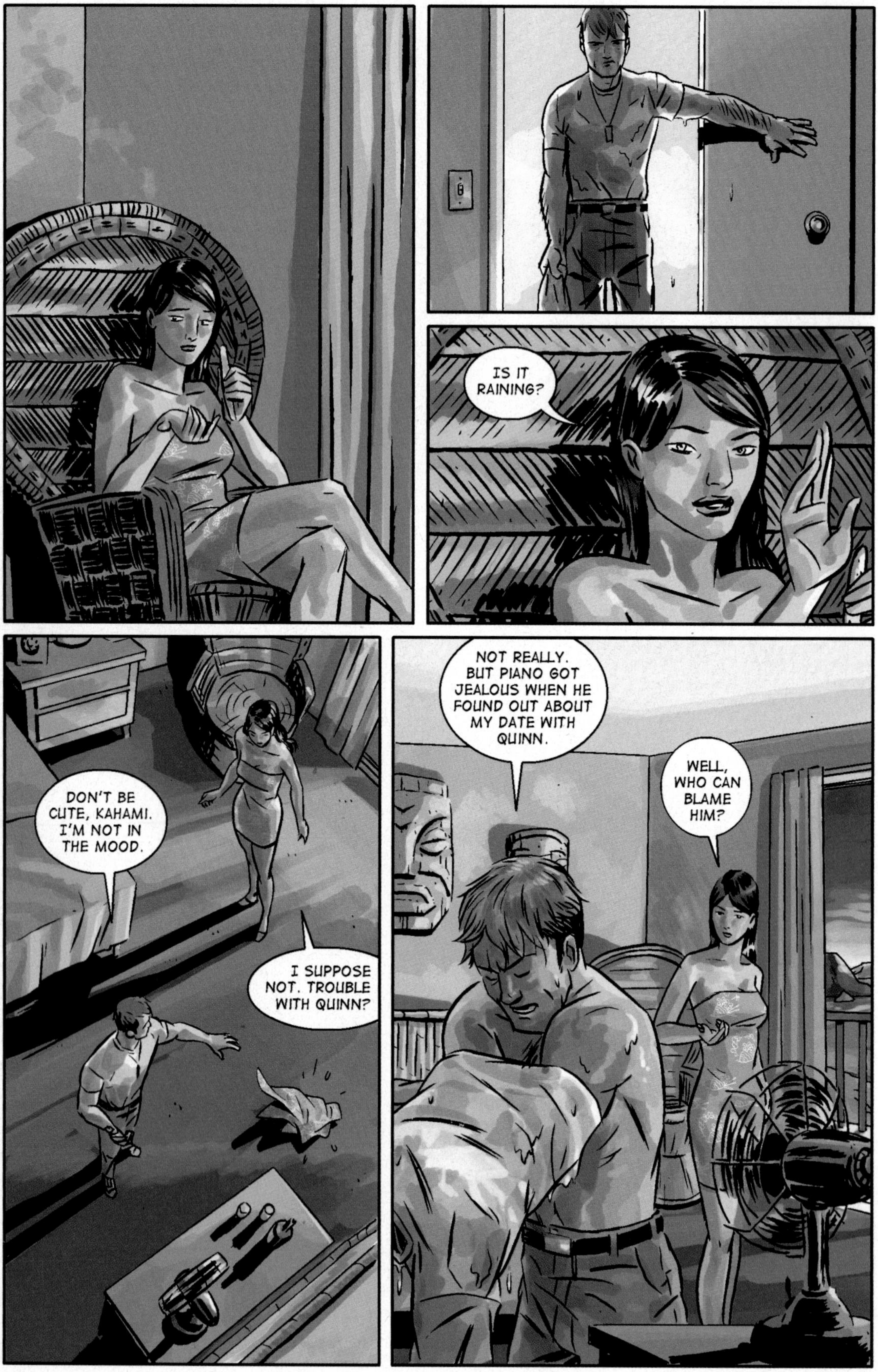
IS IT RAINING?
DON'T BE CUTE, KAHAMI. I'M NOT IN THE MOOD.
I SUPPOSE NOT. TROUBLE WITH QUINN?
NOT REALLY. BUT PIANO GOT JEALOUS WHEN HE FOUND OUT ABOUT MY DATE WITH QUINN.
WELL, WHO CAN BLAME HIM?

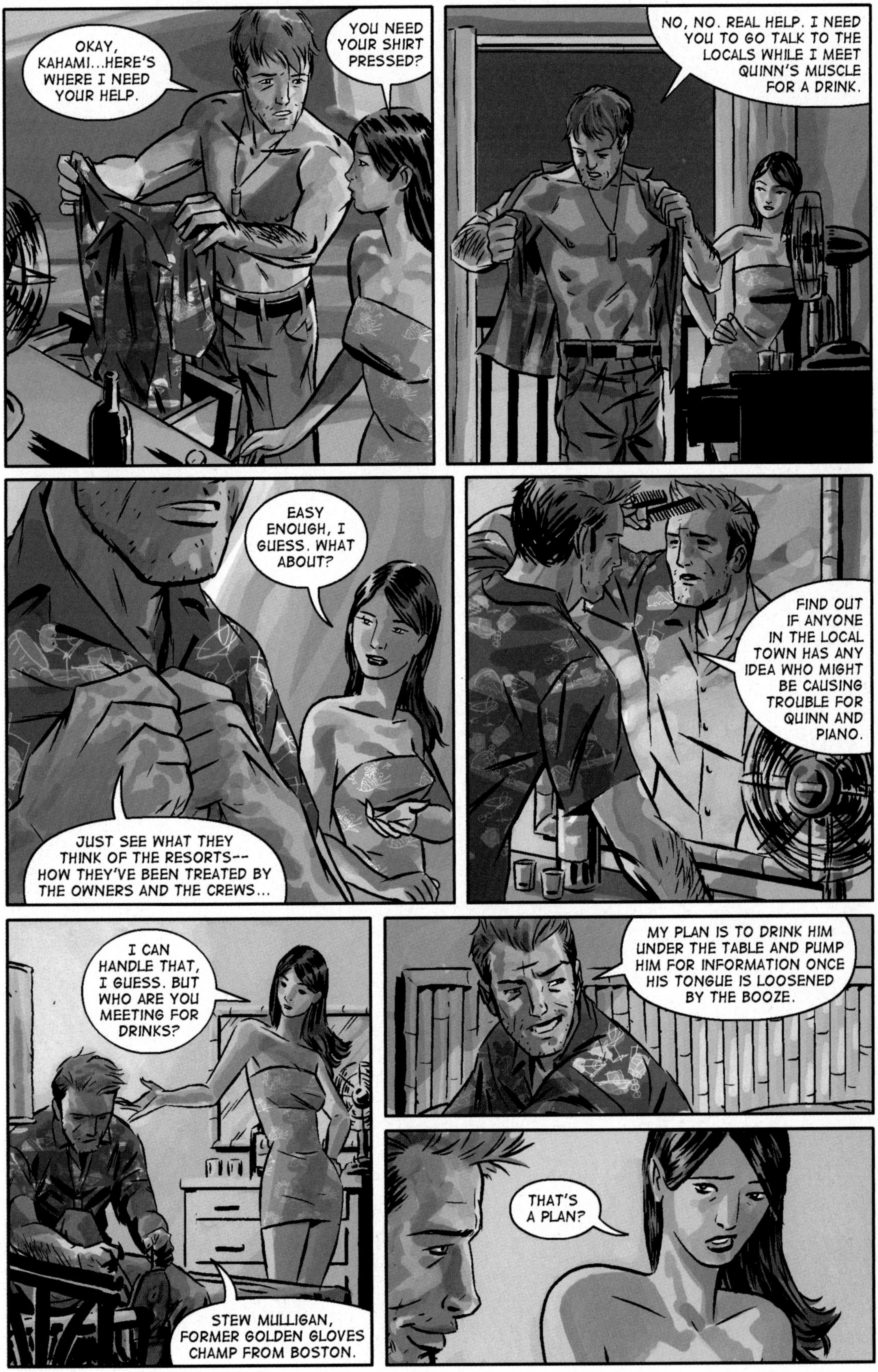
OKAY, KAHAMI...HERE'S WHERE I NEED YOUR HELP.
YOU NEED YOUR SHIRT PRESSED?
NO, NO. REAL HELP. I NEED YOU TO GO TALK TO THE LOCALS WHILE I MEET QUINN'S MUSCLE FOR A DRINK.
EASY ENOUGH, I GUESS. WHAT ABOUT?
JUST SEE WHAT THEY THINK OF THE RESORTS-- HOW THEY'VE BEEN TREATED BY THE OWNERS AND THE CREWS...
FIND OUT IF ANYONE IN THE LOCAL TOWN HAS ANY IDEA WHO MIGHT BE CAUSING TROUBLE FOR QUINN AND PIANO.
I CAN HANDLE THAT, I GUESS. BUT WHO ARE YOU MEETING FOR DRINKS?
STEW MULLIGAN, FORMER GOLDEN GLOVES CHAMP FROM BOSTON.
MY PLAN IS TO DRINK HIM UNDER THE TABLE AND PUMP HIM FOR INFORMATION ONCE HIS TONGUE IS LOOSENED BY THE BOOZE.
THAT'S A PLAN?

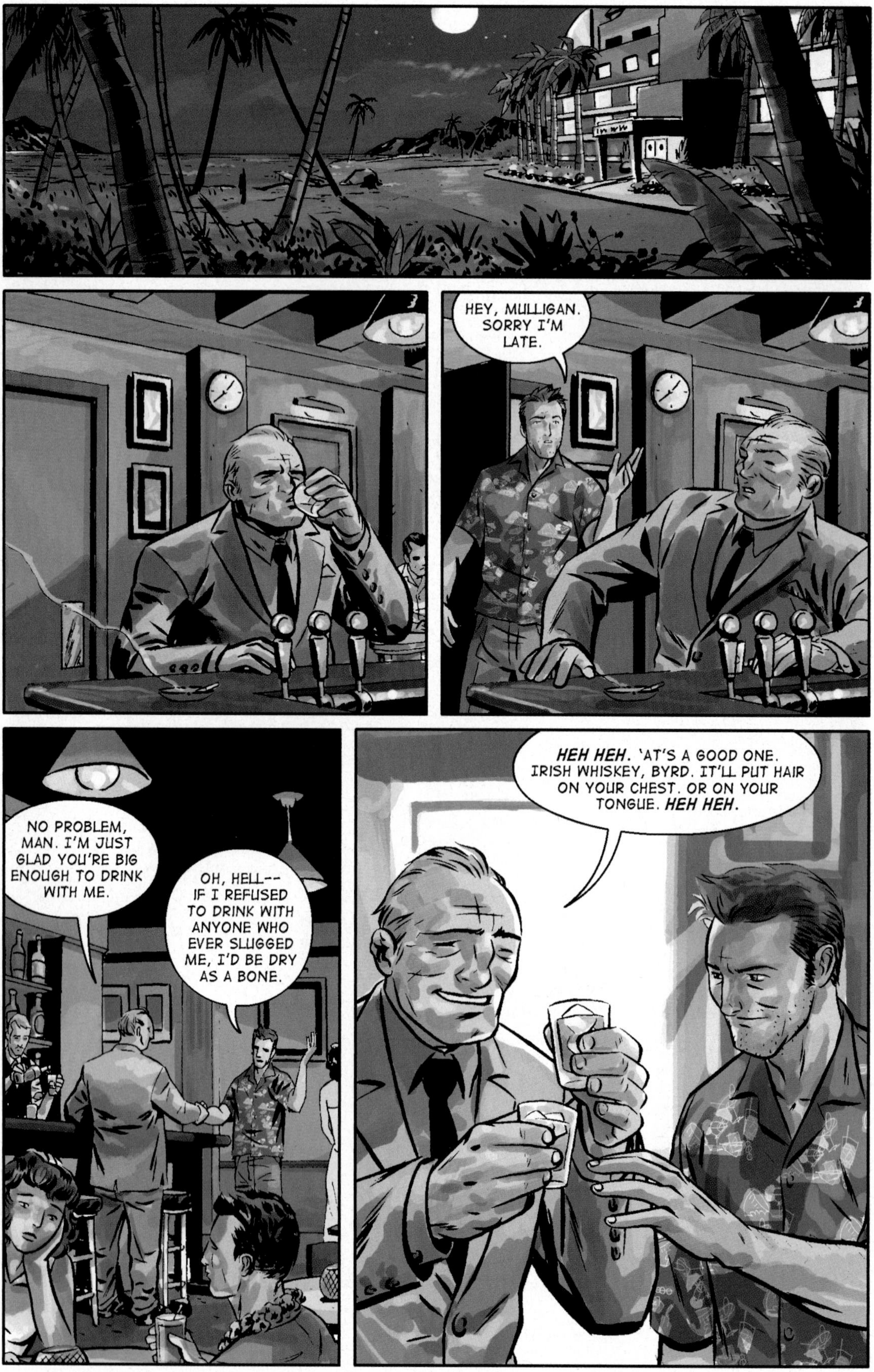
HEY, MULLIGAN. SORRY I'M LATE.
NO PROBLEM, MAN. I'M JUST GLAD YOU'RE BIG ENOUGH TO DRINK WITH ME.
OH, HELL-- IF I REFUSED TO DRINK WITH ANYONE WHO EVER SLUGGED ME, I'D BE DRY AS A BONE.
HEH HEH. 'AT'S A GOOD ONE. IRISH WHISKEY, BYRD. IT'LL PUT HAIR ON YOUR CHEST. OR ON YOUR TONGUE. HEH HEH.

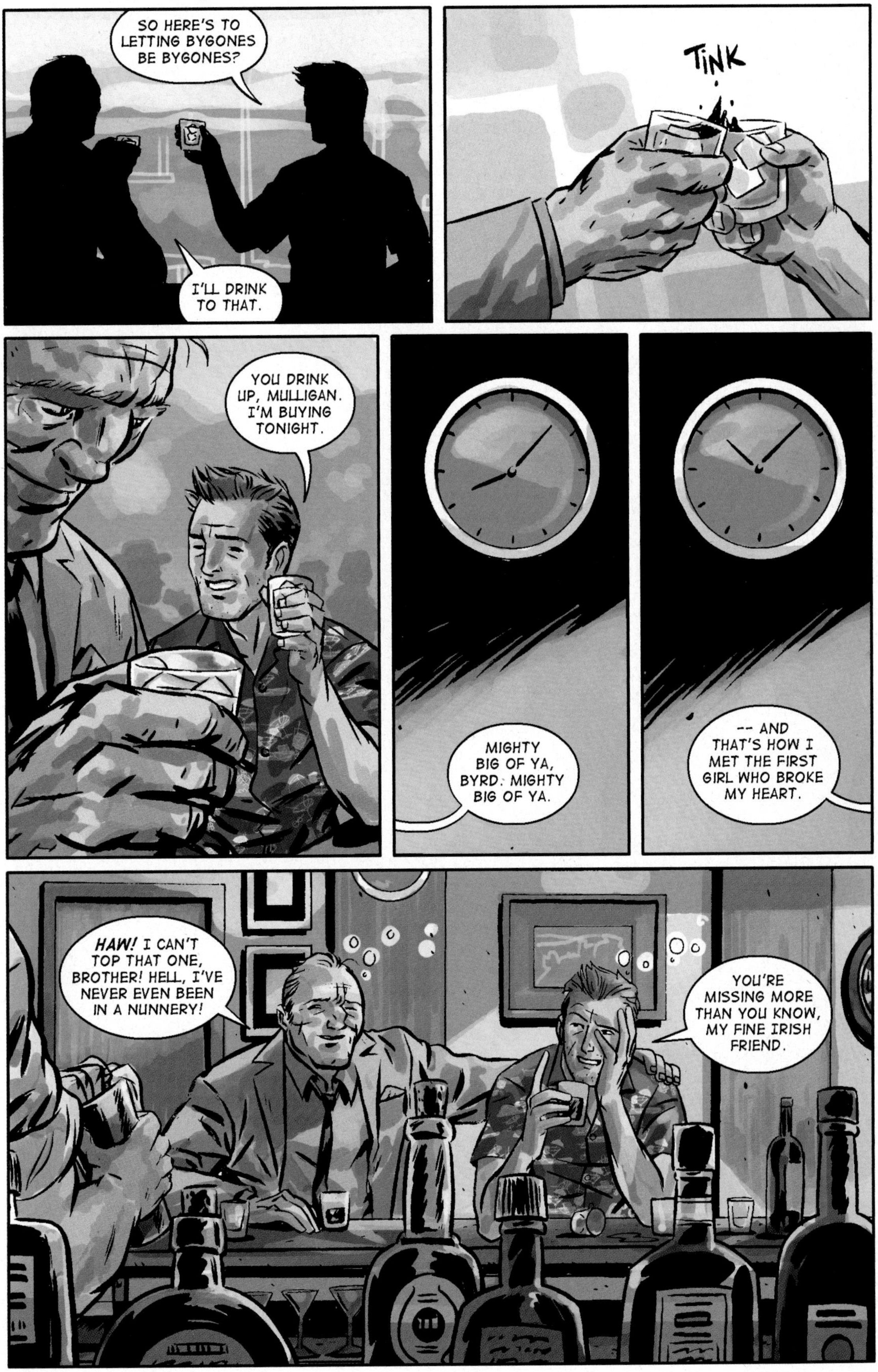
SO HERE'S TO LETTING BYGONES BE BYGONES?
I'LL DRINK TO THAT.
TINK
YOU DRINK UP, MULLIGAN. I'M BUYING TONIGHT.
MIGHTY BIG OF YA, BYRD. MIGHTY BIG OF YA.
-- AND THAT'S HOW I MET THE FIRST GIRL WHO BROKE MY HEART.
HAW! I CAN'T TOP THAT ONE, BROTHER! HELL, I'VE NEVER EVEN BEEN IN A NUNNERY!
YOU'RE MISSING MORE THAN YOU KNOW, MY FINE IRISH FRIEND.

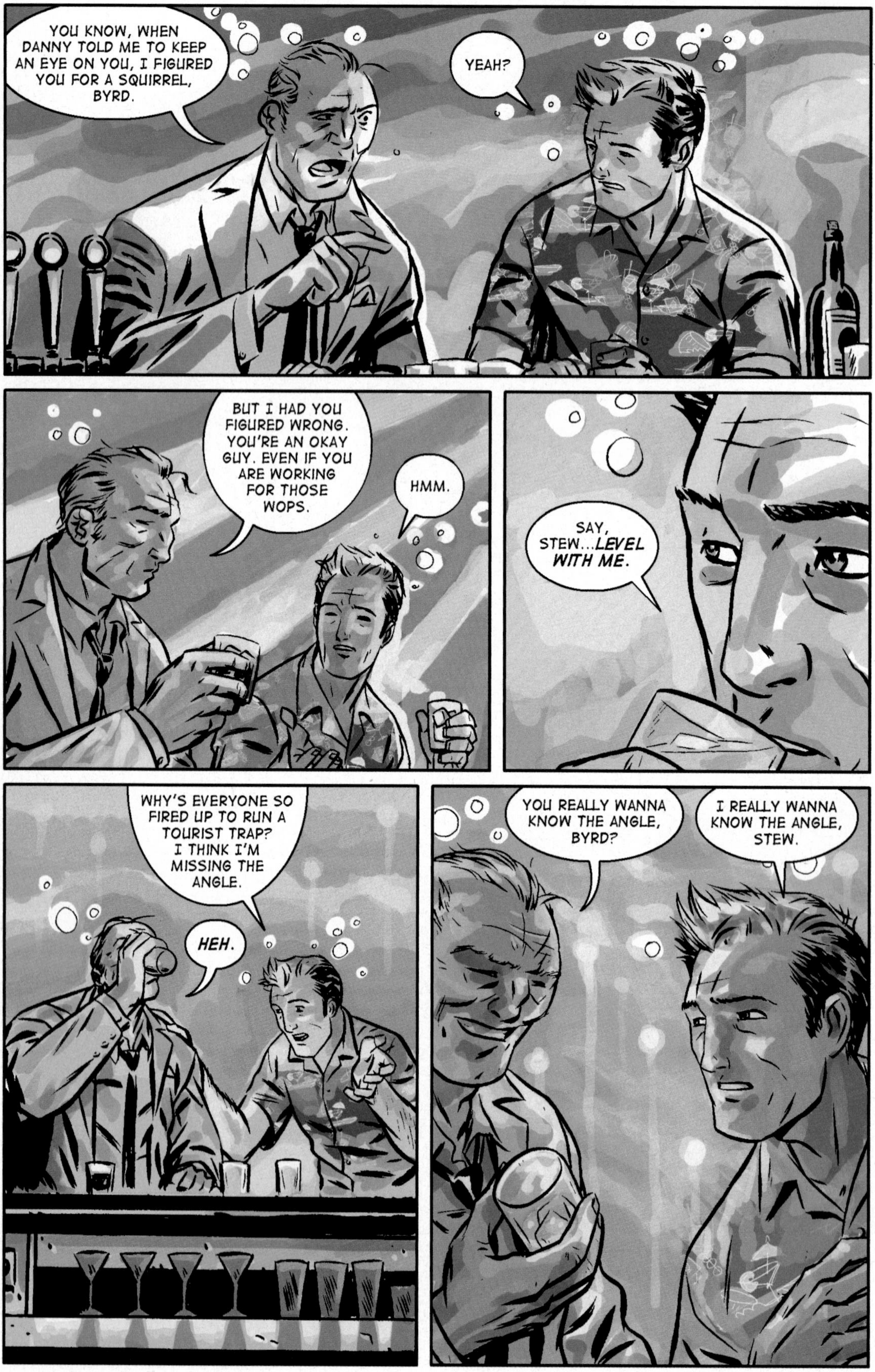
YOU KNOW, WHEN DANNY TOLD ME TO KEEP AN EYE ON YOU, I FIGURED YOU FOR A SQUIRREL, BYRD.
YEAH?
BUT I HAD YOU FIGURED WRONG. YOU'RE AN OKAY GUY. EVEN IF YOU ARE WORKING FOR THOSE WOPS.
HMM.
SAY, STEW...LEVEL WITH ME.
WHY'S EVERYONE SO FIRED UP TO RUN A TOURIST TRAP? I THINK I'M MISSING THE ANGLE.
HEH.
YOU REALLY WANNA KNOW THE ANGLE, BYRD?
I REALLY WANNA KNOW THE ANGLE, STEW.

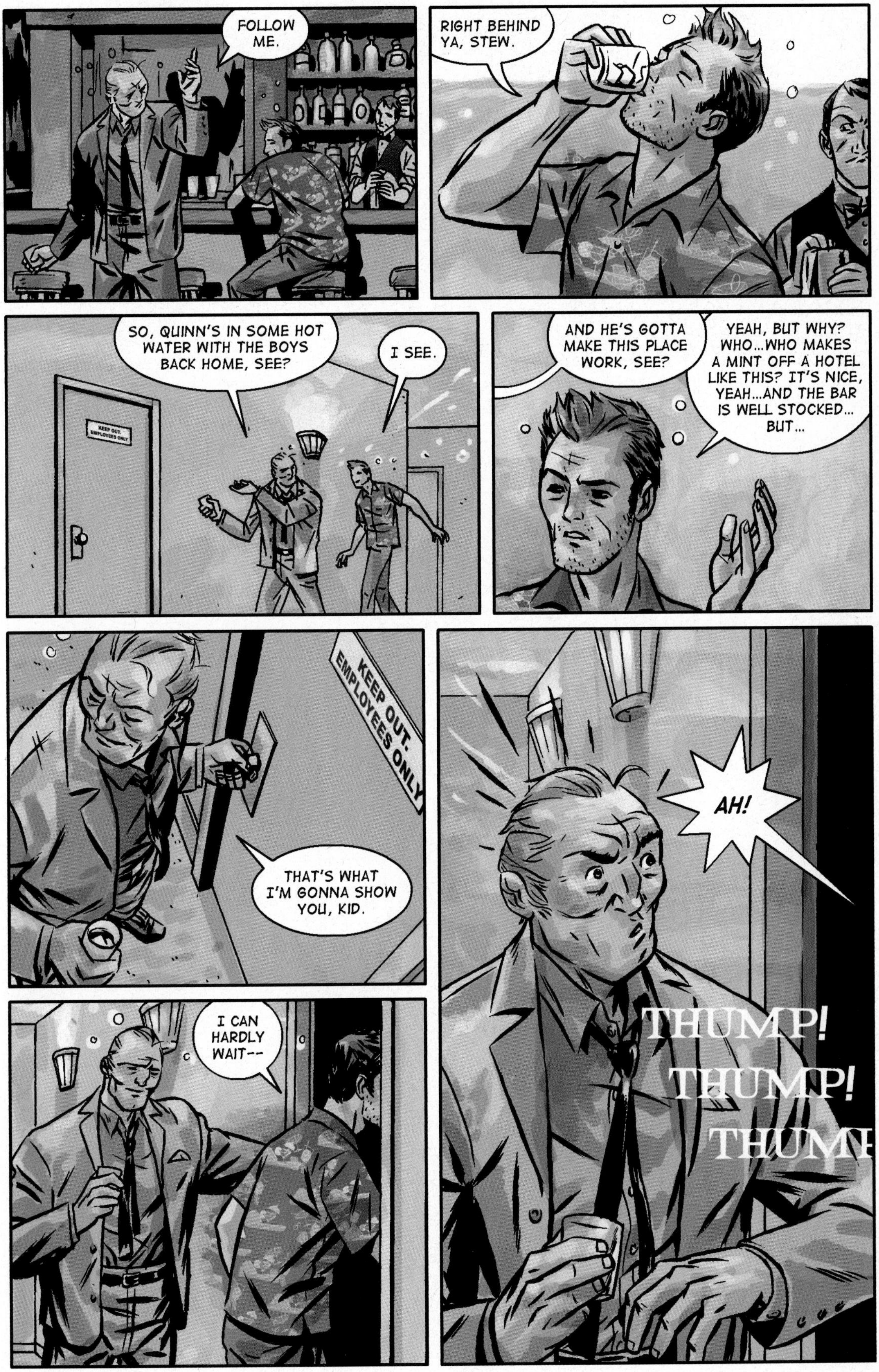
FOLLOW ME.
RIGHT BEHIND YA, STEW.
SO, QUINN'S IN SOME HOT WATER WITH THE BOYS BACK HOME, SEE?
I SEE.
KEEP OUT. EMPLOYEES ONLY
AND HE'S GOTTA MAKE THIS PLACE WORK, SEE?
YEAH, BUT WHY? WHO...WHO MAKES A MINT OFF A HOTEL LIKE THIS? IT'S NICE, YEAH...AND THE BAR IS WELL STOCKED... BUT...
KEEP OUT. EMPLOYEES ONLY
THAT'S WHAT I'M GONNA SHOW YOU, KID.
I CAN HARDLY WAIT--
AH!
THUMP!
THUMP!

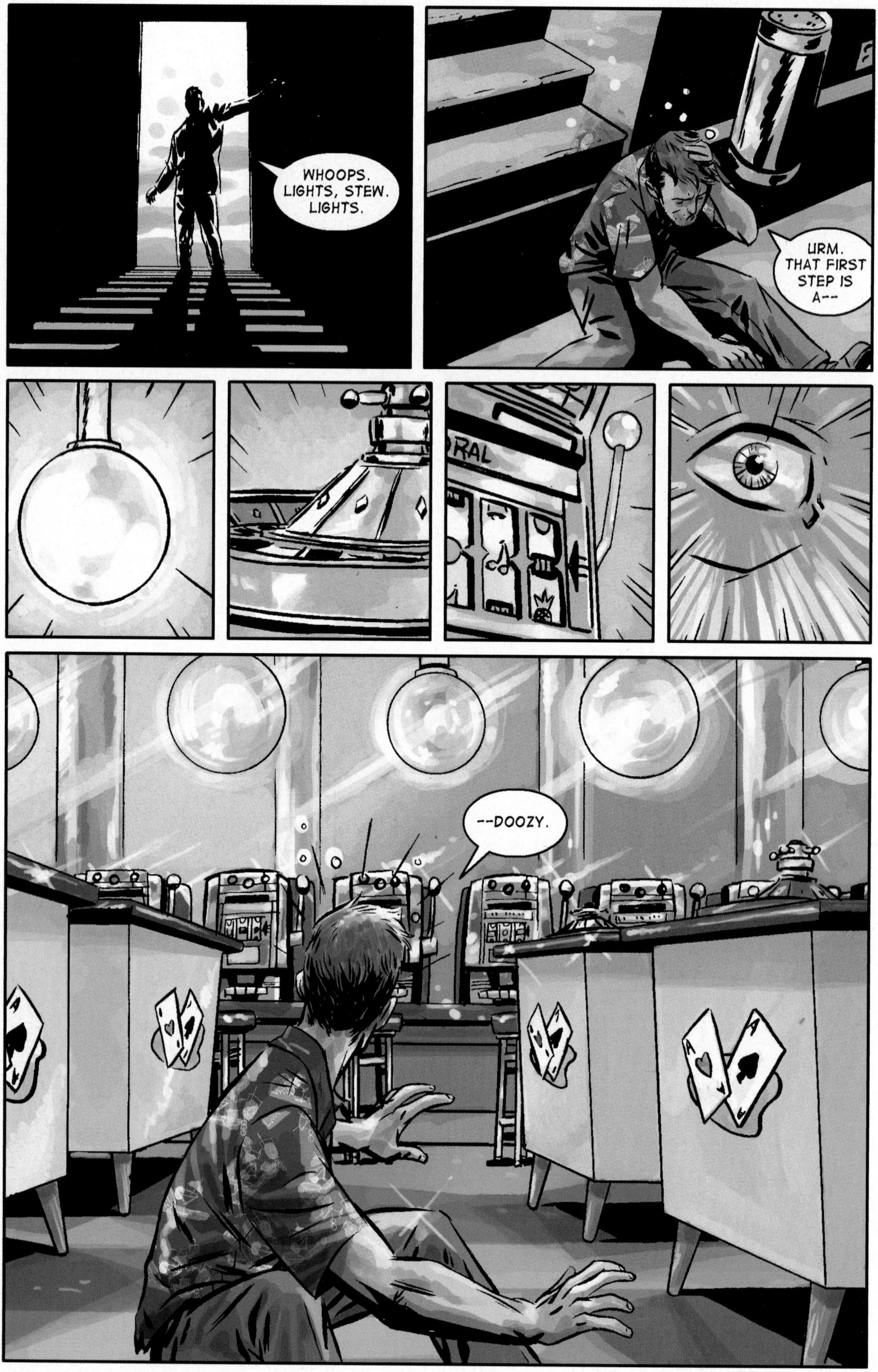
WHOOPS. LIGHTS, STEW. LIGHTS.
URM. THAT FIRST STEP IS A--
RAL
--DOOZY.

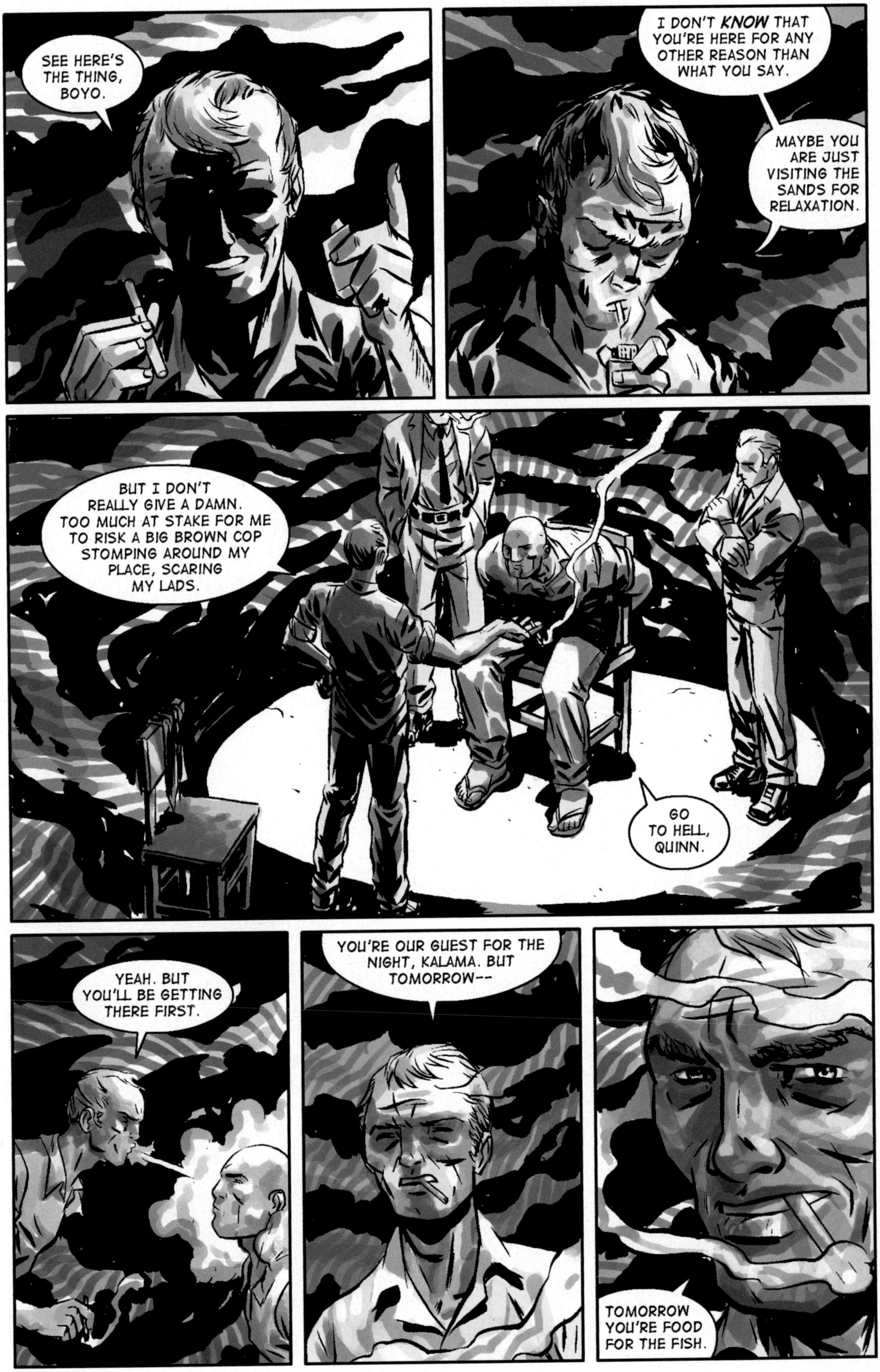
SEE HERE'S THE THING, BOYO.
I DON'T KNOW THAT YOU'RE HERE FOR ANY OTHER REASON THAN WHAT YOU SAY.
MAYBE YOU ARE JUST VISITING THE SANDS FOR RELAXATION.
BUT I DON'T REALLY GIVE A DAMN. TOO MUCH AT STAKE FOR ME TO RISK A BIG BROWN COP STOMPING AROUND MY PLACE, SCARING MY LADS.
GO TO HELL, QUINN.
YEAH. BUT YOU'LL BE GETTING THERE FIRST.
YOU'RE OUR GUEST FOR THE NIGHT, KALAMA. BUT TOMORROW--
TOMORROW YOU'RE FOOD FOR THE FISH.

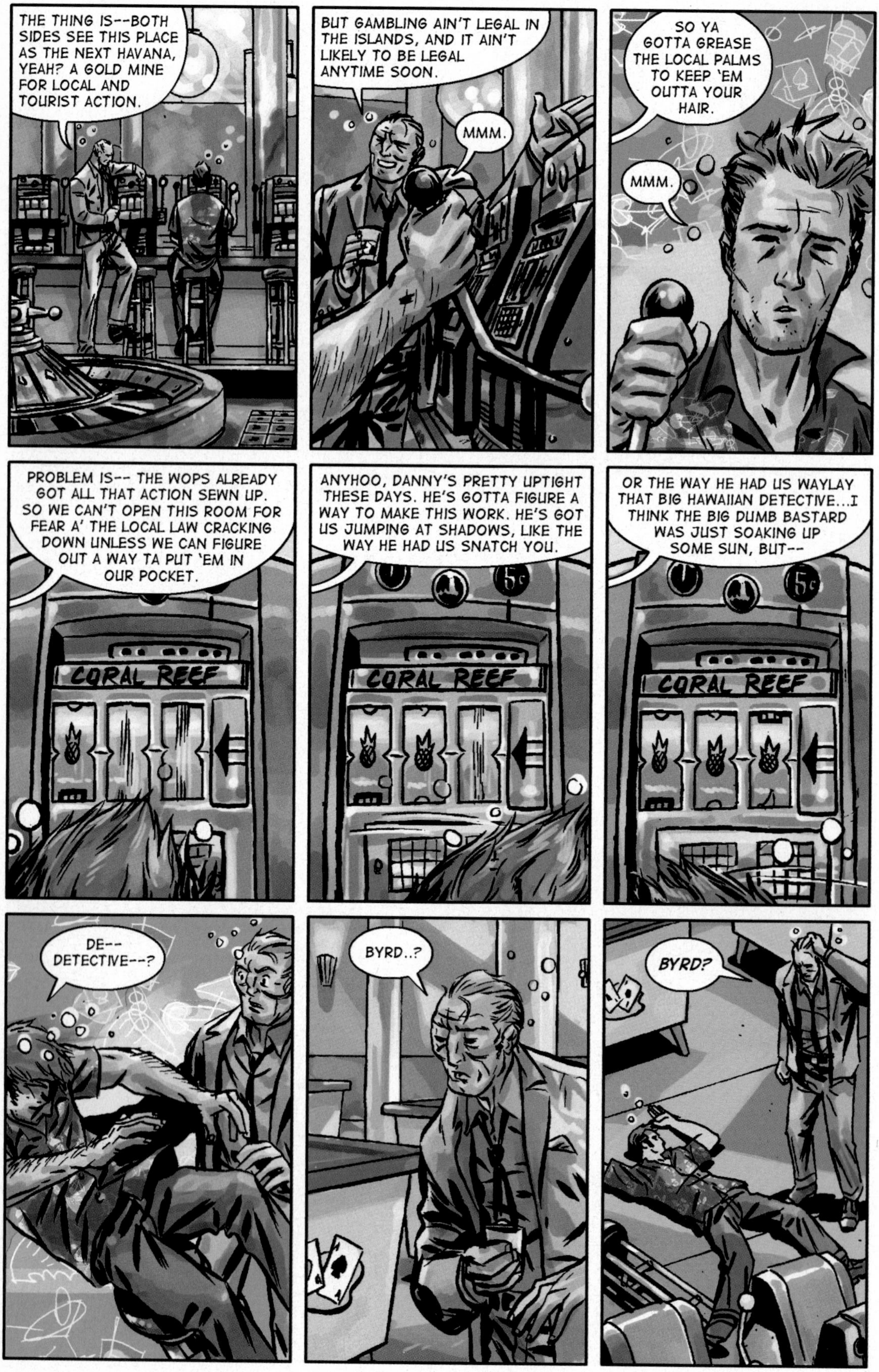
THE THING IS--BOTH SIDES SEE THIS PLACE AS THE NEXT HAVANA, YEAH? A GOLD MINE FOR LOCAL AND TOURIST ACTION.
BUT GAMBLING AIN'T LEGAL IN THE ISLANDS, AND IT AIN'T LIKELY TO BE LEGAL ANYTIME SOON.
MMM.
SO YA GOTTA GREASE THE LOCAL PALMS TO KEEP 'EM OUTTA YOUR HAIR.
MMM.
PROBLEM IS-- THE WOPS ALREADY GOT ALL THAT ACTION SEWN UP. SO WE CAN'T OPEN THIS ROOM FOR FEAR A' THE LOCAL LAW CRACKING DOWN UNLESS WE CAN FIGURE OUT A WAY TA PUT 'EM IN OUR POCKET.
CORAL REEF
ANYHOO, DANNY'S PRETTY UPTIGHT THESE DAYS. HE'S GOTTA FIGURE A WAY TO MAKE THIS WORK. HE'S GOT US JUMPING AT SHADOWS, LIKE THE WAY HE HAD US SNATCH YOU.
CORAL REEF
OR THE WAY HE HAD US WAYLAY THAT BIG HAWAIIAN DETECTIVE...I THINK THE BIG DUMB BASTARD WAS JUST SOAKING UP SOME SUN, BUT--
CORAL REEF
DE-- DETECTIVE--?
BYRD..?
BYRD?

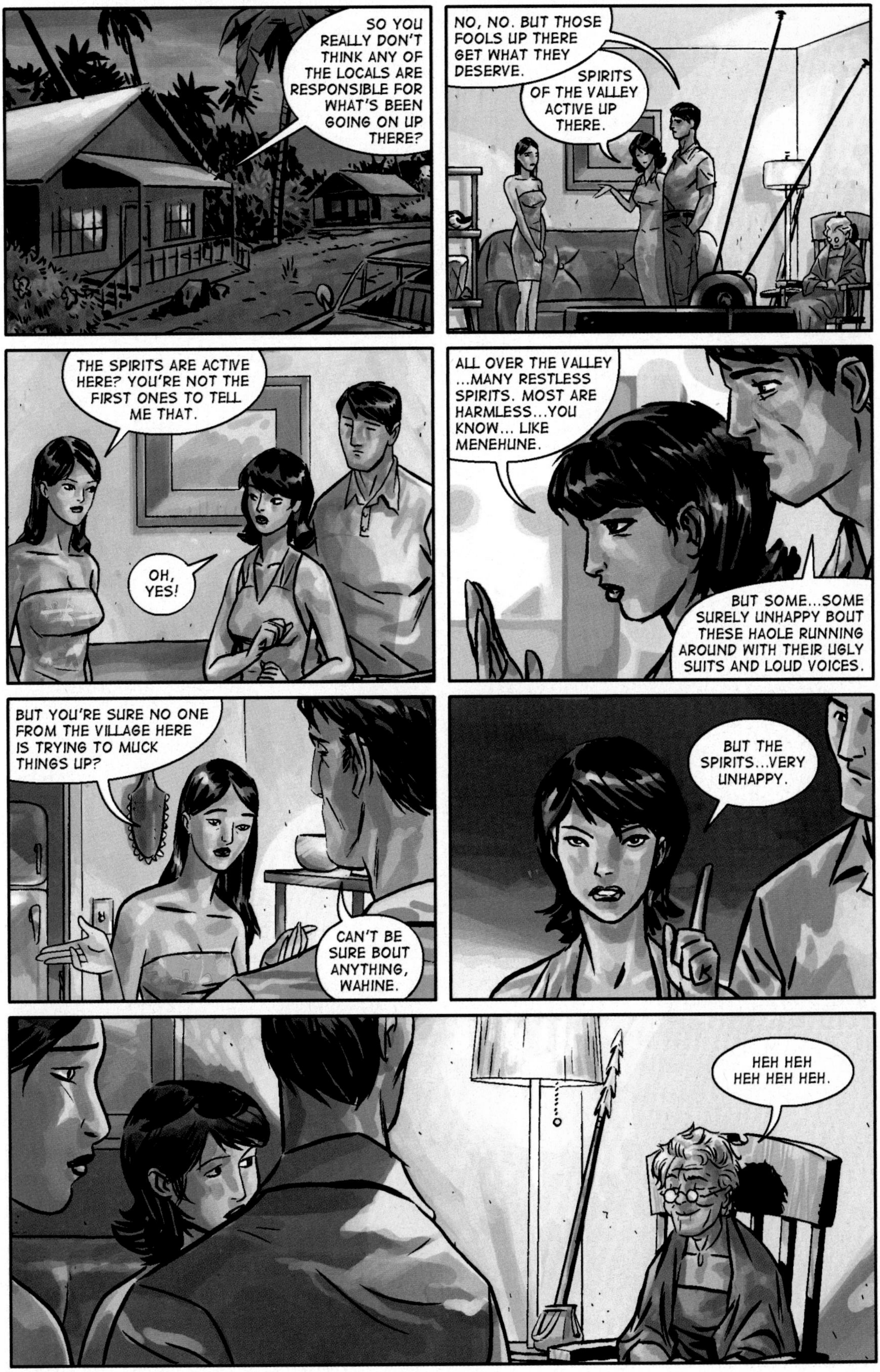

SO YOU REALLY DON'T THINK ANY OF THE LOCALS ARE RESPONSIBLE FOR WHAT'S BEEN GOING ON UP THERE?
NO, NO. BUT THOSE FOOLS UP THERE GET WHAT THEY DESERVE.
SPIRITS OF THE VALLEY ACTIVE UP THERE.
THE SPIRITS ARE ACTIVE HERE? YOU'RE NOT THE FIRST ONES TO TELL ME THAT.
OH, YES!
ALL OVER THE VALLEY ...MANY RESTLESS SPIRITS. MOST ARE HARMLESS...YOU KNOW... LIKE MENEHUNE.
BUT SOME...SOME SURELY UNHAPPY BOUT THESE HAOLE RUNNING AROUND WITH THEIR UGLY SUITS AND LOUD VOICES.
BUT YOU'RE SURE NO ONE FROM THE VILLAGE HERE IS TRYING TO MUCK THINGS UP?
CAN'T BE SURE BOUT ANYTHING, WAHINE.
BUT THE SPIRITS...VERY UNHAPPY.
HEH HEH HEH HEH HEH.

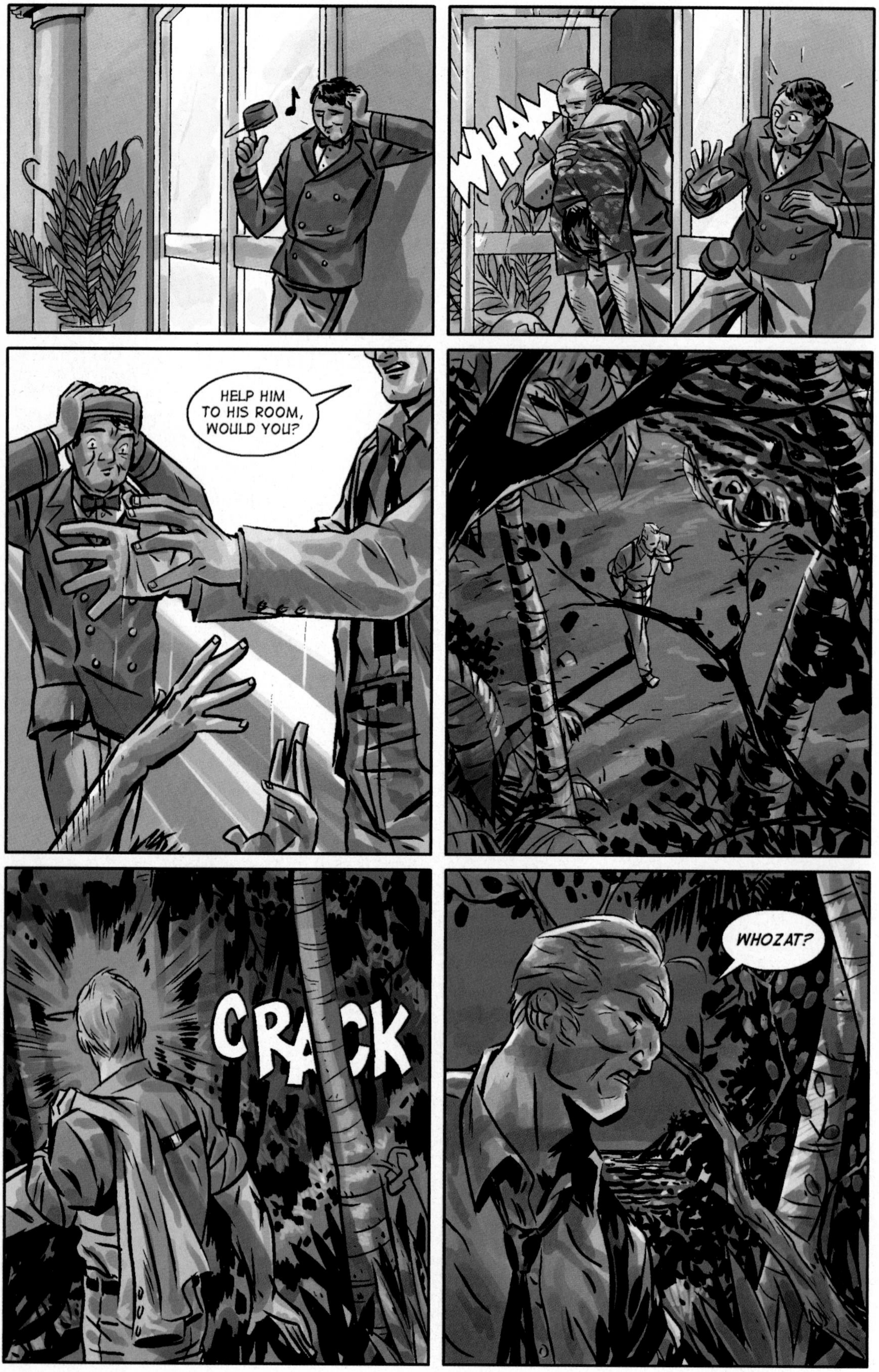
WHAM
HELP HIM TO HIS ROOM, WOULD YOU?
CRACK
WHOZAT?

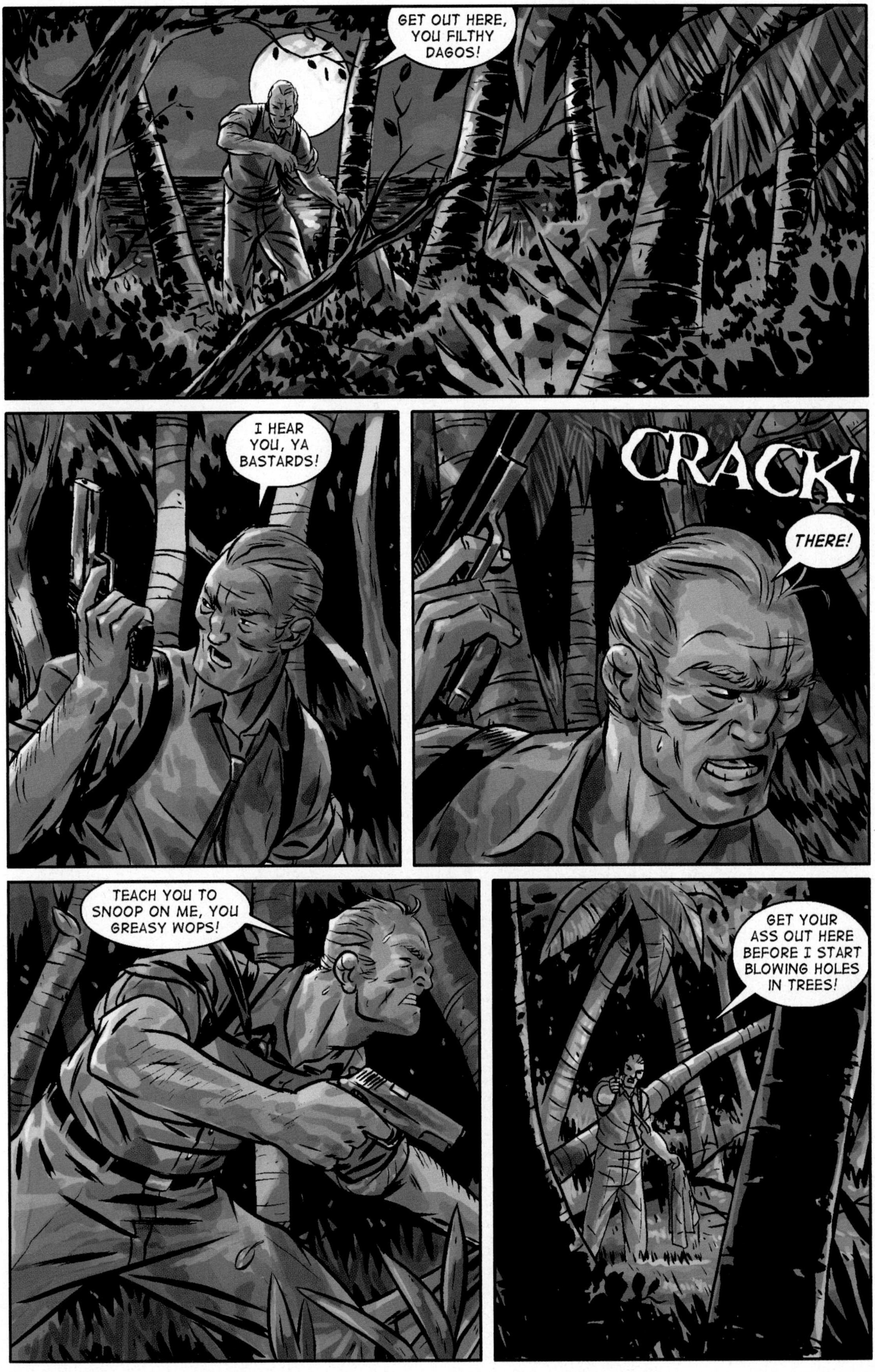
GET OUT HERE, YOU FILTHY DAGOS!
I HEAR YOU, YA BASTARDS!
CRACK!
THERE!
TEACH YOU TO SNOOP ON ME, YOU GREASY WOPS!
GET YOUR ASS OUT HERE BEFORE I START BLOWING HOLES IN TREES!

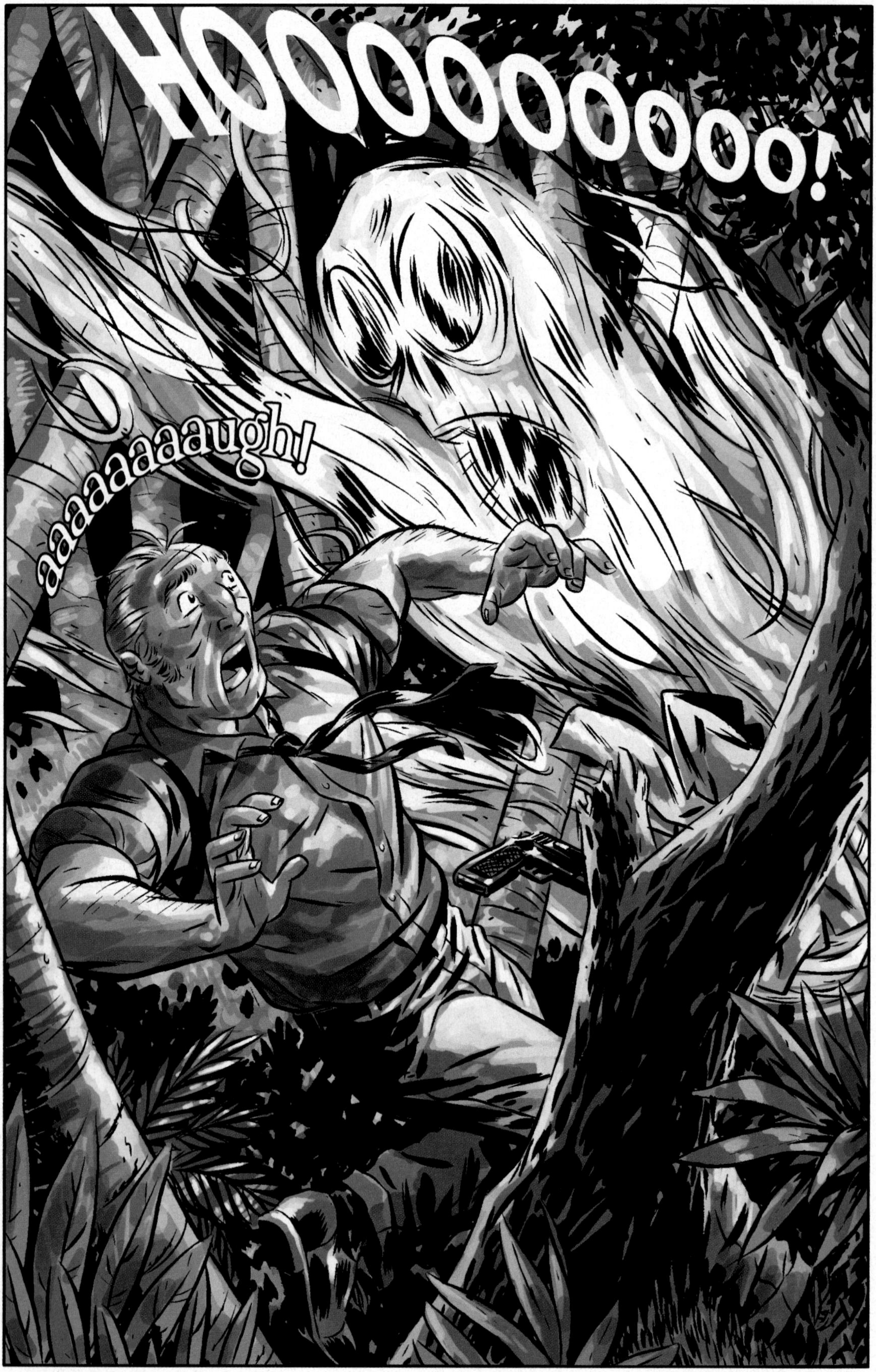
HOOOOOOOOOO!
aaaaaaaaaaugh!

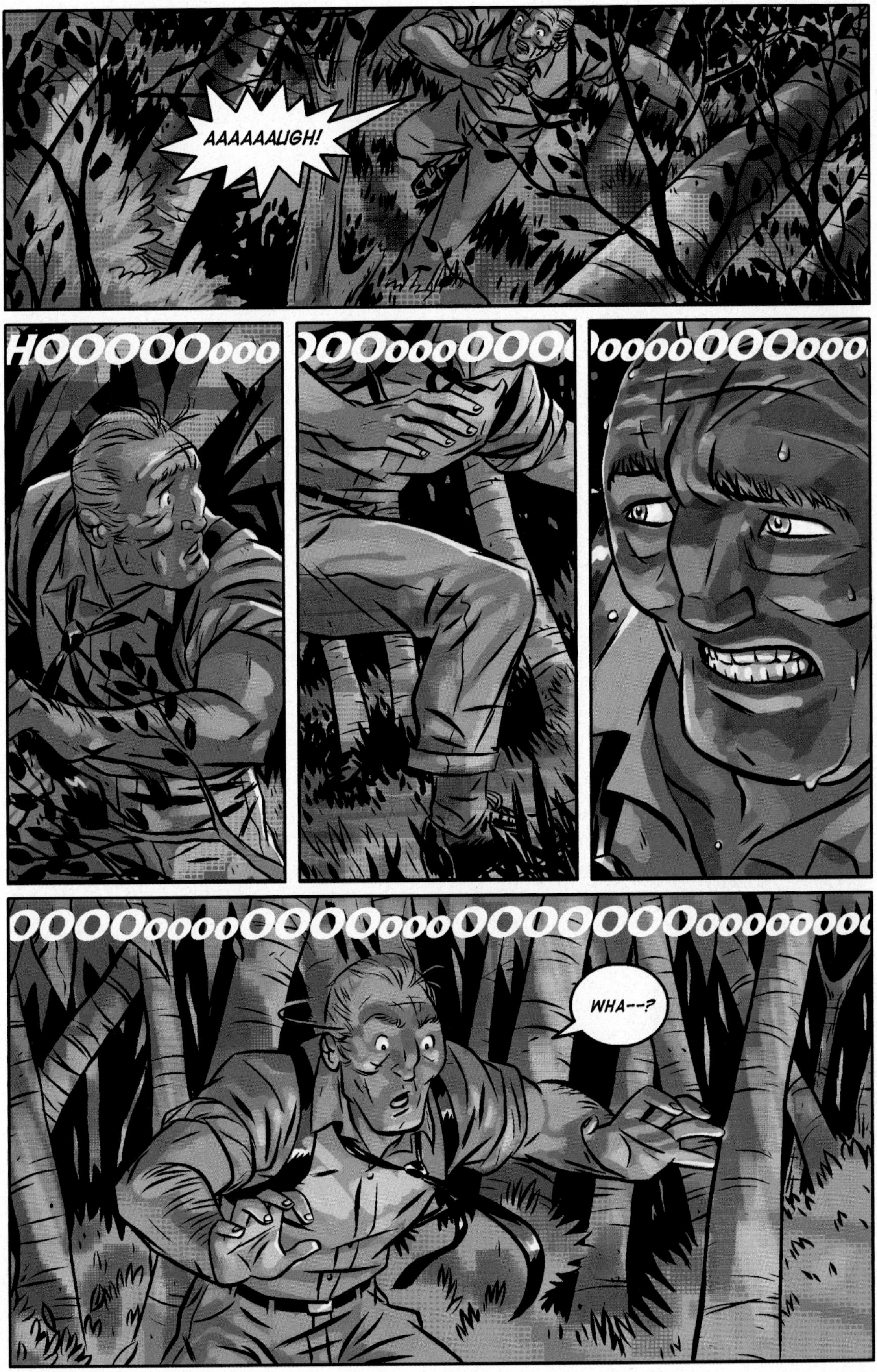
AAAAAAUGH!
HOOOOOooo
OOOoooOOOO
ooooOOOooo
OOOOooooOOOOoooOOOOOOOOooooooooo
WHA--?

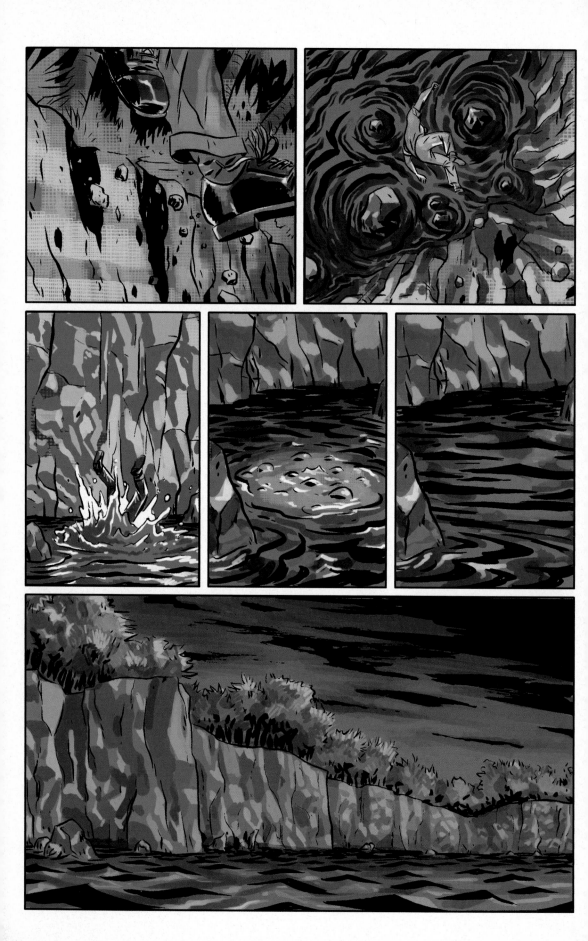

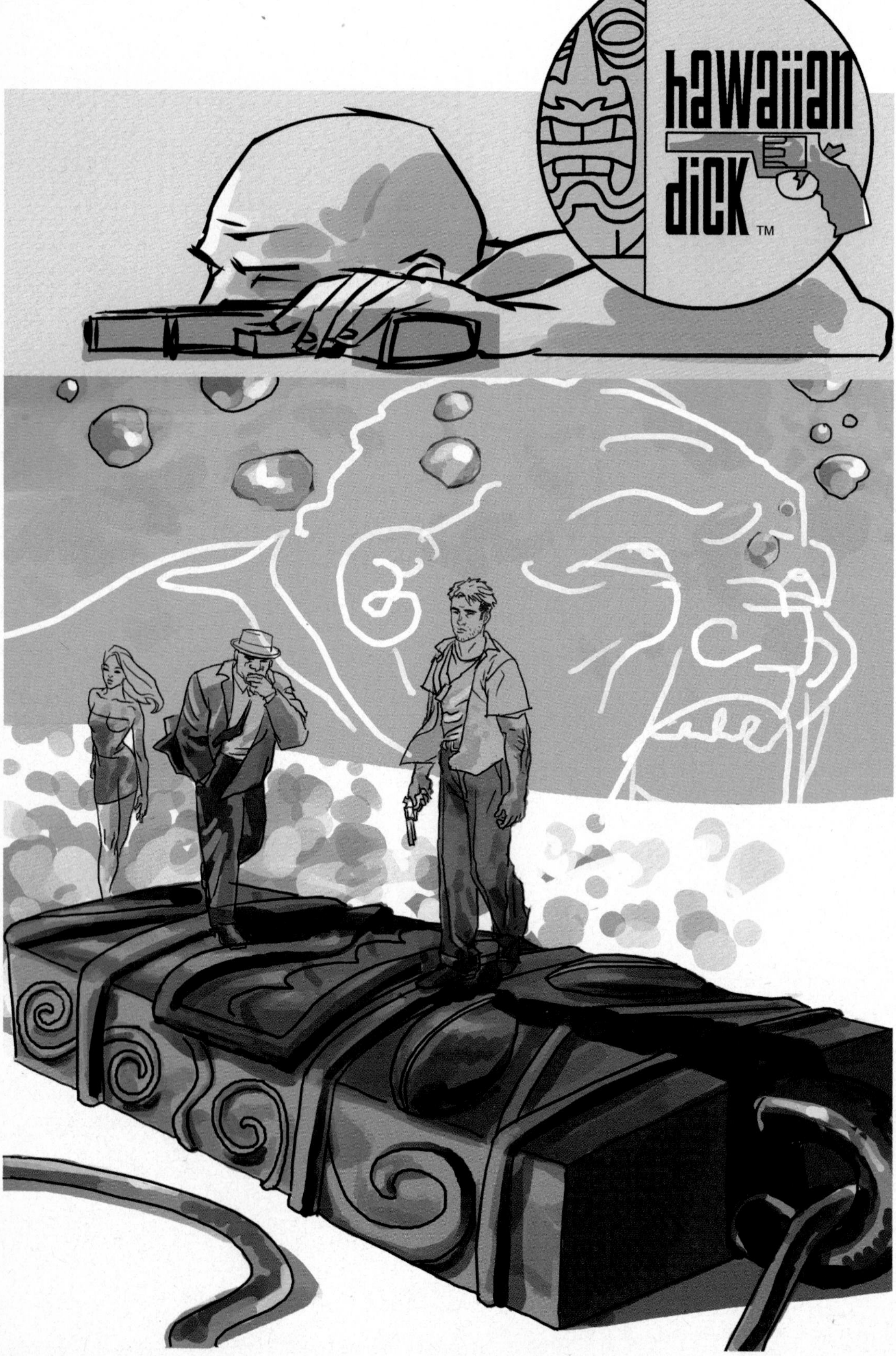
hawaiian dick TM

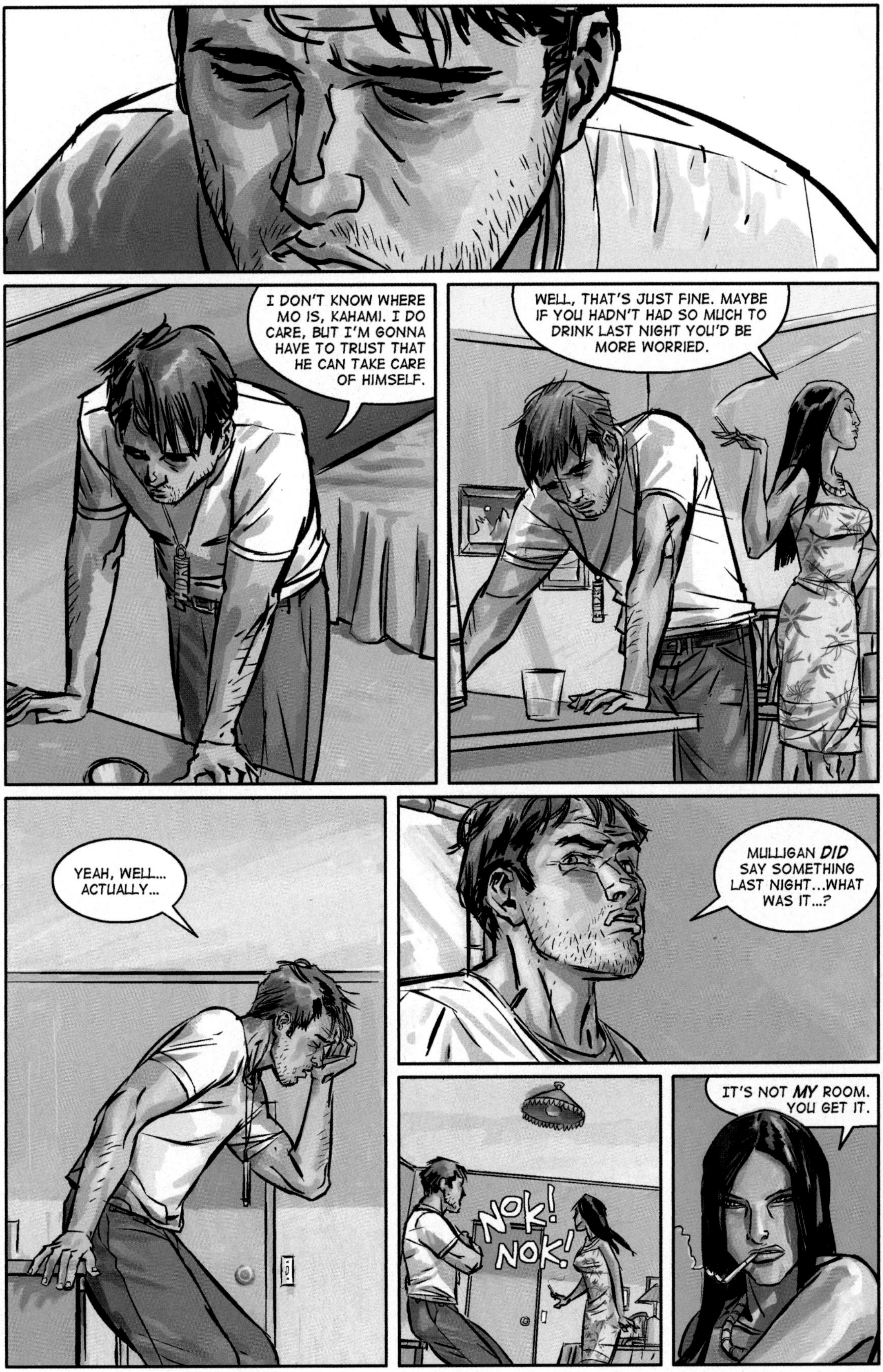
I DON'T KNOW WHERE MO IS, KAHAMI. I DO CARE, BUT I'M GONNA HAVE TO TRUST THAT HE CAN TAKE CARE OF HIMSELF.
WELL, THAT'S JUST FINE. MAYBE IF YOU HADN'T HAD SO MUCH TO DRINK LAST NIGHT YOU'D BE MORE WORRIED.
YEAH, WELL... ACTUALLY...
MULLIGAN *DID* SAY SOMETHING LAST NIGHT...WHAT WAS IT...?
NOK! NOK!
IT'S NOT *MY* ROOM. YOU GET IT.

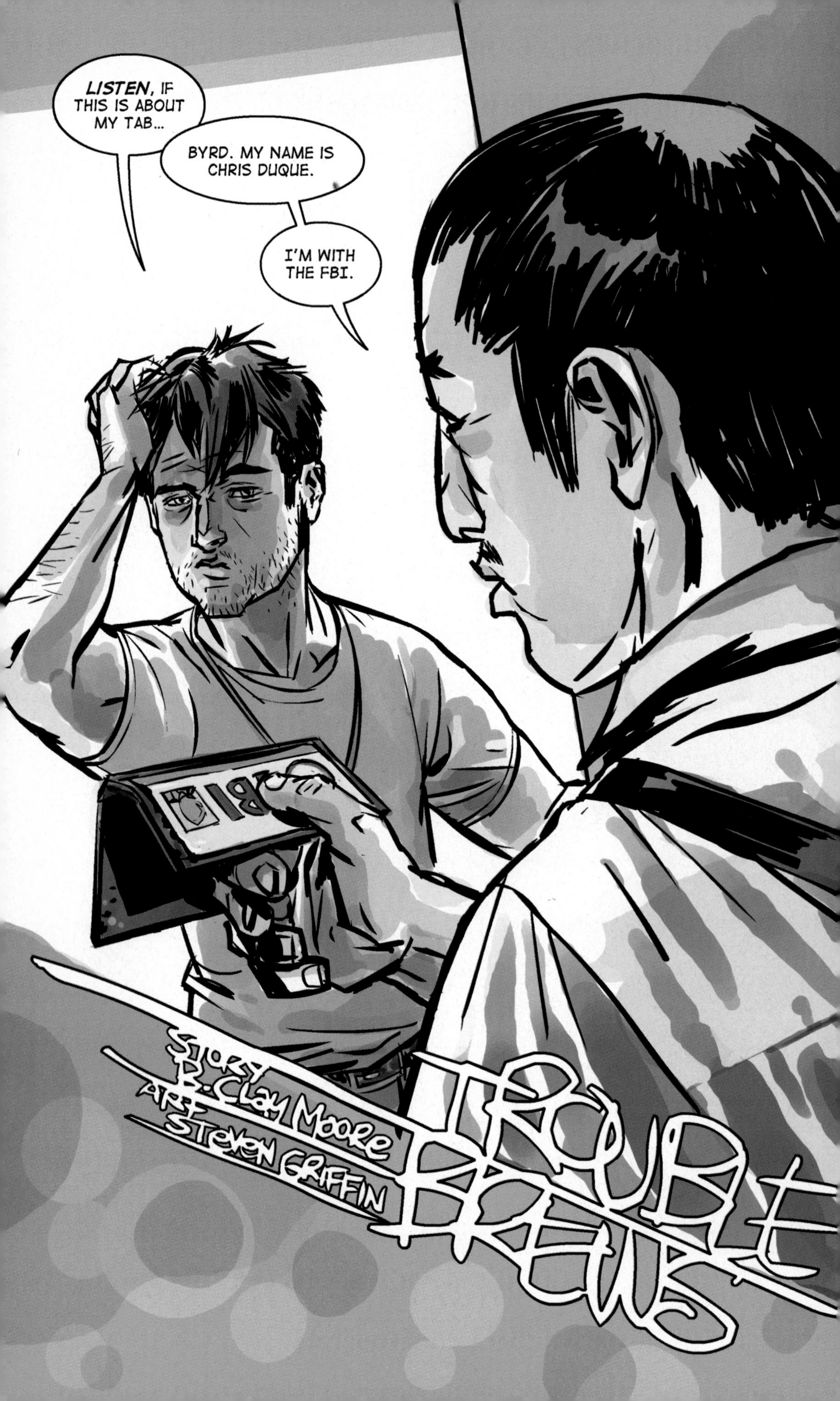

LISTEN, IF THIS IS ABOUT MY TAB...
BYRD. MY NAME IS CHRIS DUQUE.
I'M WITH THE FBI.
FBI
Story B. Clay Moore
Art Steven Griffin
TROUBLE BREWS

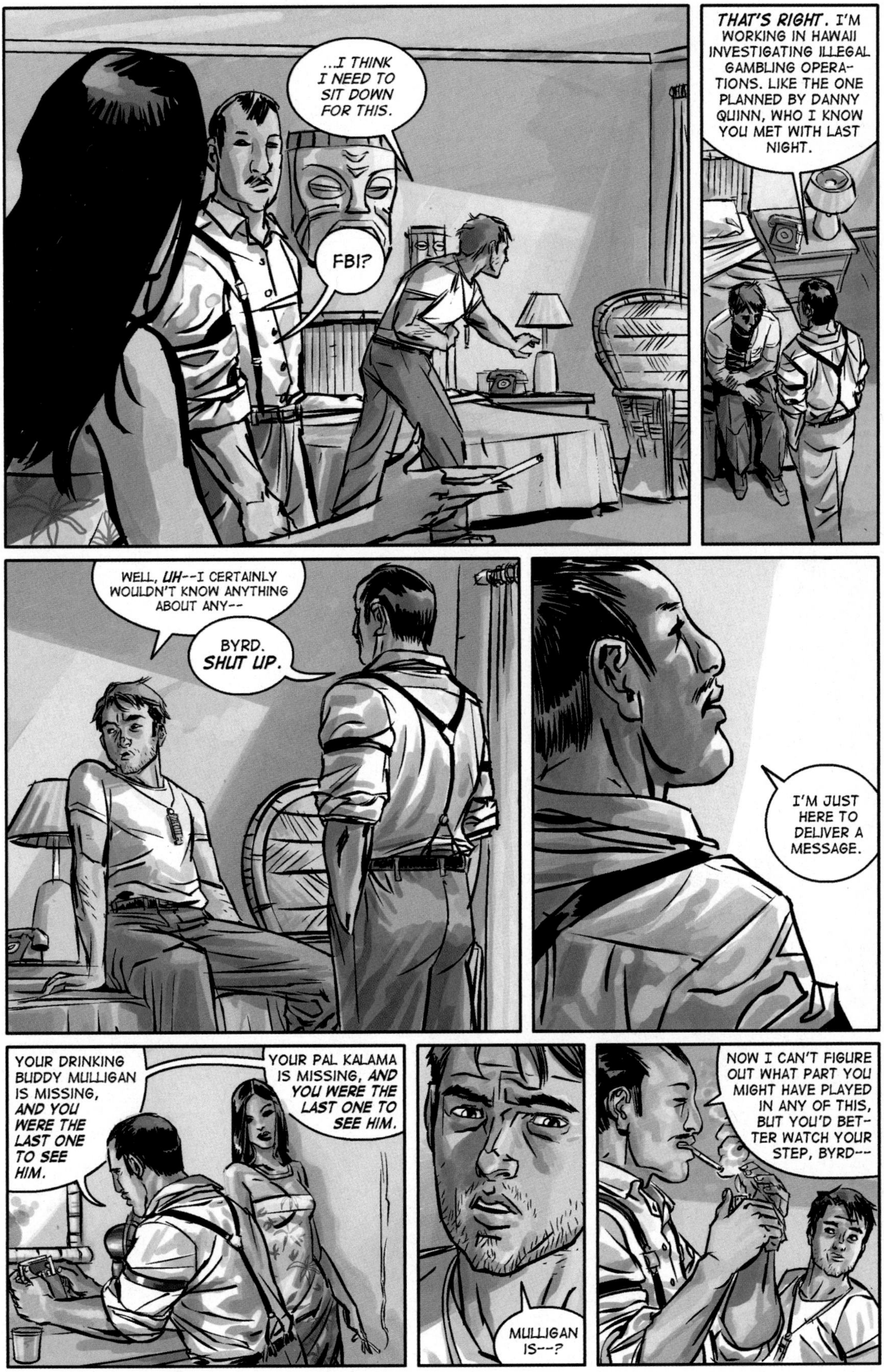
...I THINK I NEED TO SIT DOWN FOR THIS.
FBI?
THAT'S RIGHT. I'M WORKING IN HAWAII INVESTIGATING ILLEGAL GAMBLING OPERATIONS. LIKE THE ONE PLANNED BY DANNY QUINN, WHO I KNOW YOU MET WITH LAST NIGHT.
WELL, UH--I CERTAINLY WOULDN'T KNOW ANYTHING ABOUT ANY--
BYRD. SHUT UP.
I'M JUST HERE TO DELIVER A MESSAGE.
YOUR DRINKING BUDDY MULLIGAN IS MISSING, AND YOU WERE THE LAST ONE TO SEE HIM.
YOUR PAL KALAMA IS MISSING, AND YOU WERE THE LAST ONE TO SEE HIM.
MULLIGAN IS--?
NOW I CAN'T FIGURE OUT WHAT PART YOU MIGHT HAVE PLAYED IN ANY OF THIS, BUT YOU'D BETTER WATCH YOUR STEP, BYRD--

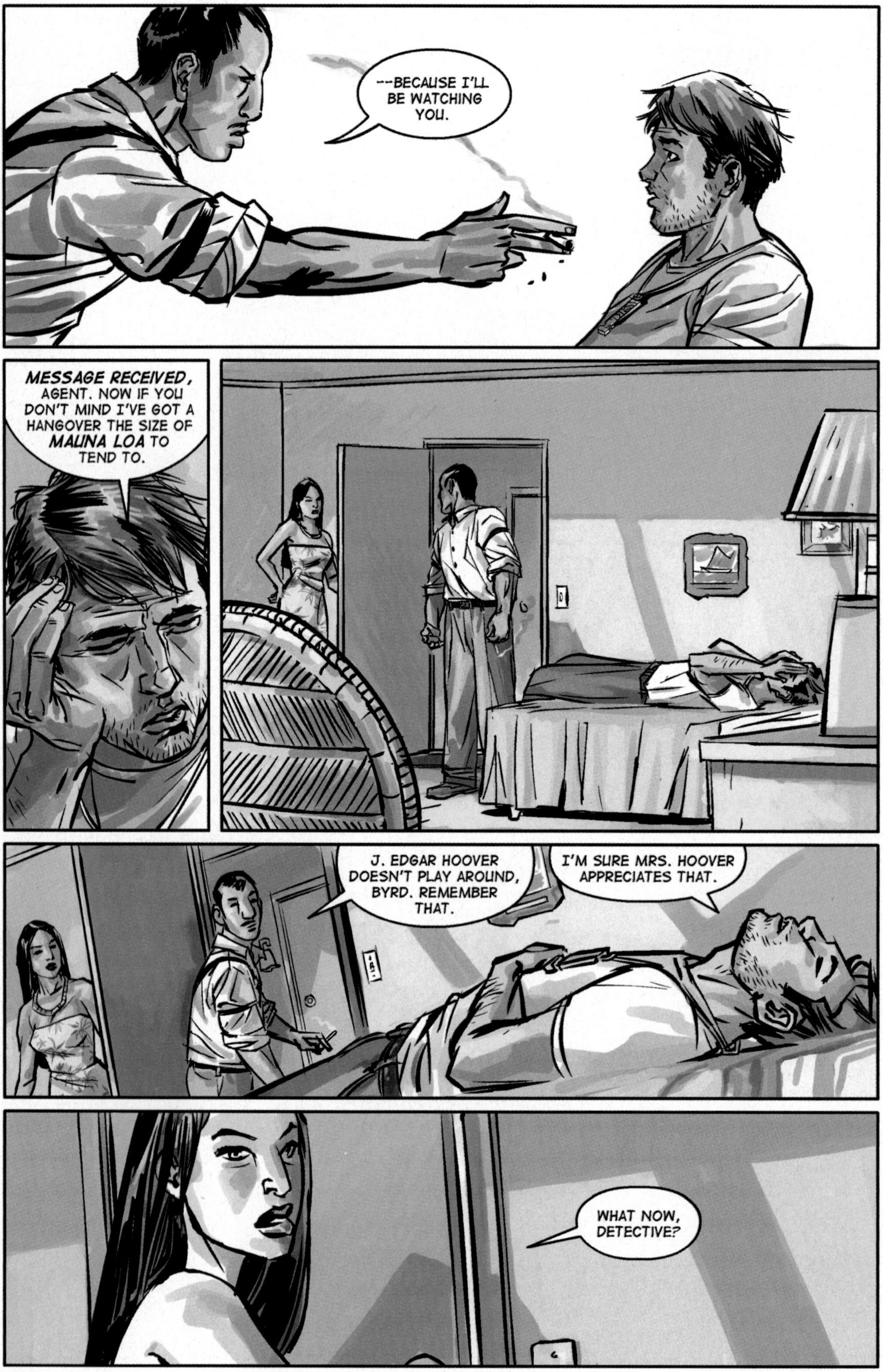
--BECAUSE I'LL BE WATCHING YOU.
MESSAGE RECEIVED, AGENT. NOW IF YOU DON'T MIND I'VE GOT A HANGOVER THE SIZE OF MAUNA LOA TO TEND TO.
J. EDGAR HOOVER DOESN'T PLAY AROUND, BYRD. REMEMBER THAT.
I'M SURE MRS. HOOVER APPRECIATES THAT.
WHAT NOW, DETECTIVE?

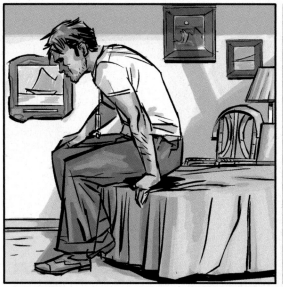

FIRST OF ALL, HAVE YOU SEEN MY SUNGLASSES? I'M NOT SURE I CAN FACE THE HAWAIIAN SUN THIS MORNING.

THANKS. MY NEXT STEP IS TO GO SEE PIANO AGAIN AND TELL HIM WHAT I FOUND OUT ABOUT QUINN.

OR WHAT I CAN REMEMBER ABOUT IT. AND I NEED TO FIGURE OUT WHERE THEY'VE GOT MO...

AND THEN..?

I DON'T KNOW, KAHAMI. I'VE NOTICED WHAT I PLAN RARELY HAS A THING TO DO WITH WHAT ACTUALLY HAPPENS. WE'LL PLAY IT BY EAR.

FEH. I'M GOING SUNBATHING.

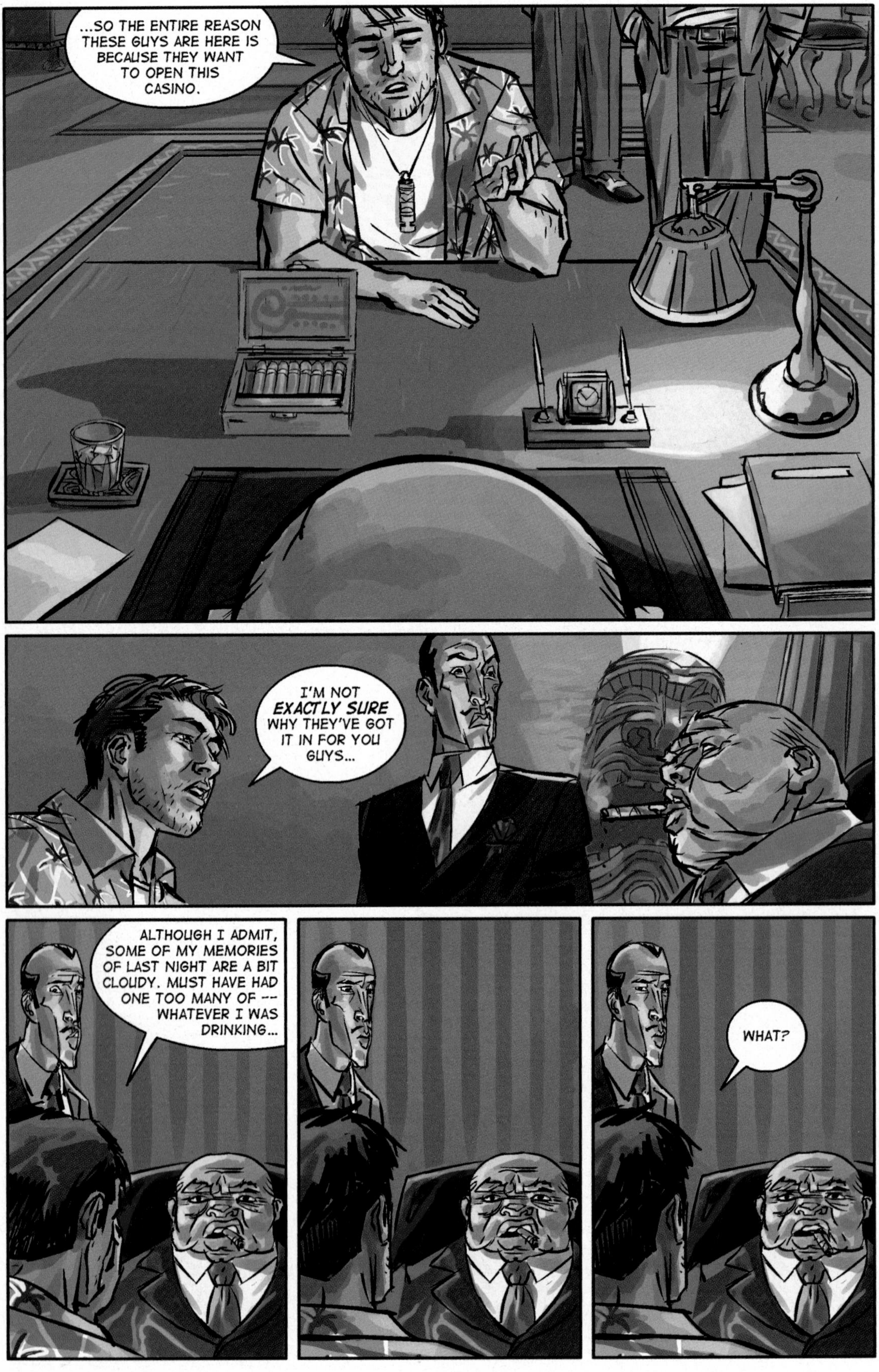
...SO THE ENTIRE REASON THESE GUYS ARE HERE IS BECAUSE THEY WANT TO OPEN THIS CASINO.
I'M NOT *EXACTLY SURE* WHY THEY'VE GOT IT IN FOR YOU GUYS...
ALTHOUGH I ADMIT, SOME OF MY MEMORIES OF LAST NIGHT ARE A BIT CLOUDY. MUST HAVE HAD ONE TOO MANY OF -- WHATEVER I WAS DRINKING...
WHAT?

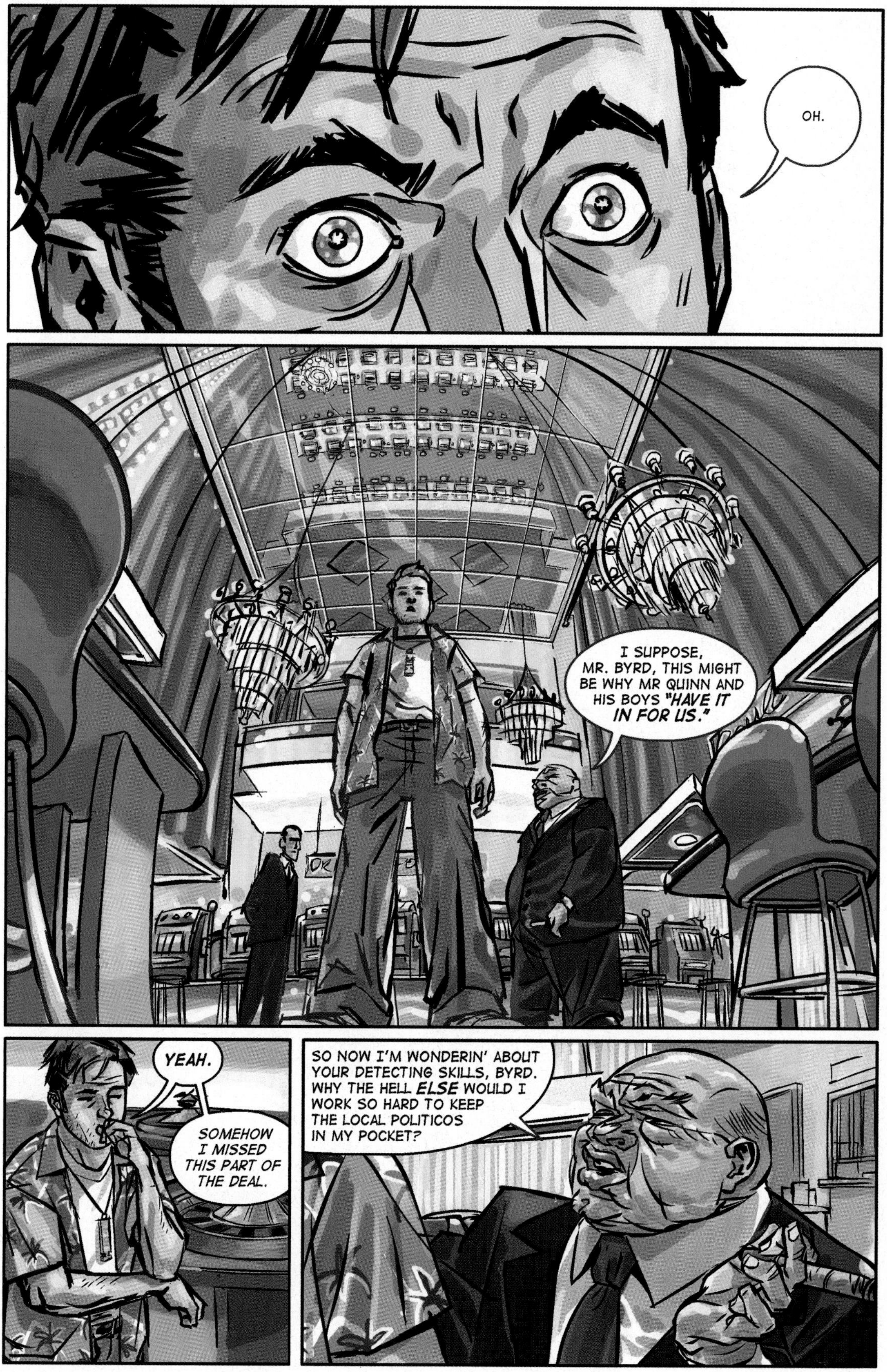
OH.
I SUPPOSE, MR. BYRD, THIS MIGHT BE WHY MR QUINN AND HIS BOYS "HAVE IT IN FOR US."
YEAH.
SOMEHOW I MISSED THIS PART OF THE DEAL.
SO NOW I'M WONDERIN' ABOUT YOUR DETECTING SKILLS, BYRD. WHY THE HELL ELSE WOULD I WORK SO HARD TO KEEP THE LOCAL POLITICOS IN MY POCKET?

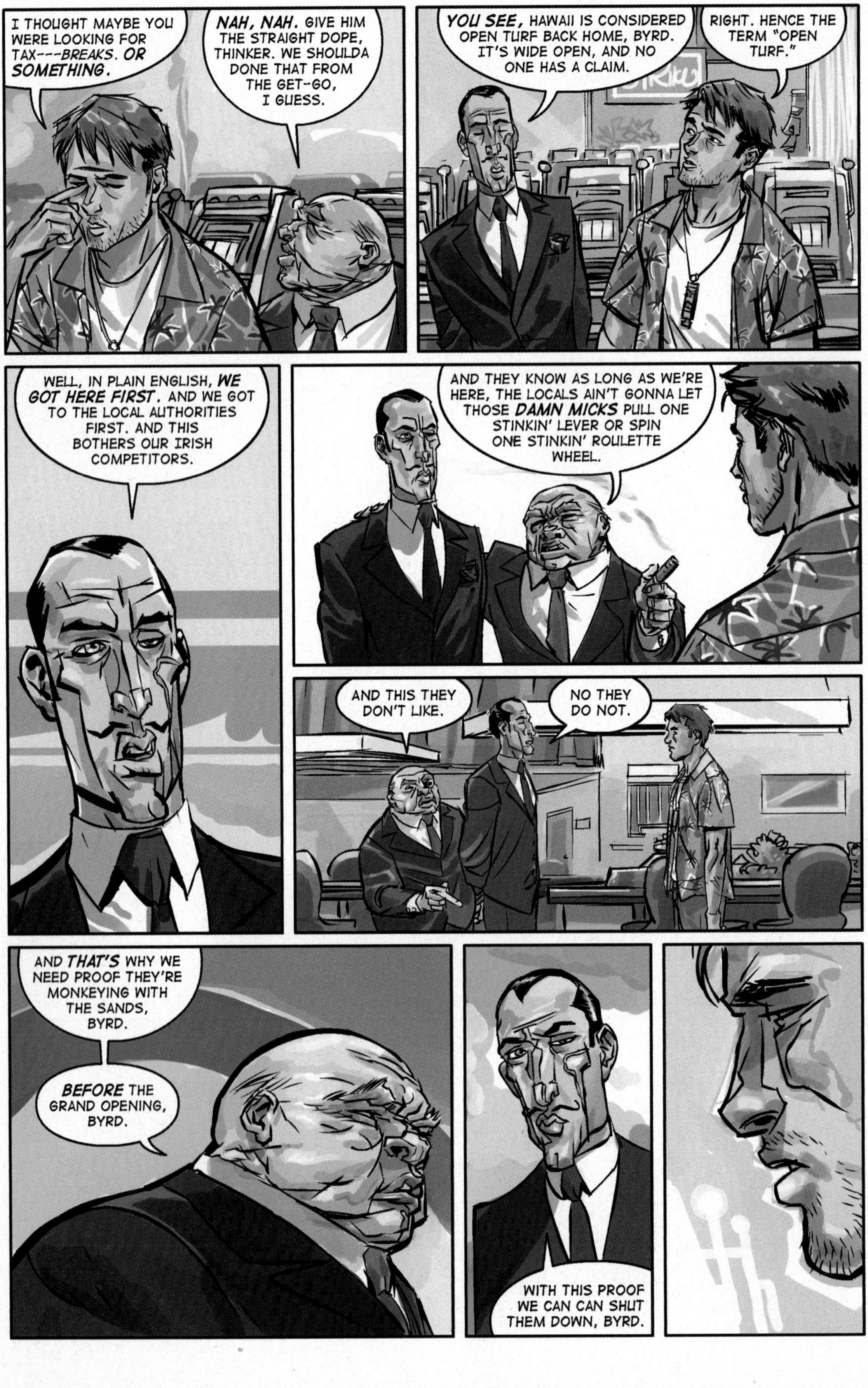

I THOUGHT MAYBE YOU WERE LOOKING FOR TAX---BREAKS. OR SOMETHING.
NAH, NAH. GIVE HIM THE STRAIGHT DOPE, THINKER. WE SHOULDA DONE THAT FROM THE GET-GO, I GUESS.
YOU SEE, HAWAII IS CONSIDERED OPEN TURF BACK HOME, BYRD. IT'S WIDE OPEN, AND NO ONE HAS A CLAIM.
RIGHT. HENCE THE TERM "OPEN TURF."
WELL, IN PLAIN ENGLISH, WE GOT HERE FIRST. AND WE GOT TO THE LOCAL AUTHORITIES FIRST. AND THIS BOTHERS OUR IRISH COMPETITORS.
AND THEY KNOW AS LONG AS WE'RE HERE, THE LOCALS AIN'T GONNA LET THOSE DAMN MICKS PULL ONE STINKIN' LEVER OR SPIN ONE STINKIN' ROULETTE WHEEL.
AND THIS THEY DON'T LIKE.
NO THEY DO NOT.
AND THAT'S WHY WE NEED PROOF THEY'RE MONKEYING WITH THE SANDS, BYRD.
BEFORE THE GRAND OPENING, BYRD.
WITH THIS PROOF WE CAN CAN SHUT THEM DOWN, BYRD.

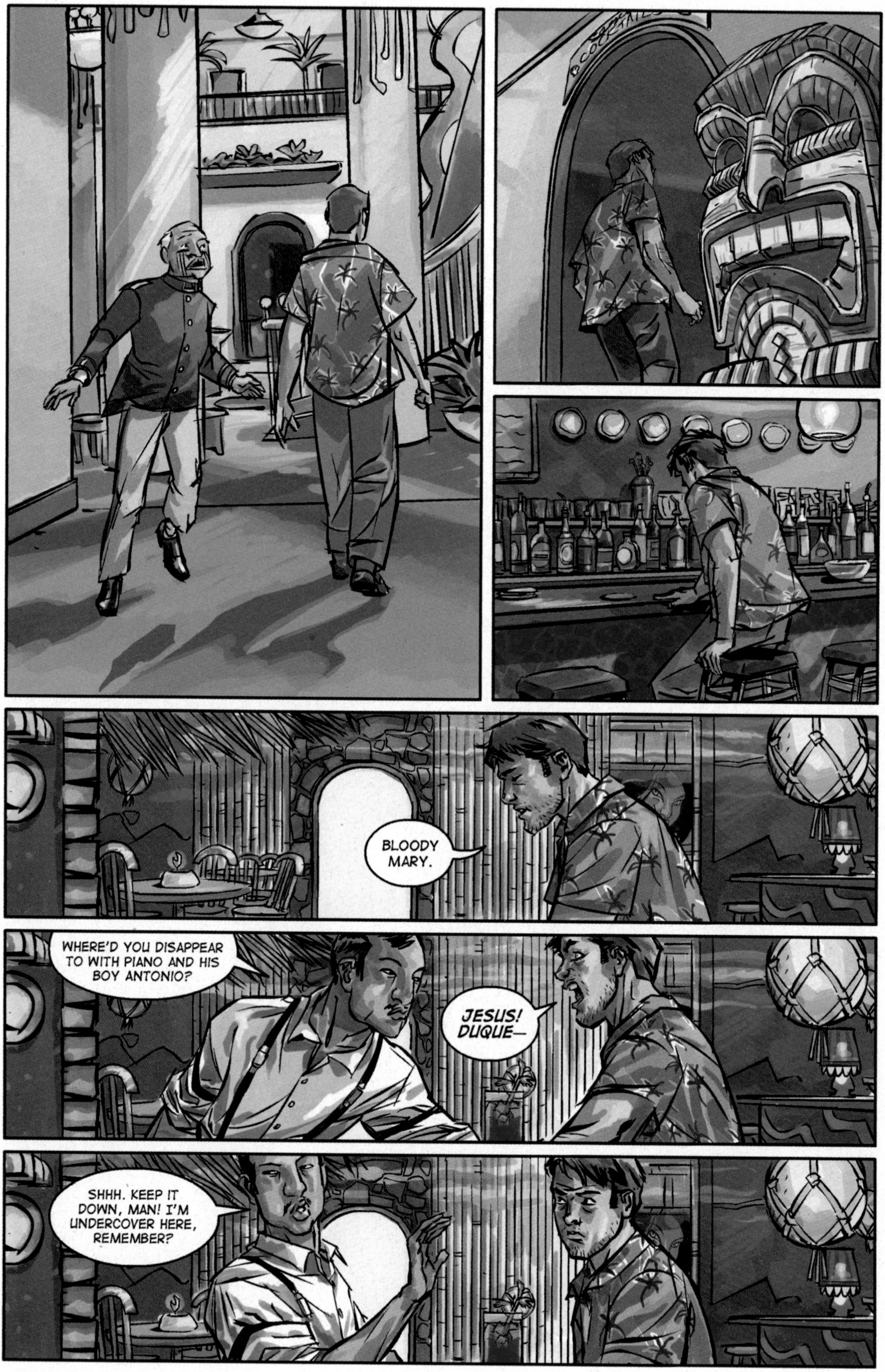
BLOODY MARY.
WHERE'D YOU DISAPPEAR TO WITH PIANO AND HIS BOY ANTONIO?
JESUS! DUQUE—
SHHH. KEEP IT DOWN, MAN! I'M UNDERCOVER HERE, REMEMBER?

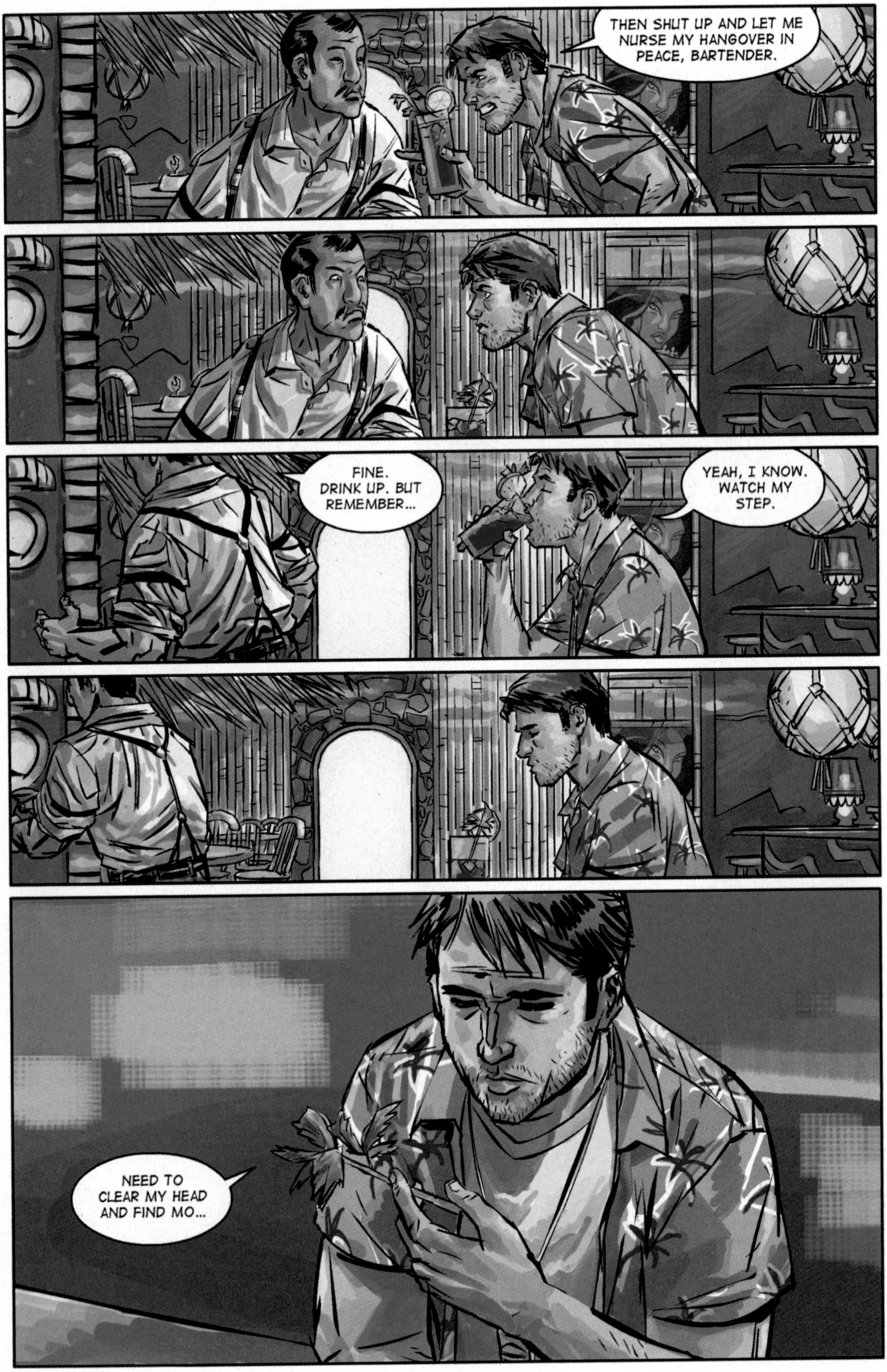
THEN SHUT UP AND LET ME NURSE MY HANGOVER IN PEACE, BARTENDER.
FINE. DRINK UP. BUT REMEMBER...
YEAH, I KNOW. WATCH MY STEP.
NEED TO CLEAR MY HEAD AND FIND MO...

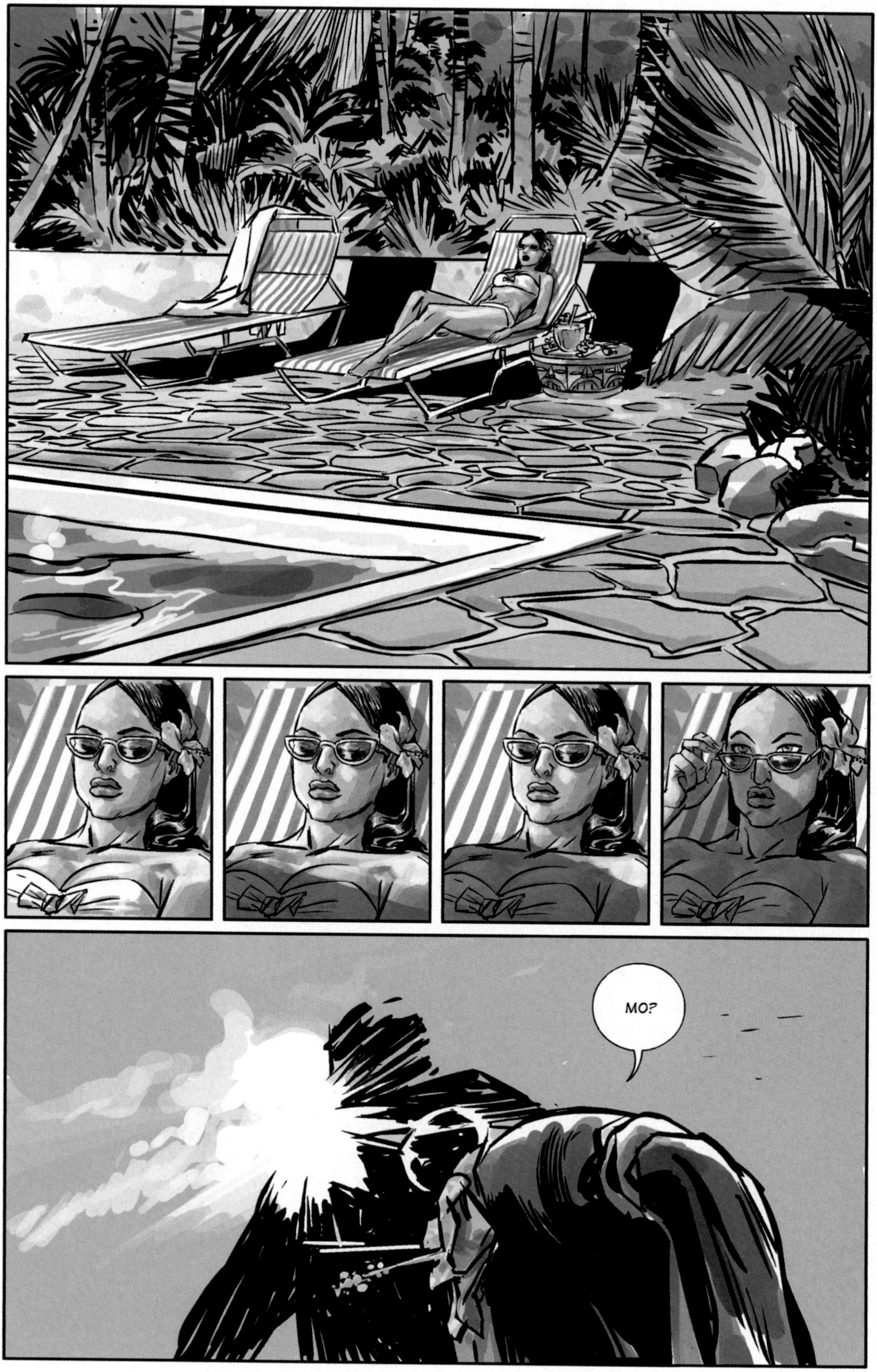
MO?

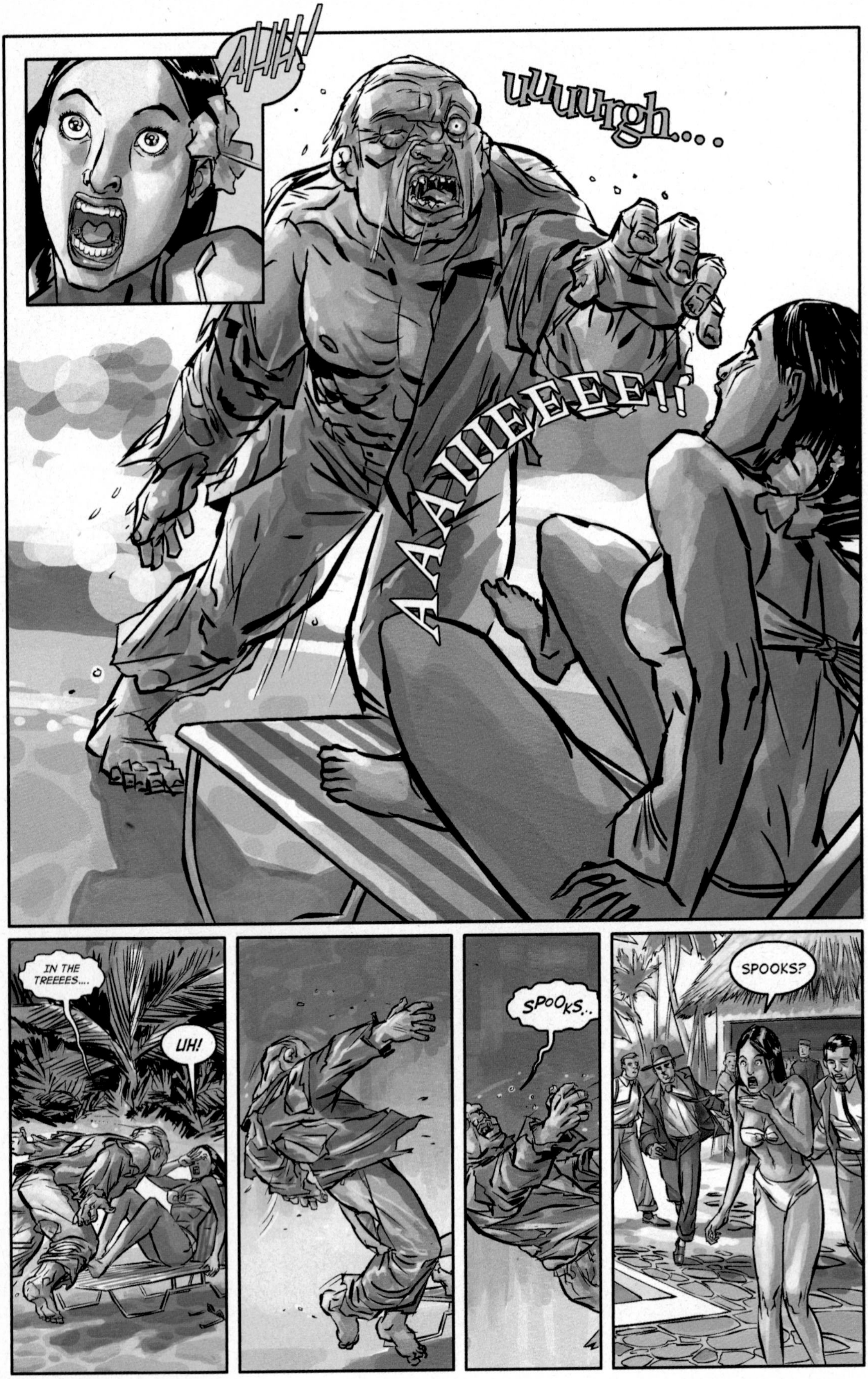
AHH!
uuuurgh....
AAAIIEEEEE!!
IN THE TREEEES....
UH!
SPOOKS..
SPOOKS?

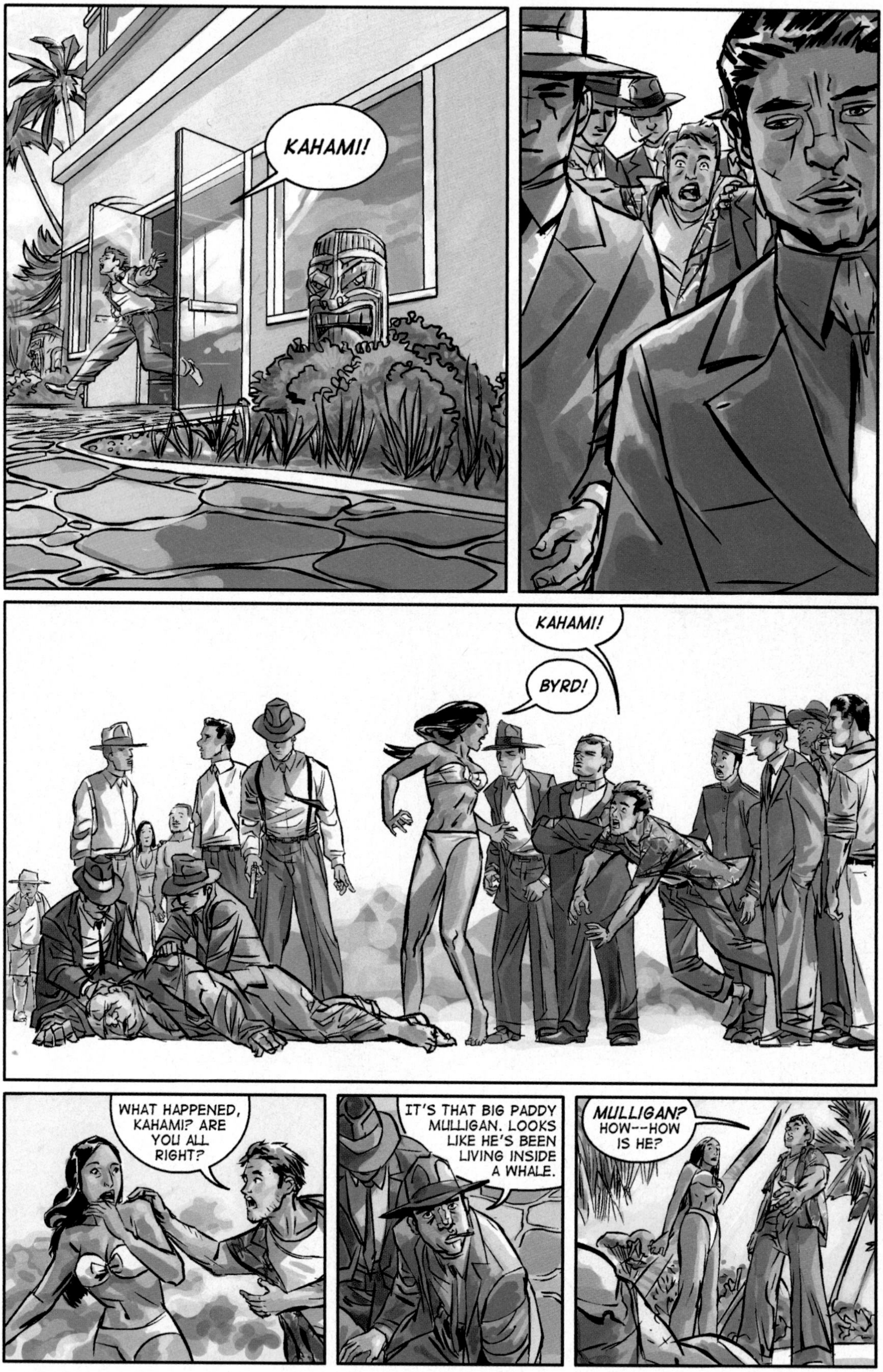
KAHAMI!
KAHAMI!
BYRD!
WHAT HAPPENED, KAHAMI? ARE YOU ALL RIGHT?
IT'S THAT BIG PADDY MULLIGAN. LOOKS LIKE HE'S BEEN LIVING INSIDE A WHALE.
MULLIGAN? HOW--HOW IS HE?

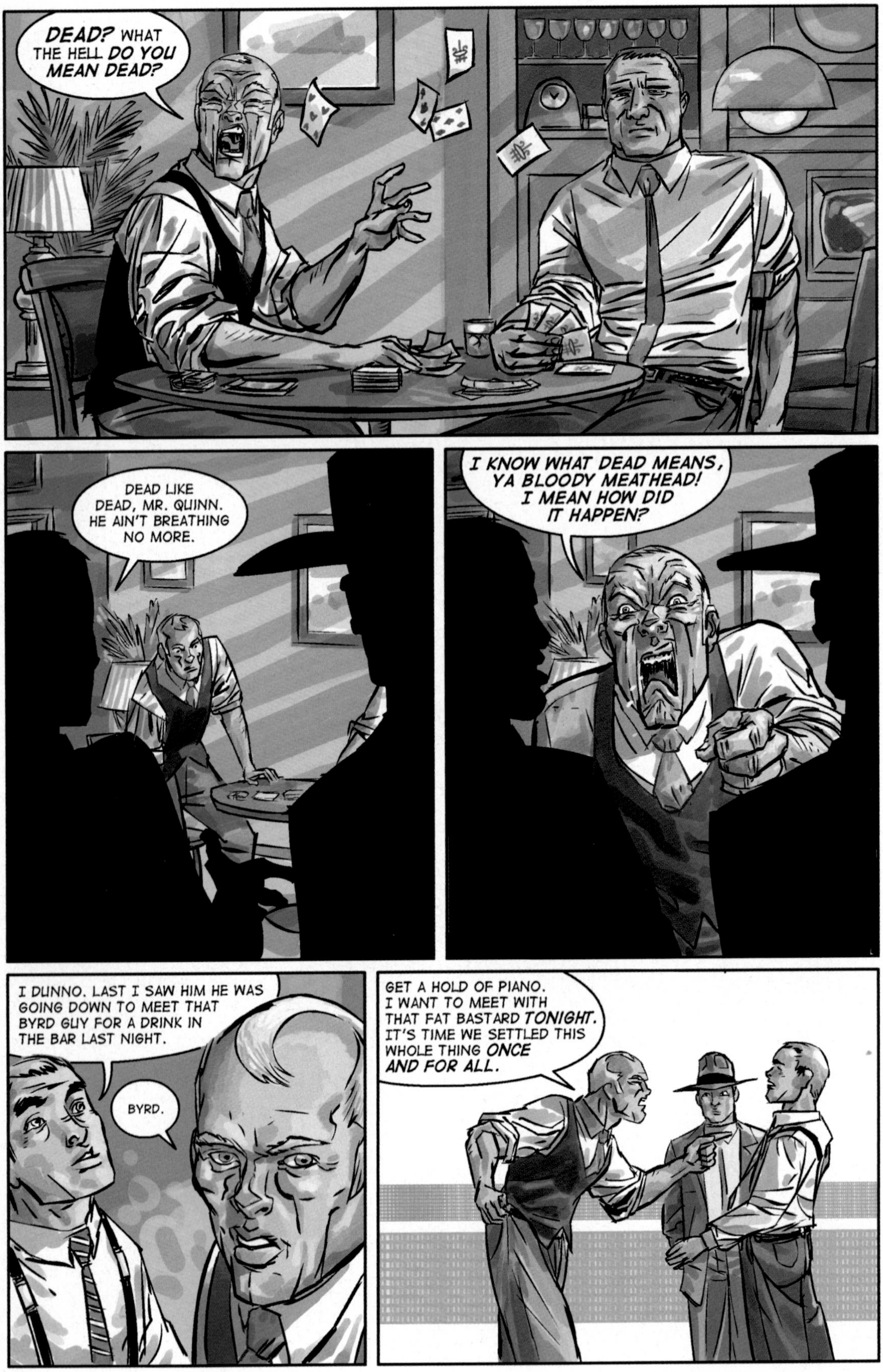
DEAD? WHAT THE HELL DO YOU MEAN DEAD?
DEAD LIKE DEAD, MR. QUINN. HE AIN'T BREATHING NO MORE.
I KNOW WHAT DEAD MEANS, YA BLOODY MEATHEAD! I MEAN HOW DID IT HAPPEN?
I DUNNO. LAST I SAW HIM HE WAS GOING DOWN TO MEET THAT BYRD GUY FOR A DRINK IN THE BAR LAST NIGHT.
BYRD.
GET A HOLD OF PIANO. I WANT TO MEET WITH THAT FAT BASTARD TONIGHT. IT'S TIME WE SETTLED THIS WHOLE THING ONCE AND FOR ALL.

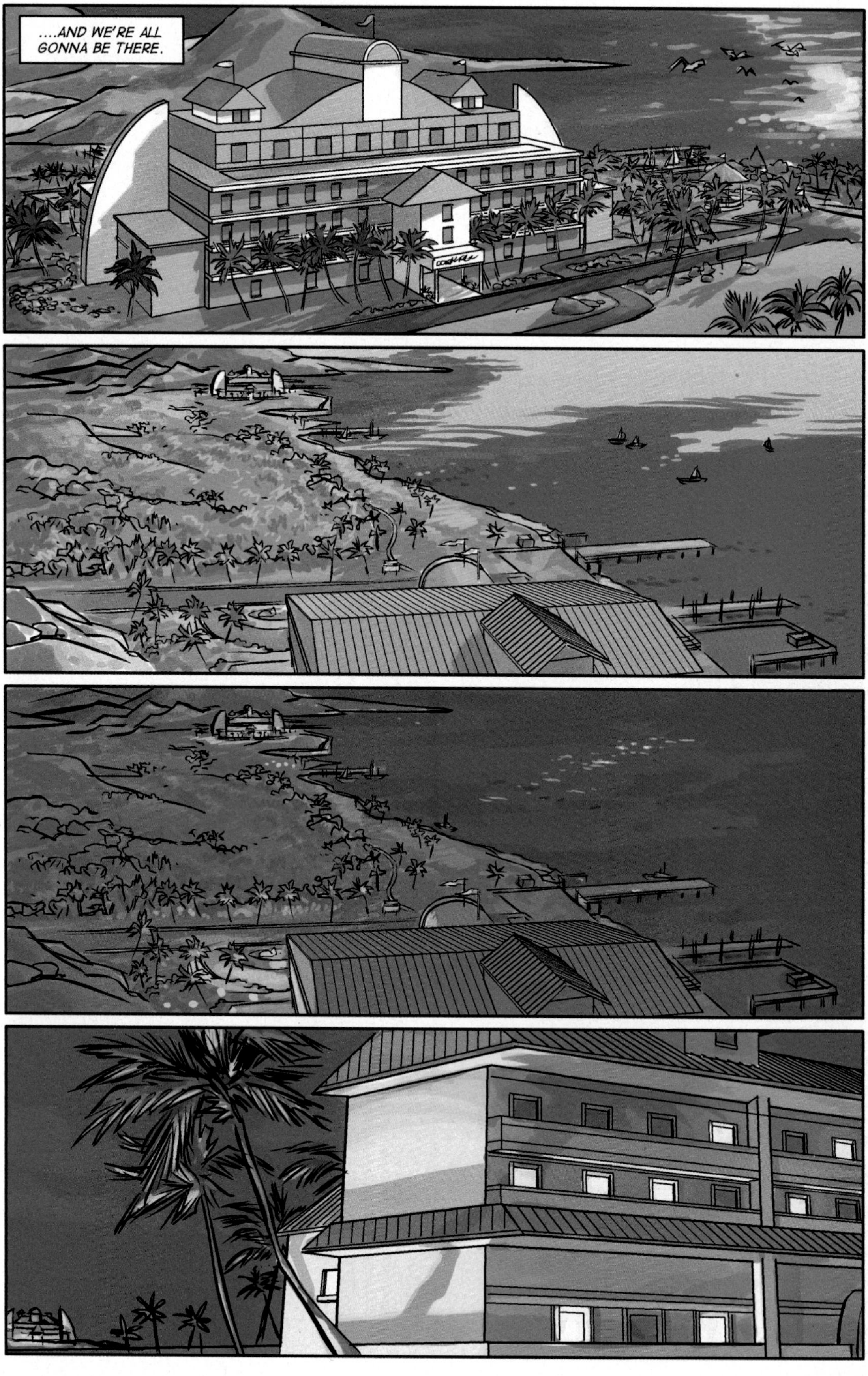
....AND WE'RE ALL GONNA BE THERE.

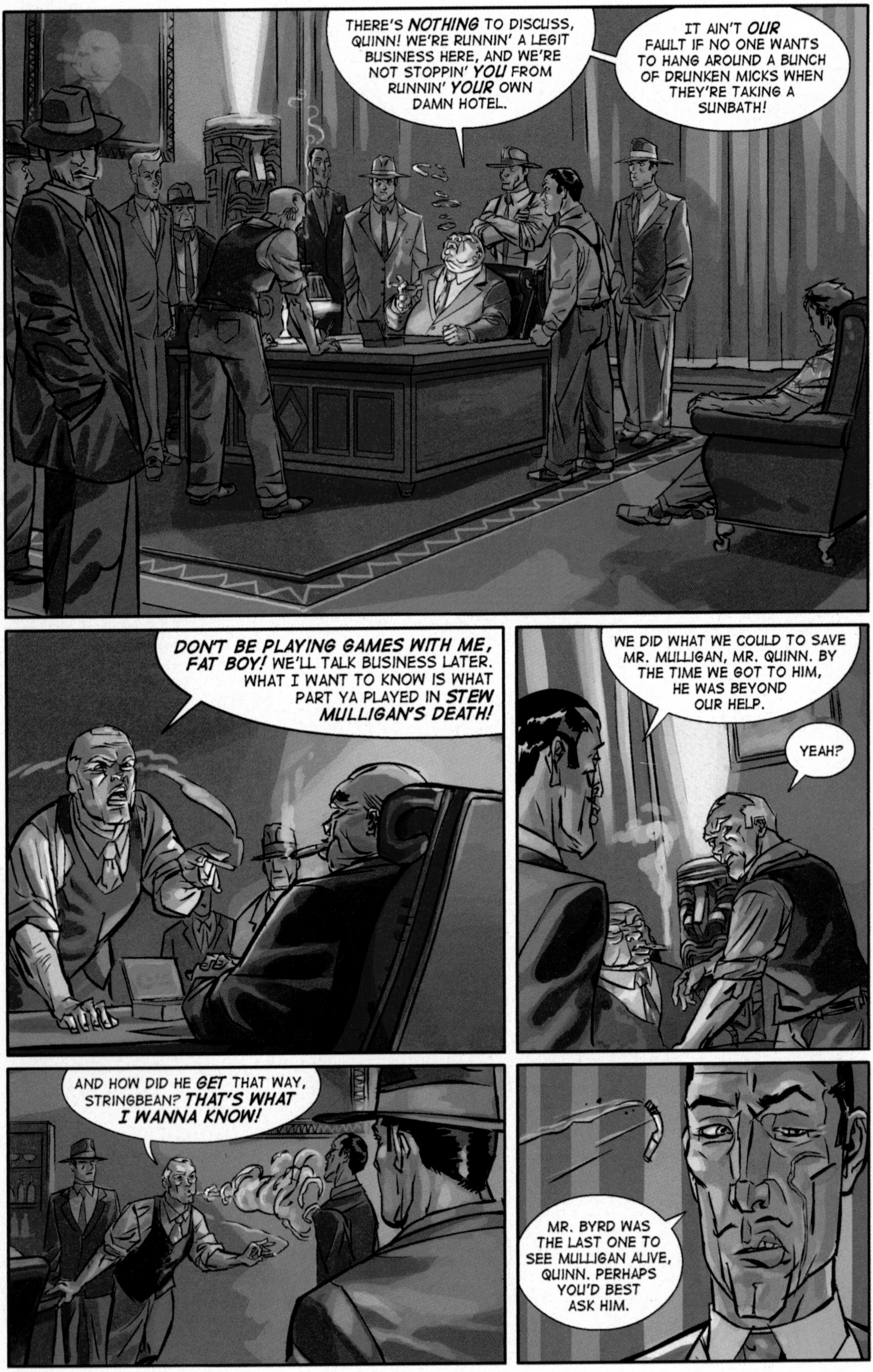
THERE'S NOTHING TO DISCUSS, QUINN! WE'RE RUNNIN' A LEGIT BUSINESS HERE, AND WE'RE NOT STOPPIN' YOU FROM RUNNIN' YOUR OWN DAMN HOTEL.
IT AIN'T OUR FAULT IF NO ONE WANTS TO HANG AROUND A BUNCH OF DRUNKEN MICKS WHEN THEY'RE TAKING A SUNBATH!
DON'T BE PLAYING GAMES WITH ME, FAT BOY! WE'LL TALK BUSINESS LATER. WHAT I WANT TO KNOW IS WHAT PART YA PLAYED IN STEW MULLIGAN'S DEATH!
WE DID WHAT WE COULD TO SAVE MR. MULLIGAN, MR. QUINN. BY THE TIME WE GOT TO HIM, HE WAS BEYOND OUR HELP.
YEAH?
AND HOW DID HE GET THAT WAY, STRINGBEAN? THAT'S WHAT I WANNA KNOW!
MR. BYRD WAS THE LAST ONE TO SEE MULLIGAN ALIVE, QUINN. PERHAPS YOU'D BEST ASK HIM.

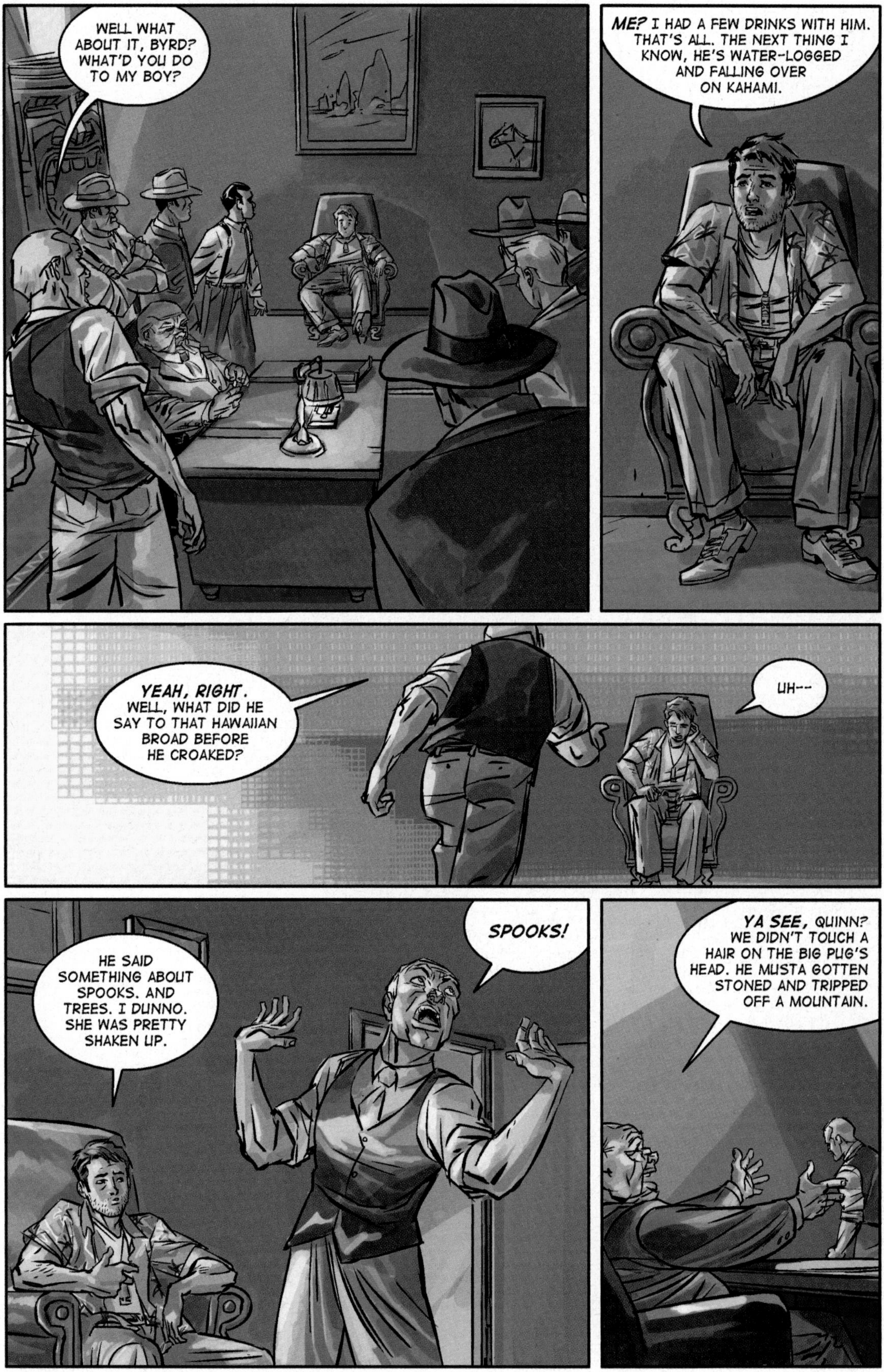
WELL WHAT ABOUT IT, BYRD? WHAT'D YOU DO TO MY BOY?
ME? I HAD A FEW DRINKS WITH HIM. THAT'S ALL. THE NEXT THING I KNOW, HE'S WATER-LOGGED AND FALLING OVER ON KAHAMI.
YEAH, RIGHT. WELL, WHAT DID HE SAY TO THAT HAWAIIAN BROAD BEFORE HE CROAKED?
UH--
HE SAID SOMETHING ABOUT SPOOKS. AND TREES. I DUNNO. SHE WAS PRETTY SHAKEN UP.
SPOOKS!
YA SEE, QUINN? WE DIDN'T TOUCH A HAIR ON THE BIG PUG'S HEAD. HE MUSTA GOTTEN STONED AND TRIPPED OFF A MOUNTAIN.

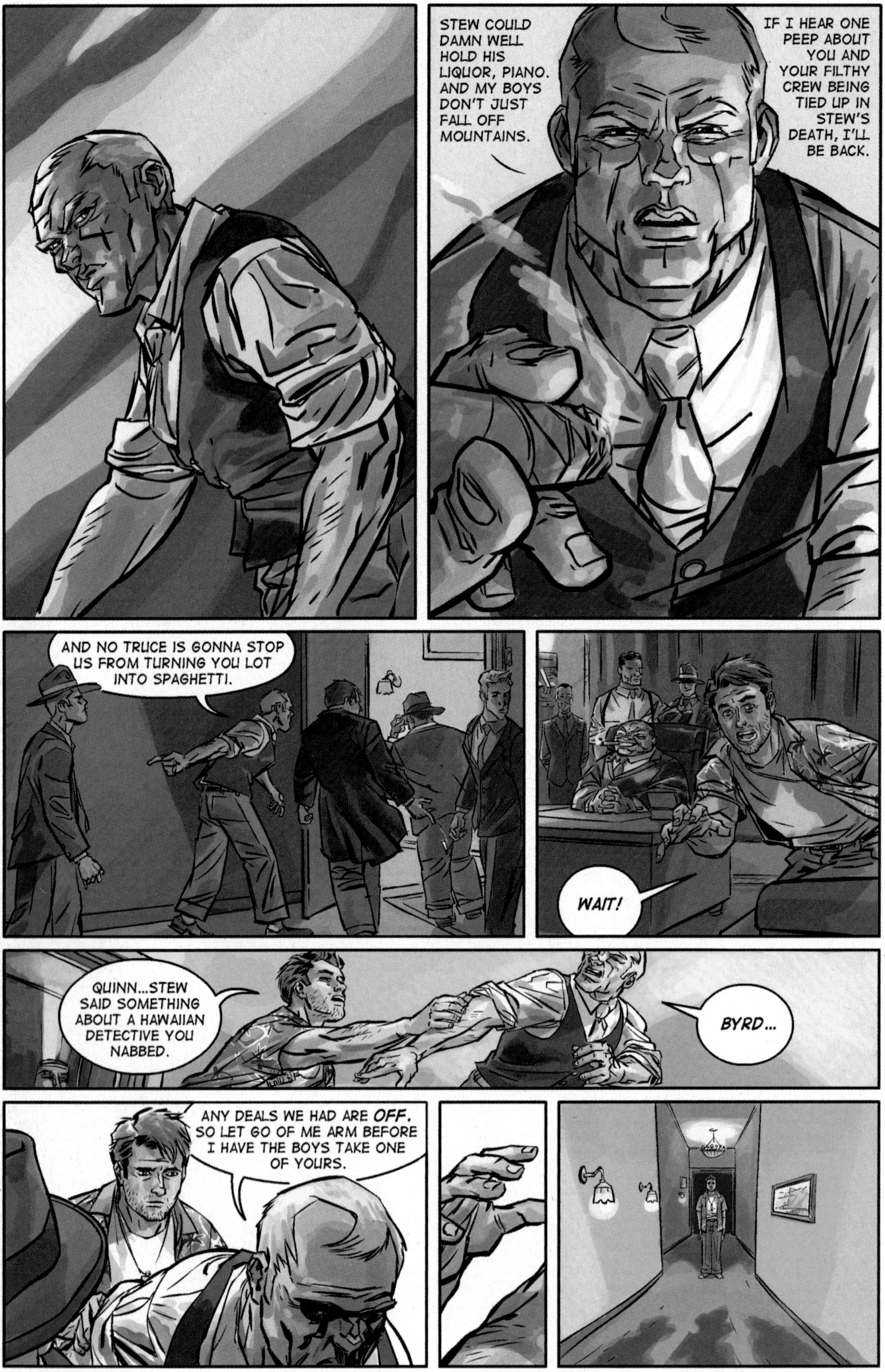
STEW COULD DAMN WELL HOLD HIS LIQUOR, PIANO. AND MY BOYS DON'T JUST FALL OFF MOUNTAINS.
IF I HEAR ONE PEEP ABOUT YOU AND YOUR FILTHY CREW BEING TIED UP IN STEW'S DEATH, I'LL BE BACK.
AND NO TRUCE IS GONNA STOP US FROM TURNING YOU LOT INTO SPAGHETTI.
WAIT!
QUINN...STEW SAID SOMETHING ABOUT A HAWAIIAN DETECTIVE YOU NABBED.
BYRD...
ANY DEALS WE HAD ARE OFF. SO LET GO OF ME ARM BEFORE I HAVE THE BOYS TAKE ONE OF YOURS.

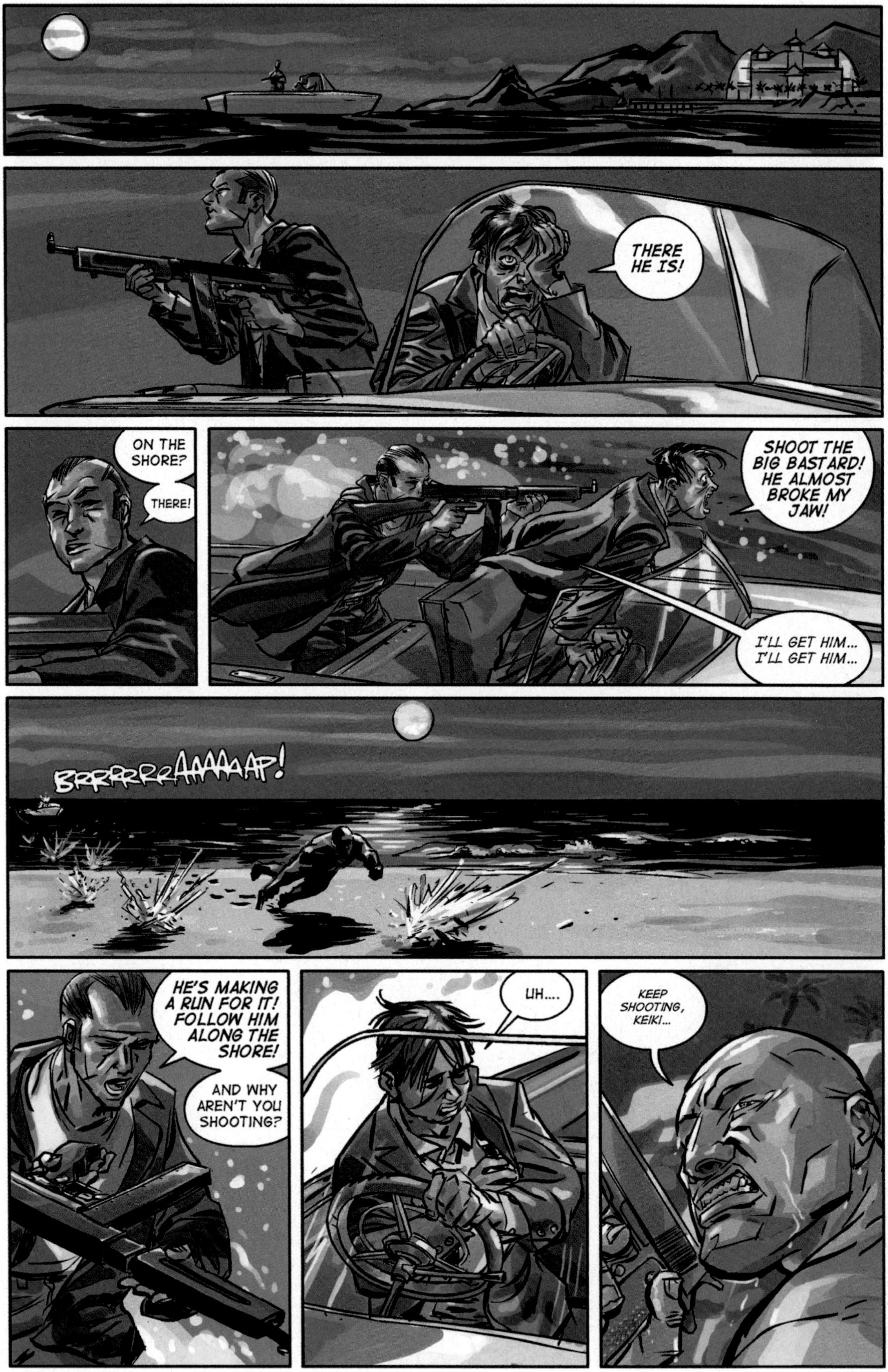
THERE HE IS!
ON THE SHORE?
THERE!
SHOOT THE BIG BASTARD! HE ALMOST BROKE MY JAW!
I'LL GET HIM... I'LL GET HIM...
BRRRRRRAAAAAAP!
HE'S MAKING A RUN FOR IT! FOLLOW HIM ALONG THE SHORE!
AND WHY AREN'T YOU SHOOTING?
UH....
KEEP SHOOTING, KEIKI...

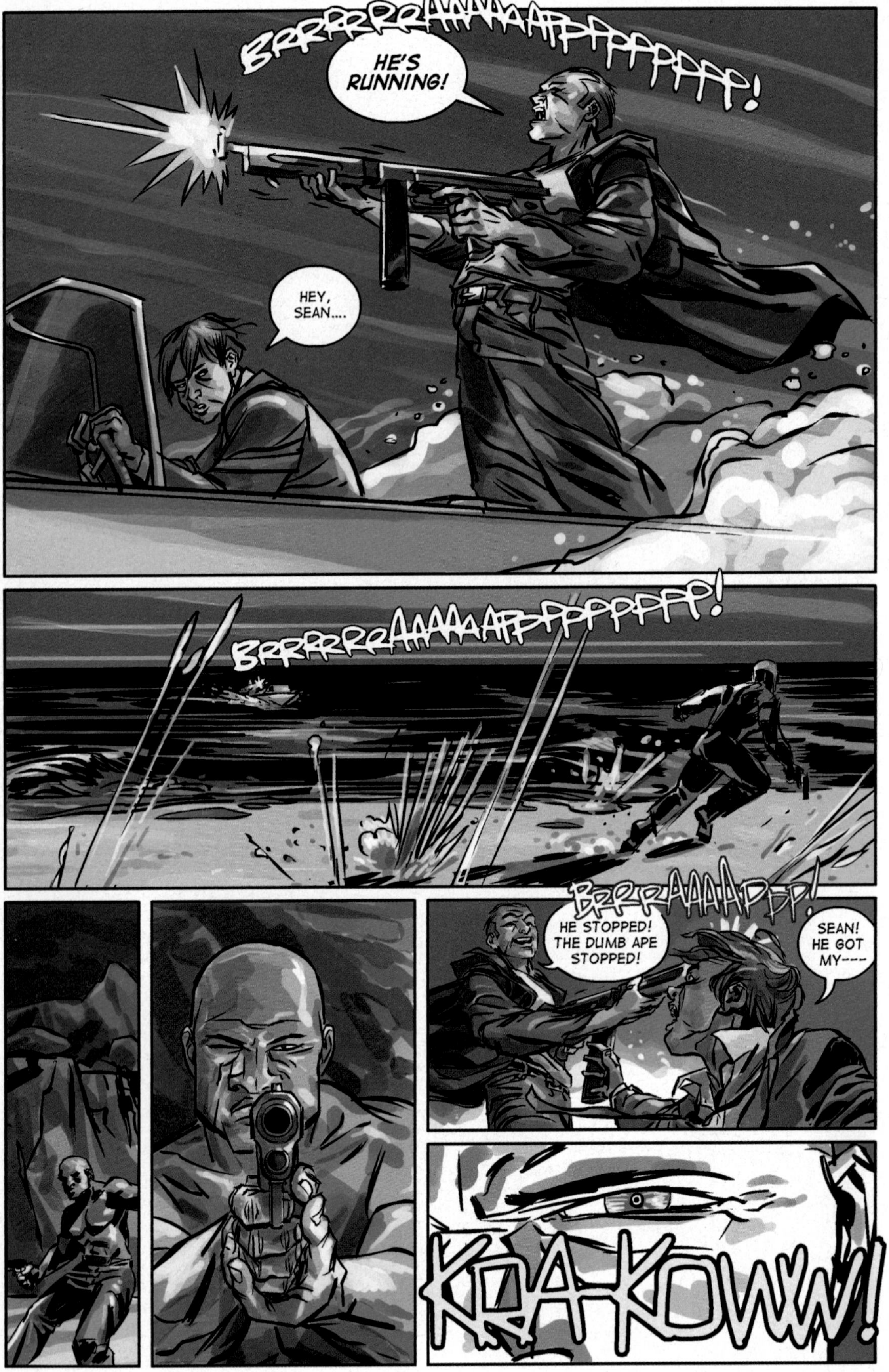
BRRRRRRAAAAAAPPPPPPPPP!
HE'S RUNNING!
HEY, SEAN....
BRRRRRRAAAAAPPPPPPPPP!
BRRRAAAAPPP!
HE STOPPED! THE DUMB APE STOPPED!
SEAN! HE GOT MY---
KRA-KOWW!

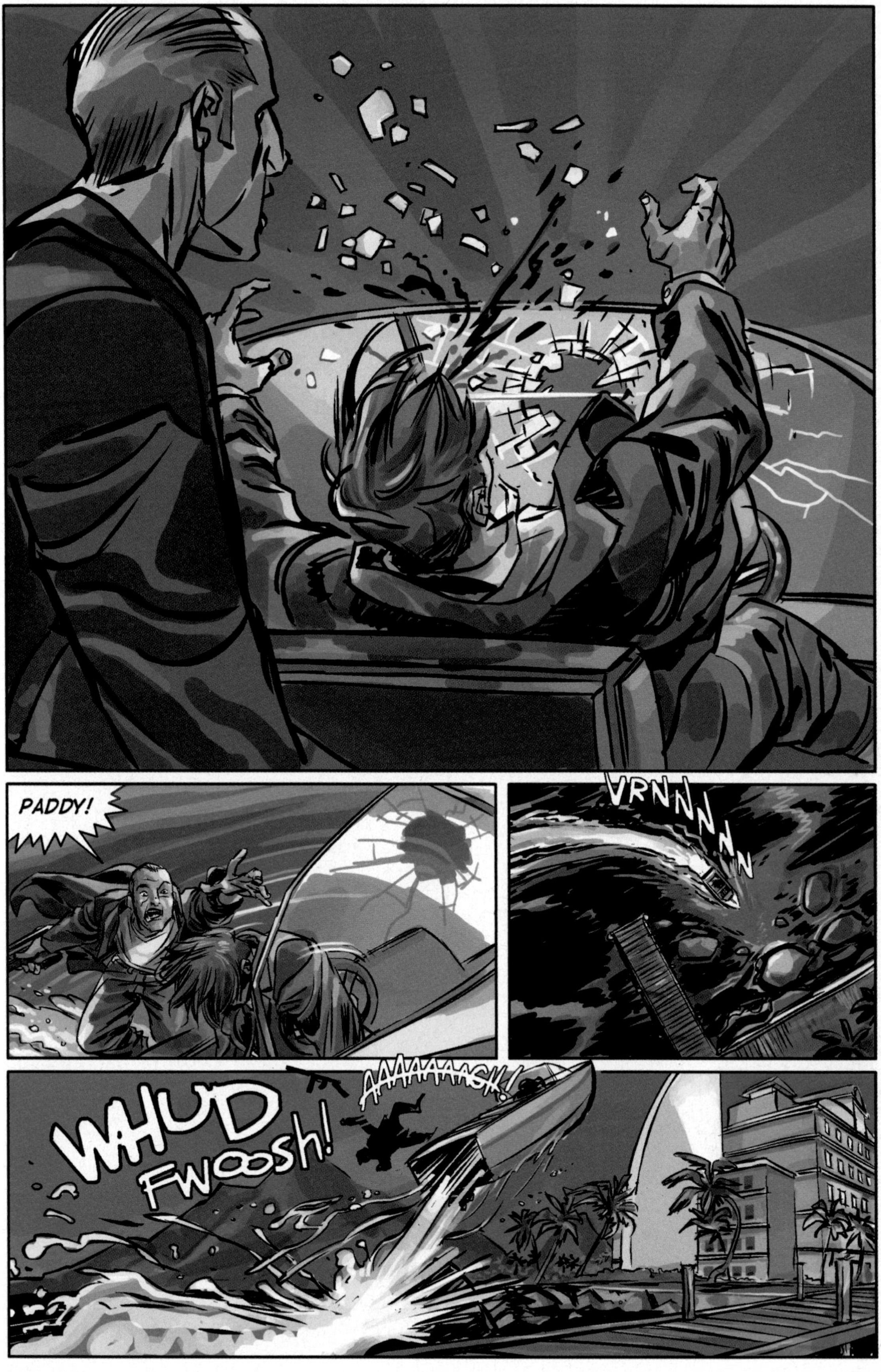
PADDY!
VRNNNNNN
WHUD
AAAAAAAAGH!
FWOOSH!

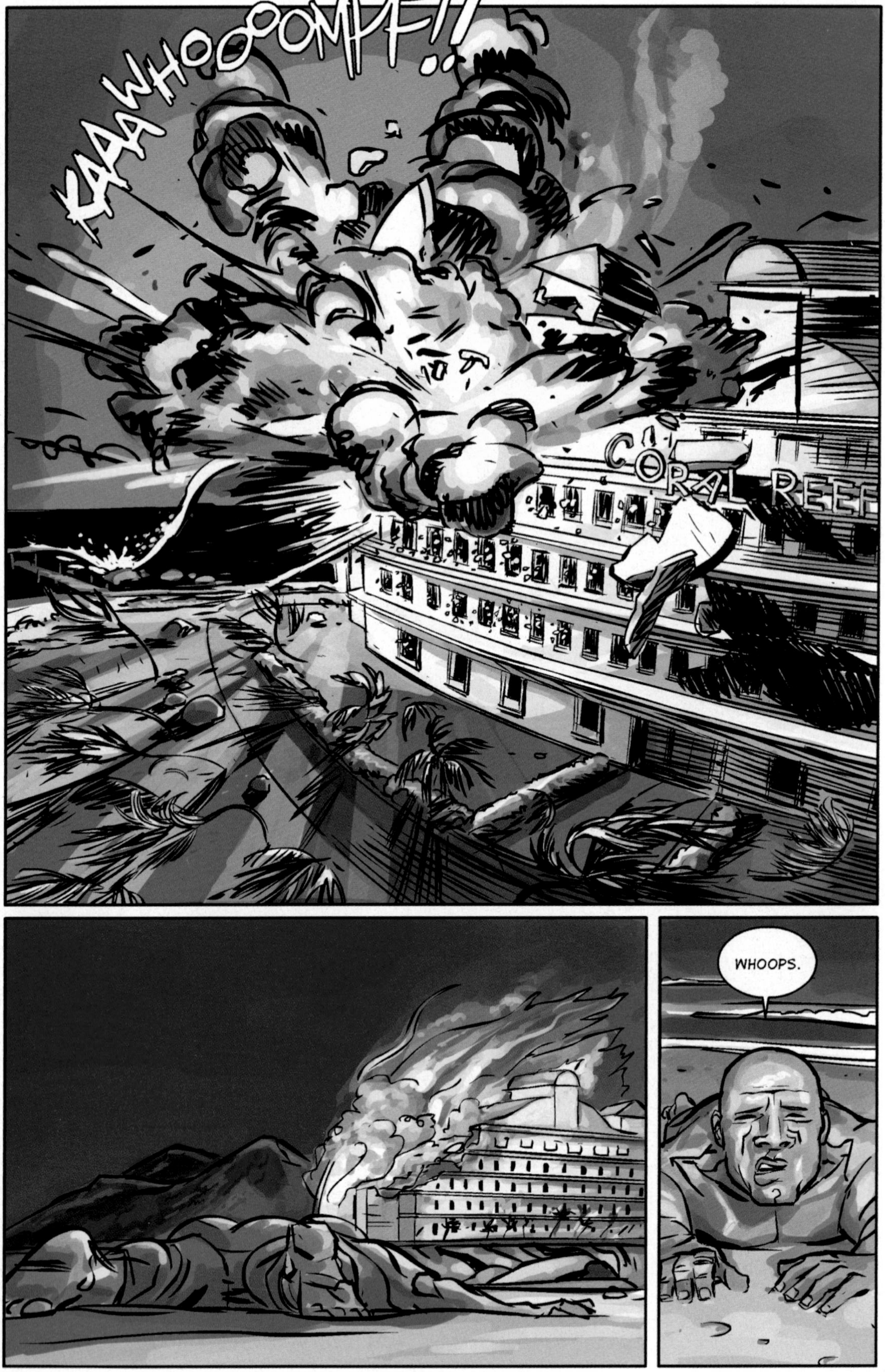
KAAAWHOOOOOMPF!!
CORAL REEF
WHOOPS.

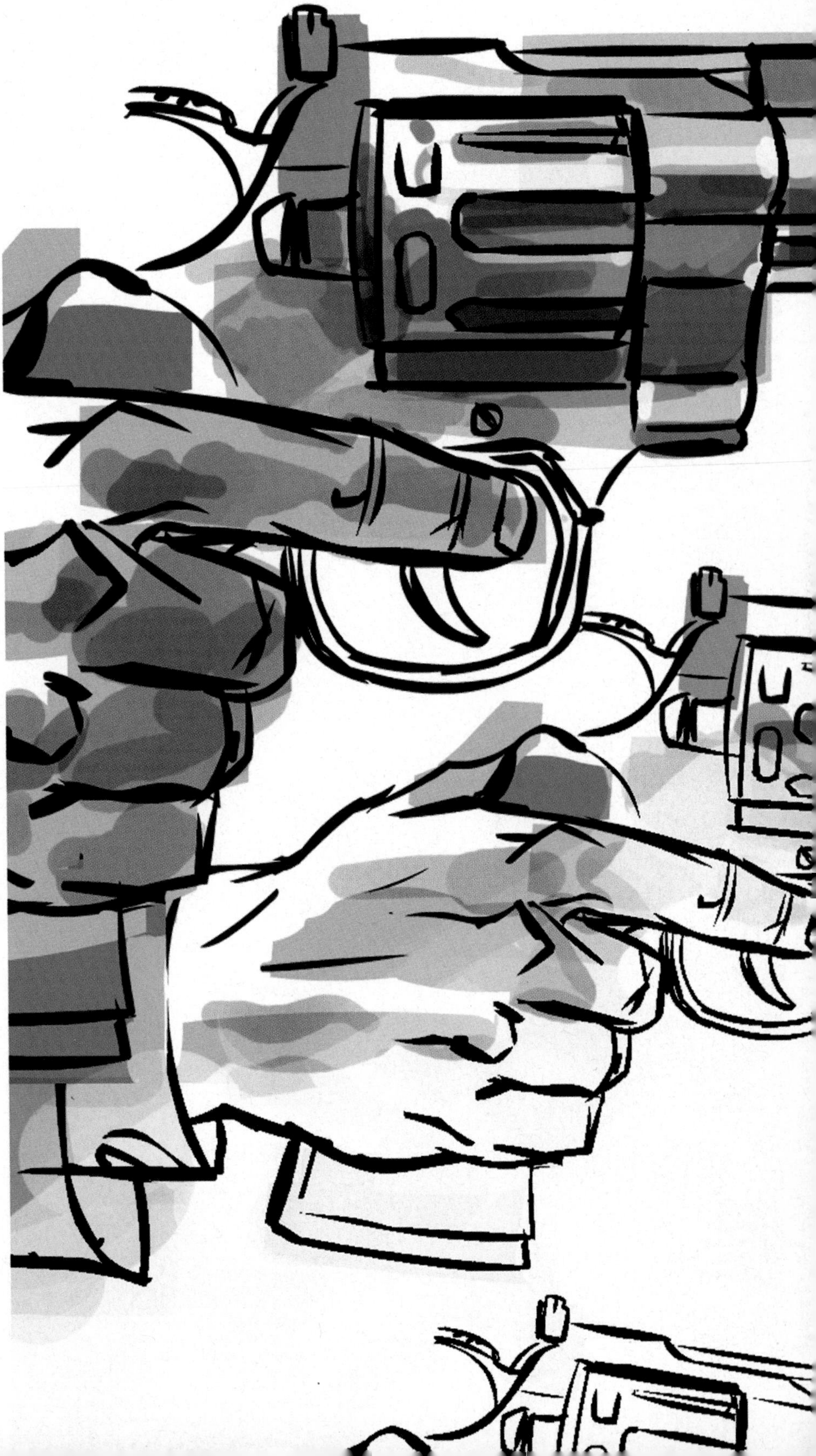

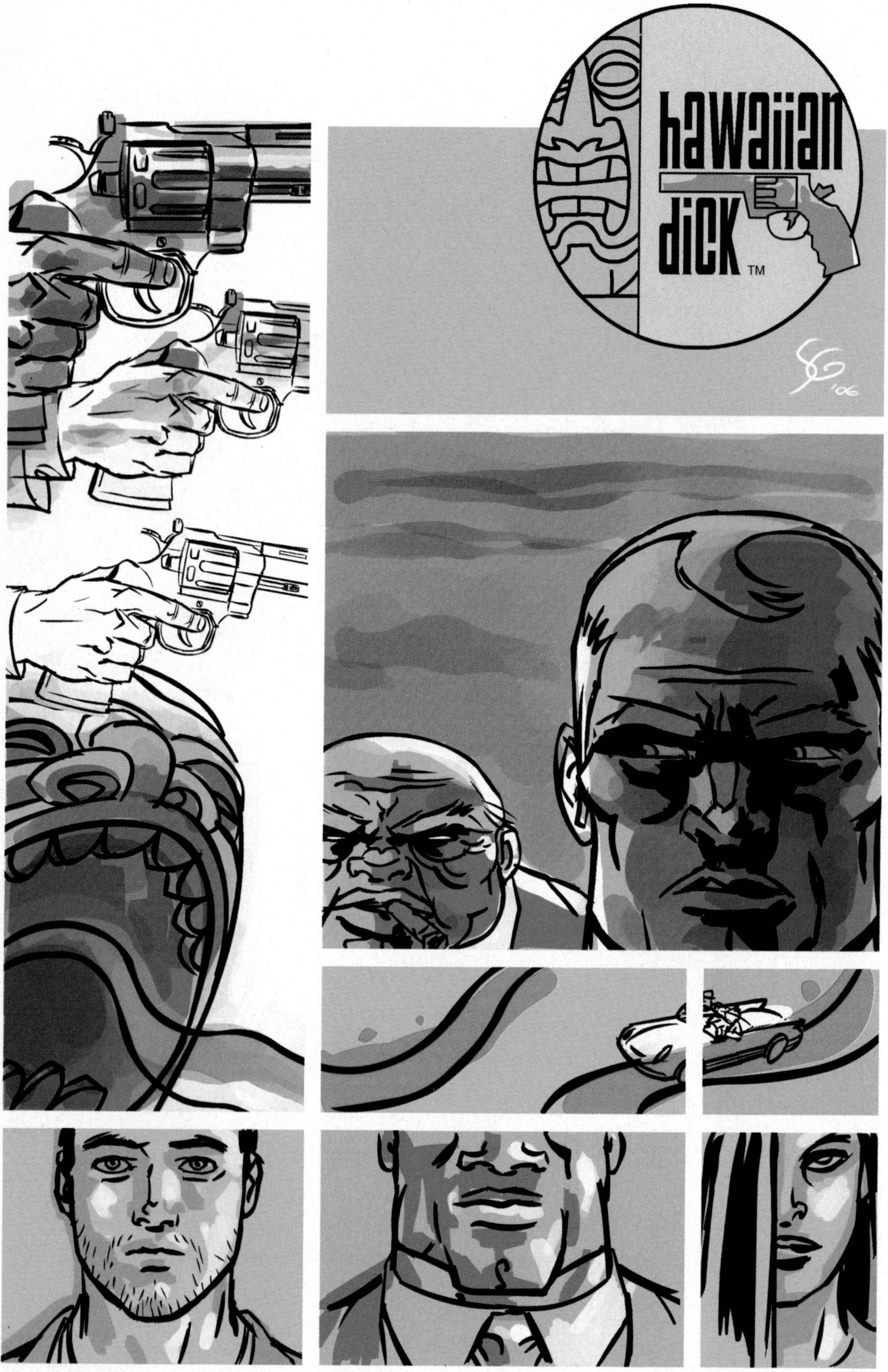

hawaiian dick TM
SG '06

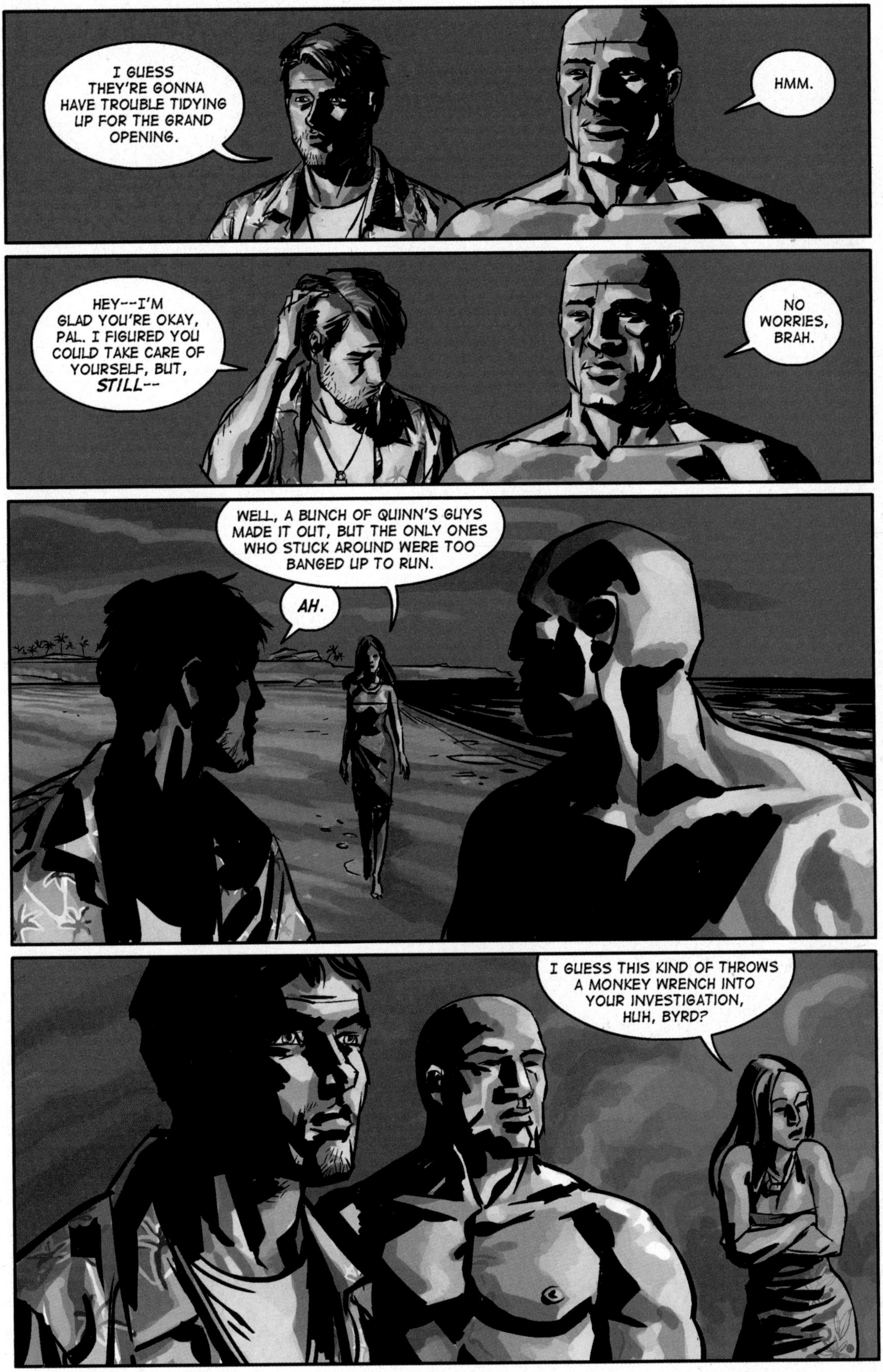
I GUESS THEY'RE GONNA HAVE TROUBLE TIDYING UP FOR THE GRAND OPENING.
HMM.
HEY--I'M GLAD YOU'RE OKAY, PAL. I FIGURED YOU COULD TAKE CARE OF YOURSELF, BUT, STILL--
NO WORRIES, BRAH.
WELL, A BUNCH OF QUINN'S GUYS MADE IT OUT, BUT THE ONLY ONES WHO STUCK AROUND WERE TOO BANGED UP TO RUN.
AH.
I GUESS THIS KIND OF THROWS A MONKEY WRENCH INTO YOUR INVESTIGATION, HUH, BYRD?

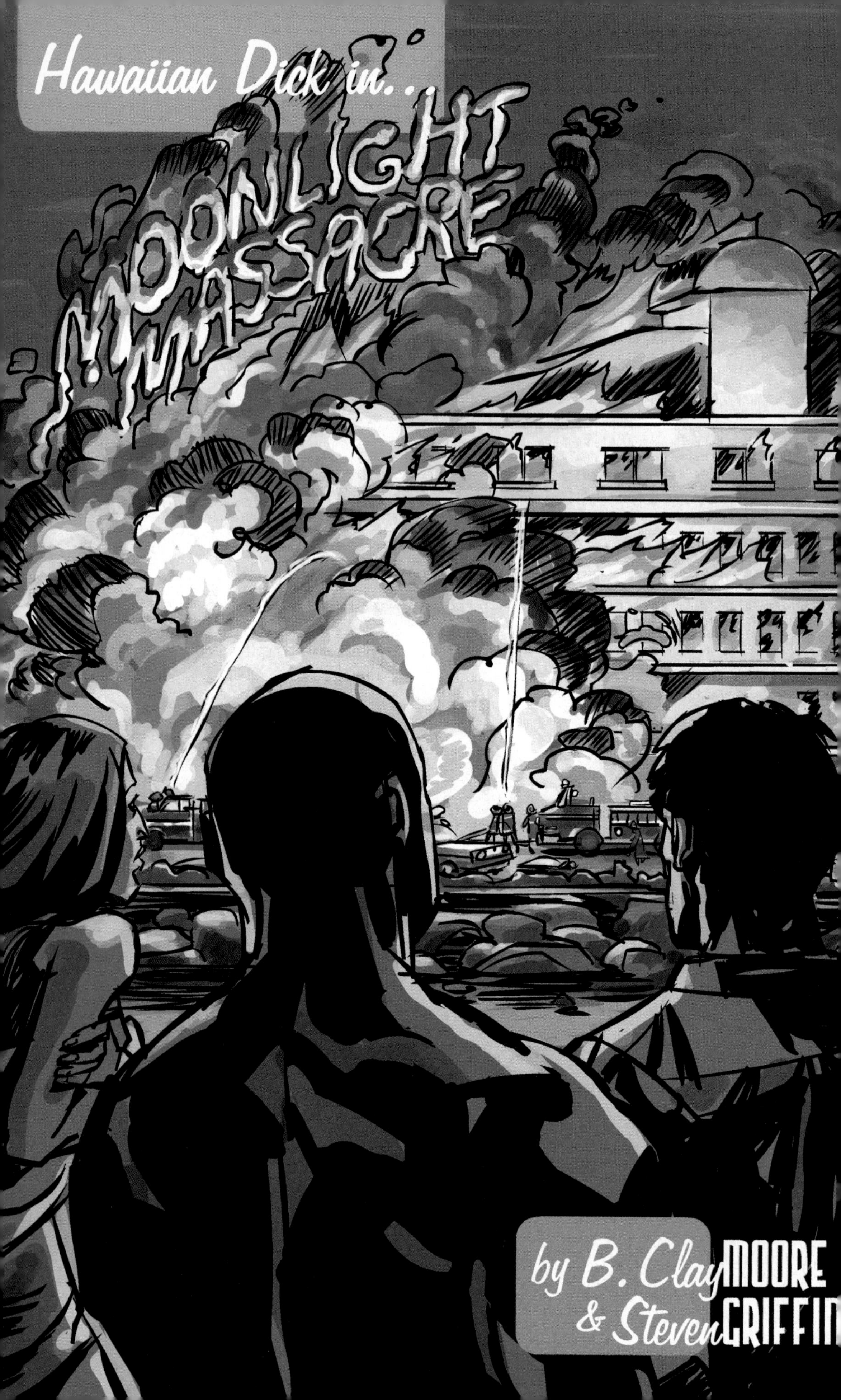

Hawaiian Dick in...
MOONLIGHT MASSACRE
by B. Clay MOORE
& Steven GRIFFIN

BYRD! BYRD, YA CRAFTY BASTARD!

AH, *GOOD*. IT'S MY FAVORITE COUPLE.

THEY'RE EVEN PRETTIER THAN YOU SAID THEY WERE.

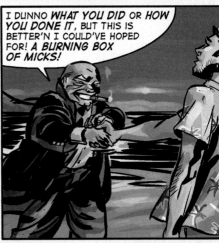

I DUNNO *WHAT YOU DID* OR *HOW YOU DONE IT*, BUT THIS IS BETTER'N I COULD'VE HOPED FOR! *A BURNING BOX OF MICKS!*

I DIDN'T HAVE ANYTHING TO DO WITH IT, PIANO. A COUPLE OF QUINN'S BOYS MANAGED TO PILOT THEIR MOTORBOAT RIGHT INTO THE DINING ROOM.

HAW!

I'M PAYING YOU ANYWAY!

HOW MANY OF THEM MADE IT OUT?

MOST OF THEM. SO I THINK MAYBE YOUR TROUBLES ARE JUST BEGINNING.

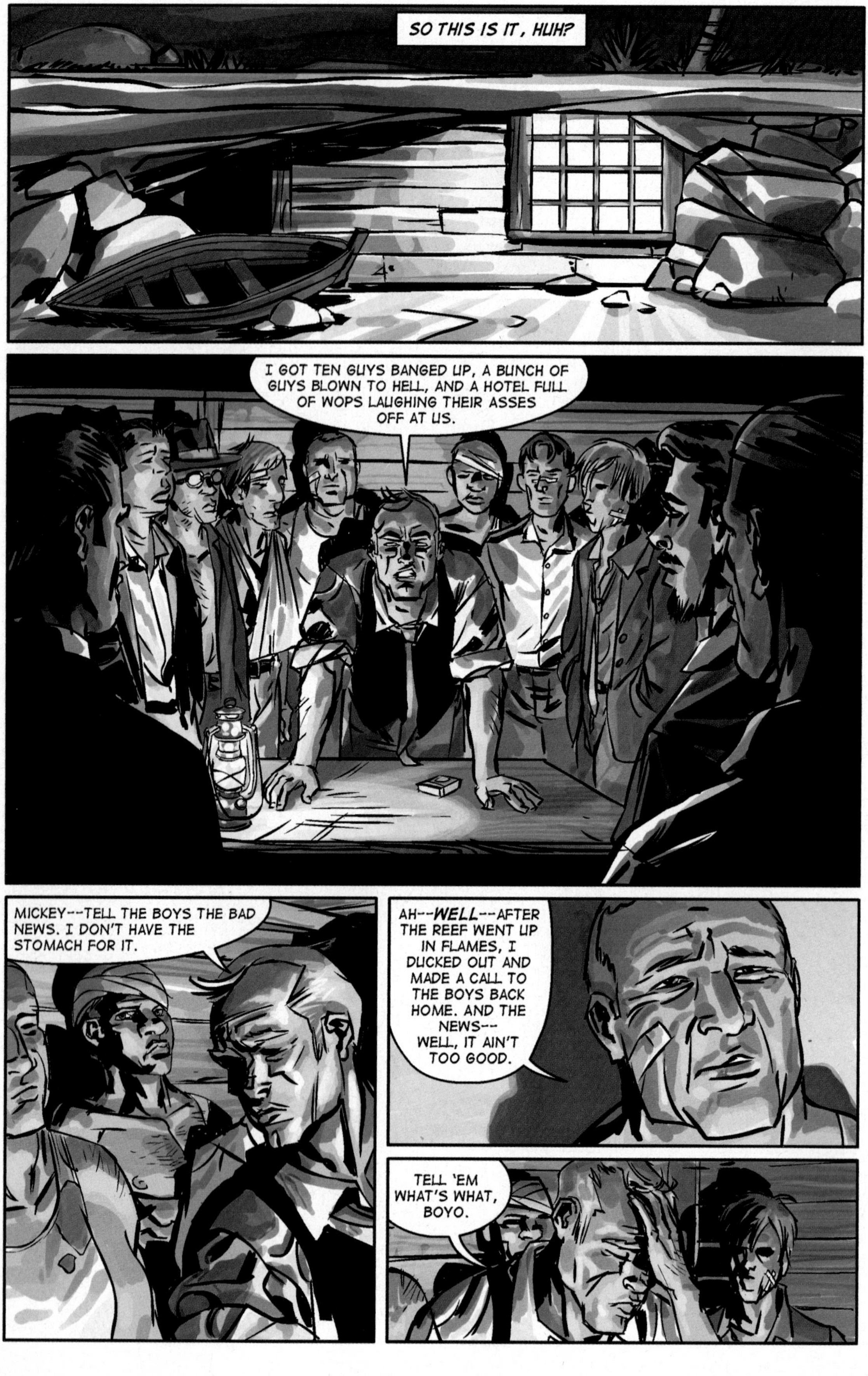
SO THIS IS IT, HUH?
I GOT TEN GUYS BANGED UP, A BUNCH OF GUYS BLOWN TO HELL, AND A HOTEL FULL OF WOPS LAUGHING THEIR ASSES OFF AT US.
MICKEY--TELL THE BOYS THE BAD NEWS. I DON'T HAVE THE STOMACH FOR IT.
AH--*WELL*--AFTER THE REEF WENT UP IN FLAMES, I DUCKED OUT AND MADE A CALL TO THE BOYS BACK HOME. AND THE NEWS-- WELL, IT AIN'T TOO GOOD.
TELL 'EM WHAT'S WHAT, BOYO.

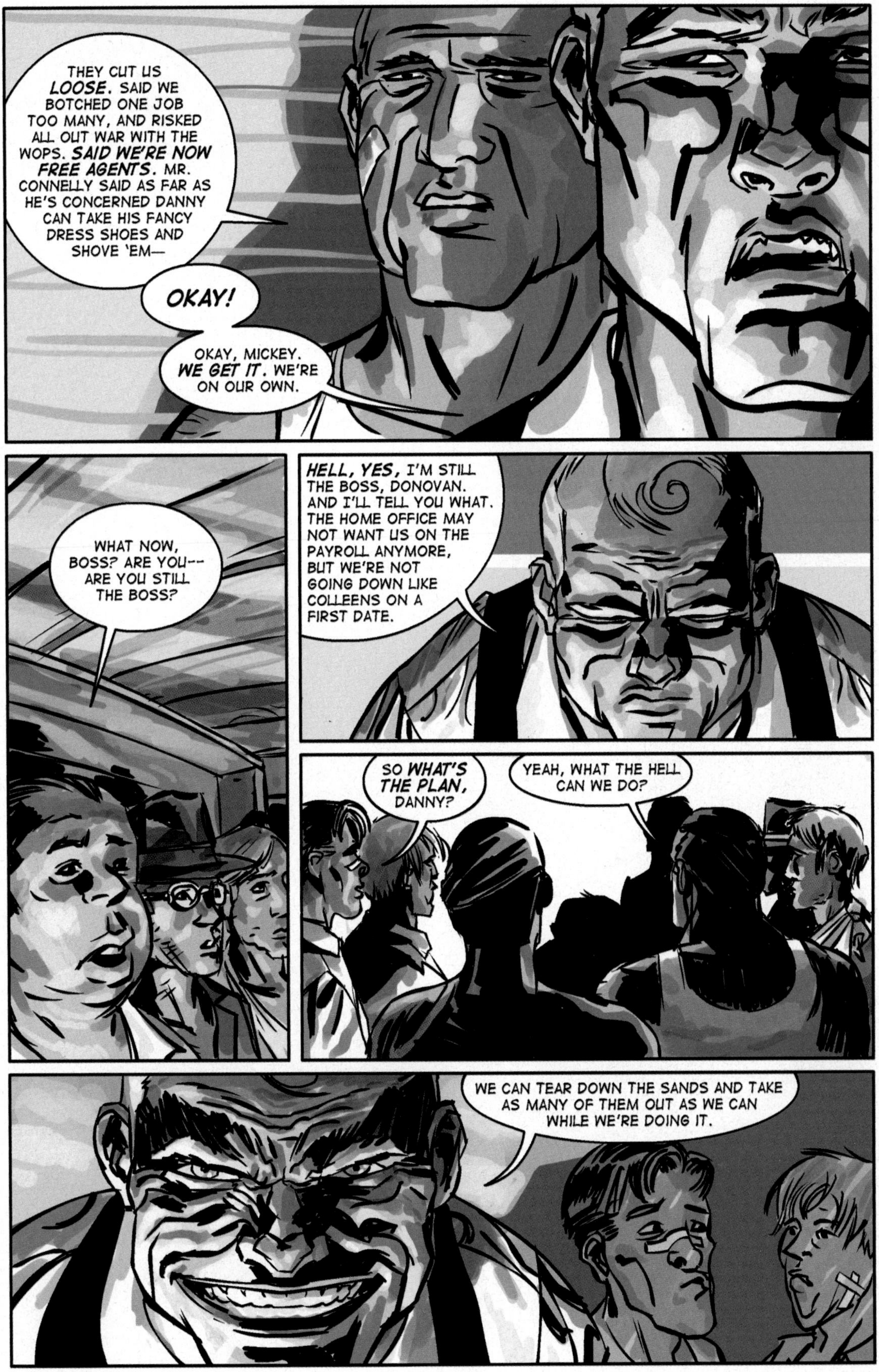
THEY CUT US LOOSE. SAID WE BOTCHED ONE JOB TOO MANY, AND RISKED ALL OUT WAR WITH THE WOPS. SAID WE'RE NOW FREE AGENTS. MR. CONNELLY SAID AS FAR AS HE'S CONCERNED DANNY CAN TAKE HIS FANCY DRESS SHOES AND SHOVE 'EM—
OKAY!
OKAY, MICKEY. WE GET IT. WE'RE ON OUR OWN.
WHAT NOW, BOSS? ARE YOU-- ARE YOU STILL THE BOSS?
HELL, YES, I'M STILL THE BOSS, DONOVAN. AND I'LL TELL YOU WHAT. THE HOME OFFICE MAY NOT WANT US ON THE PAYROLL ANYMORE, BUT WE'RE NOT GOING DOWN LIKE COLLEENS ON A FIRST DATE.
SO WHAT'S THE PLAN, DANNY?
YEAH, WHAT THE HELL CAN WE DO?
WE CAN TEAR DOWN THE SANDS AND TAKE AS MANY OF THEM OUT AS WE CAN WHILE WE'RE DOING IT.

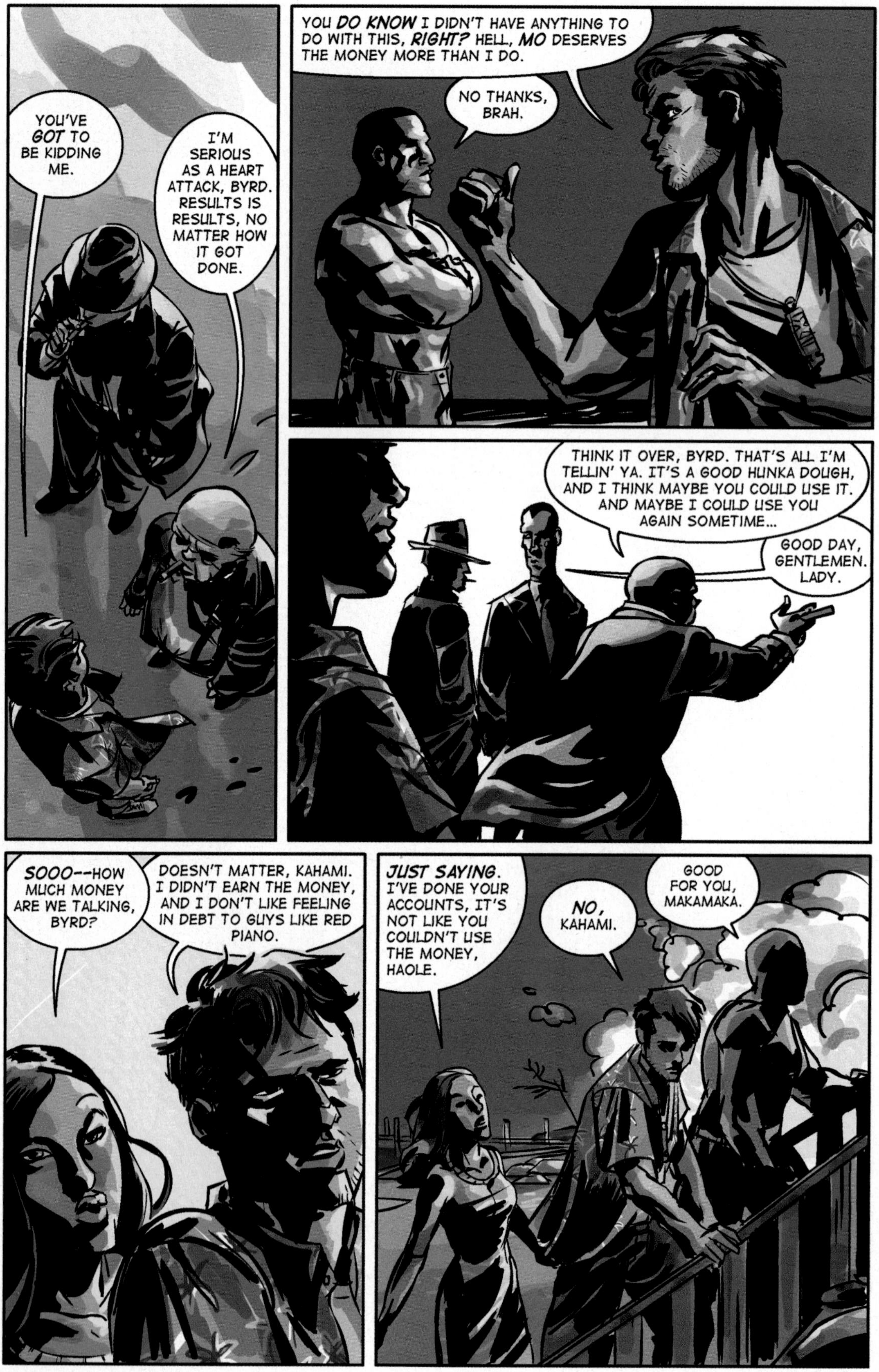
YOU'VE GOT TO BE KIDDING ME.
I'M SERIOUS AS A HEART ATTACK, BYRD. RESULTS IS RESULTS, NO MATTER HOW IT GOT DONE.
YOU DO KNOW I DIDN'T HAVE ANYTHING TO DO WITH THIS, RIGHT? HELL, MO DESERVES THE MONEY MORE THAN I DO.
NO THANKS, BRAH.
THINK IT OVER, BYRD. THAT'S ALL I'M TELLIN' YA. IT'S A GOOD HUNKA DOUGH, AND I THINK MAYBE YOU COULD USE IT. AND MAYBE I COULD USE YOU AGAIN SOMETIME...
GOOD DAY, GENTLEMEN. LADY.
SOOO--HOW MUCH MONEY ARE WE TALKING, BYRD?
DOESN'T MATTER, KAHAMI. I DIDN'T EARN THE MONEY, AND I DON'T LIKE FEELING IN DEBT TO GUYS LIKE RED PIANO.
JUST SAYING. I'VE DONE YOUR ACCOUNTS, IT'S NOT LIKE YOU COULDN'T USE THE MONEY, HAOLE.
NO, KAHAMI.
GOOD FOR YOU, MAKAMAKA.

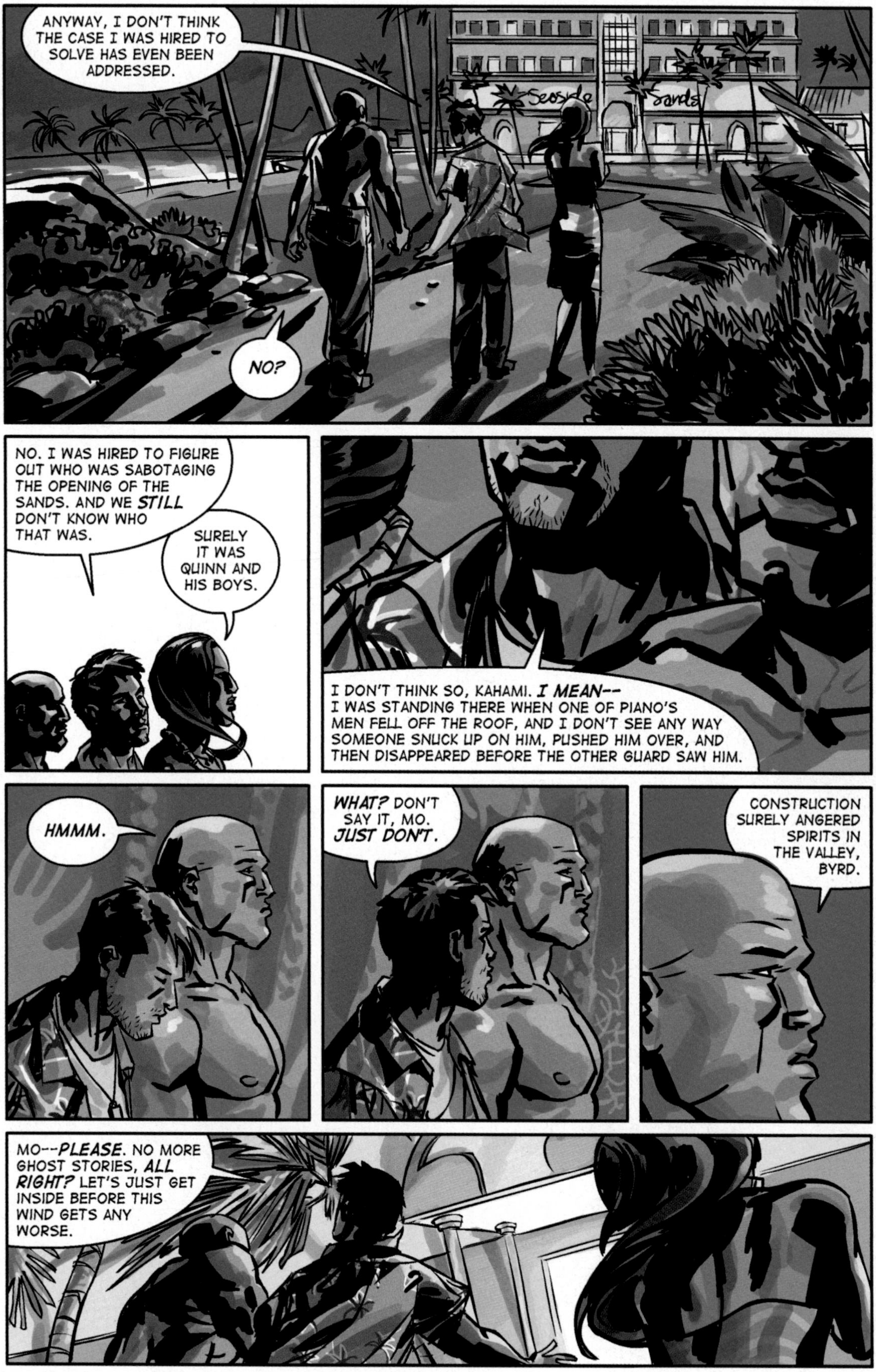

ANYWAY, I DON'T THINK THE CASE I WAS HIRED TO SOLVE HAS EVEN BEEN ADDRESSED.
NO?
NO. I WAS HIRED TO FIGURE OUT WHO WAS SABOTAGING THE OPENING OF THE SANDS. AND WE STILL DON'T KNOW WHO THAT WAS.
SURELY IT WAS QUINN AND HIS BOYS.
I DON'T THINK SO, KAHAMI. I MEAN-- I WAS STANDING THERE WHEN ONE OF PIANO'S MEN FELL OFF THE ROOF, AND I DON'T SEE ANY WAY SOMEONE SNUCK UP ON HIM, PUSHED HIM OVER, AND THEN DISAPPEARED BEFORE THE OTHER GUARD SAW HIM.
HMMM.
WHAT? DON'T SAY IT, MO. JUST DON'T.
CONSTRUCTION SURELY ANGERED SPIRITS IN THE VALLEY, BYRD.
MO--PLEASE. NO MORE GHOST STORIES, ALL RIGHT? LET'S JUST GET INSIDE BEFORE THIS WIND GETS ANY WORSE.

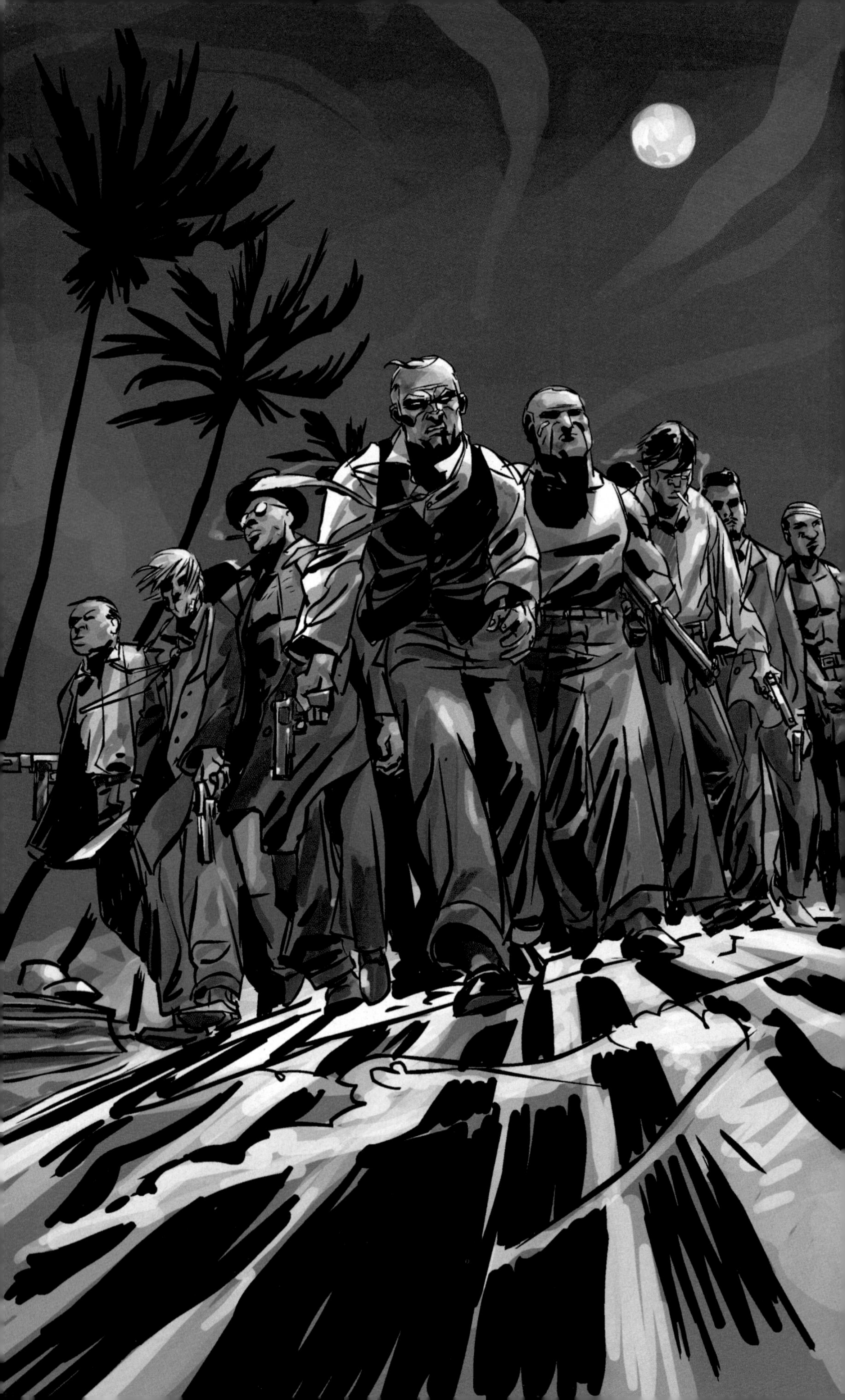

SO WHAT NOW, BYRD? I GOTTA GET BACK TO TOWN BEFORE THEY MOVE MY DESK OUTTA THE SQUADROOM.

I SHOULD GO BACK, TOO. THINK YOU COULD CRAM US BOTH INTO THAT LITTLE RED MACHINE YOU SPLURGED ON?

YEAH...I THOUGHT I'D BE BRINGING HOME MORE CASH, SO I BLEW MY WHOLE ADVANCE FROM PIANO ON THAT BABY.

YOU COULD ALWAYS TAKE PIANO UP ON HIS OFFER.

NAH. BUT A PART OF ME *DOES* WANT TO KNOW WHAT WAS REALLY HAPPENING HERE BEFORE MO BLEW UP THE IRISHMEN.

JUST SO MUCH HONOHONO, BYRD. THESE GUYS ARE LIKE CREEPING GRASS, FILLING EVERY ROTTEN CRACK IF YOU LET 'EM. MAYBE THEY WERE TEARING EACH OTHER'S PLACES UP, MAYBE THERE WAS--

I'M SORRY, MO. I *KNOW* WE'VE SEEN SOME REALLY-- *STRANGE STUFF*, BUT I CAN'T JUST WRITE IT OFF AS A CASE OF ANGRY ANCESTORS TRYING TO PUSH THE HAOLE OUT OF THEIR VALLEY.

HEY--WHAT ABOUT THAT GIRL IN WHITE? THE ONE WHO UNTIED YOU OVER AT THE REEF? EVER FIGURE OUT WHO SHE WAS?

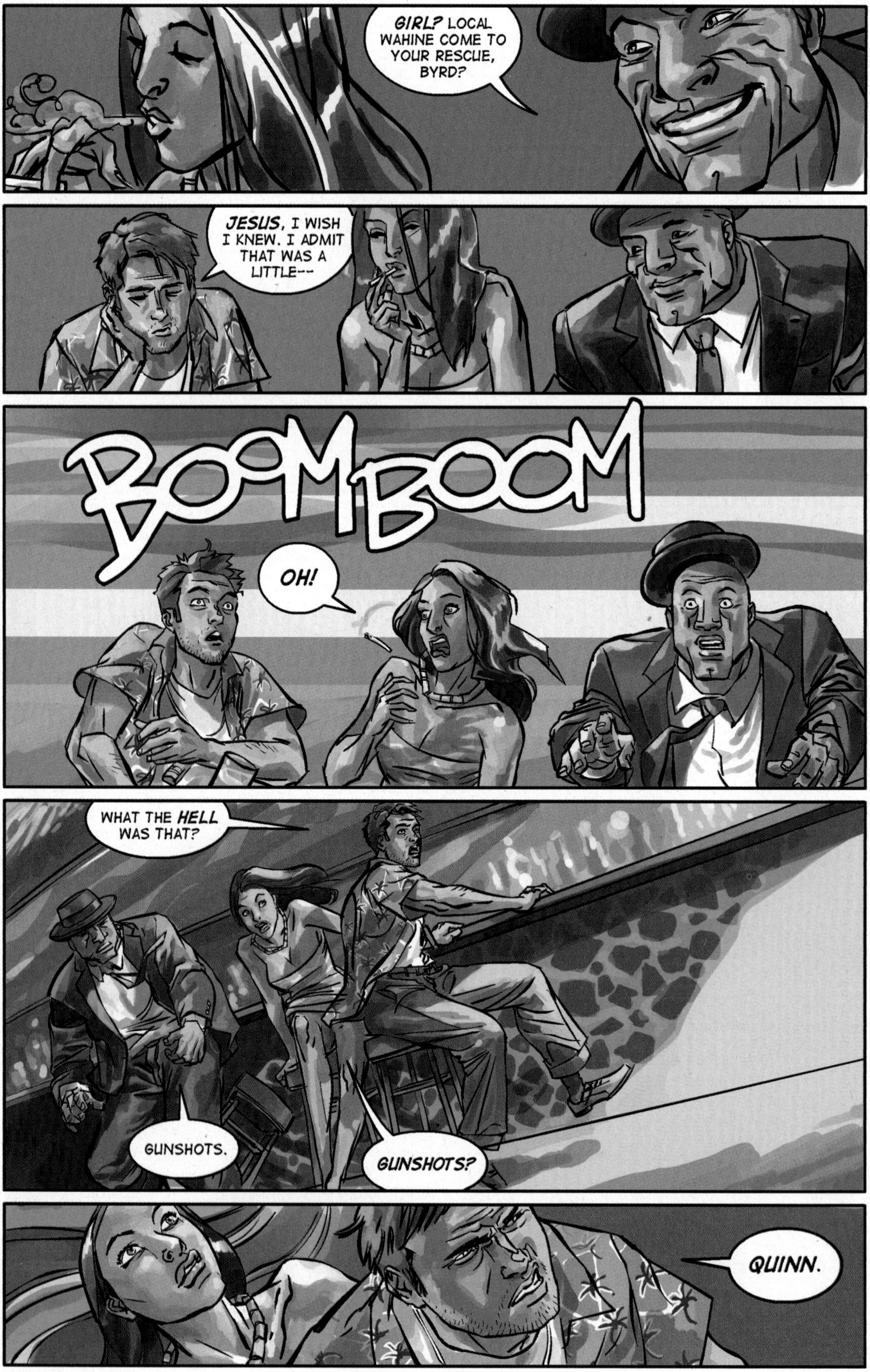
GIRL? LOCAL WAHINE COME TO YOUR RESCUE, BYRD?
JESUS, I WISH I KNEW. I ADMIT THAT WAS A LITTLE--
BOOM BOOM
OH!
WHAT THE HELL WAS THAT?
GUNSHOTS.
GUNSHOTS?
QUINN.

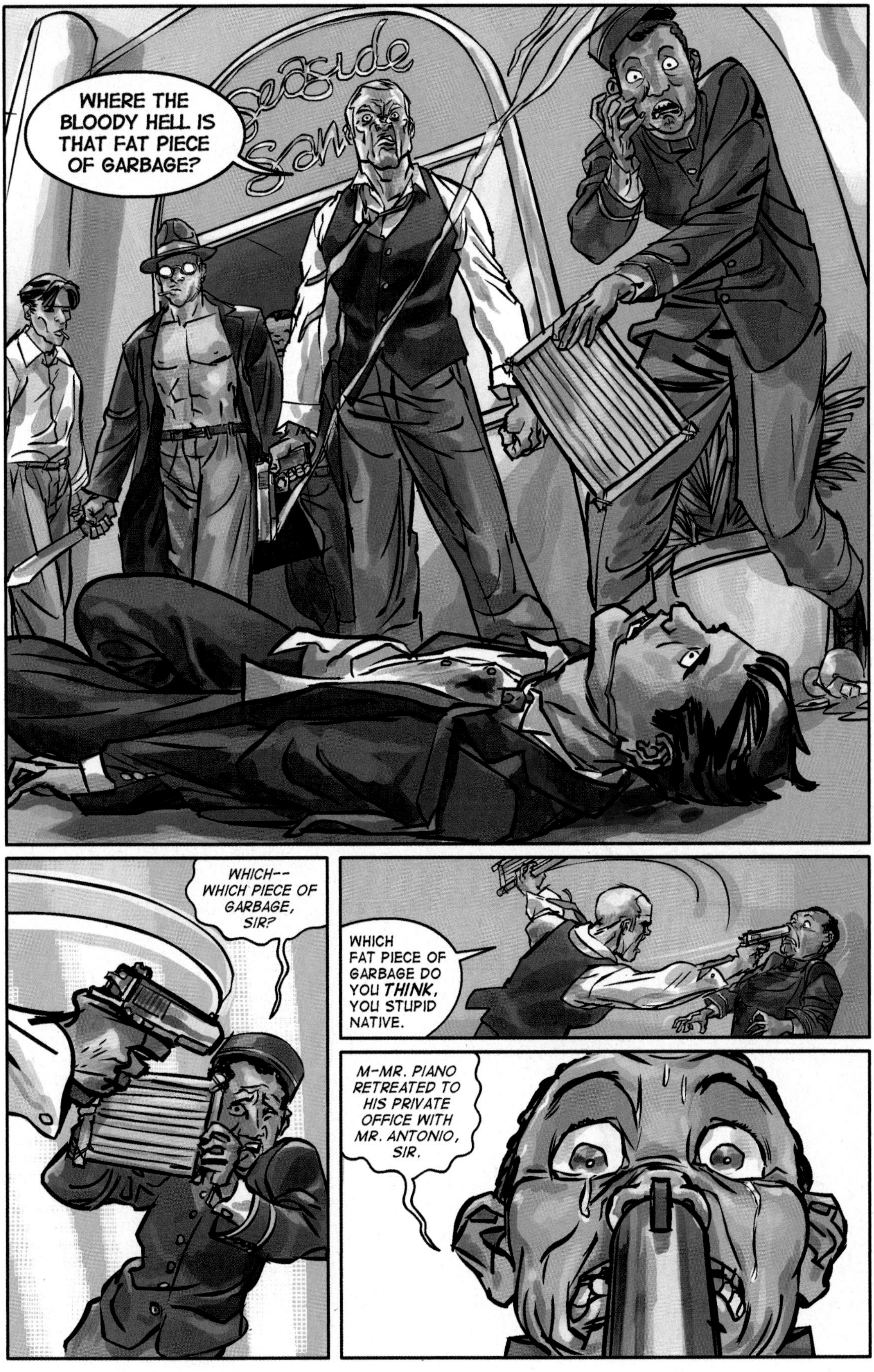
WHERE THE BLOODY HELL IS THAT FAT PIECE OF GARBAGE?
Seaside San
WHICH-- WHICH PIECE OF GARBAGE, SIR?
WHICH FAT PIECE OF GARBAGE DO YOU *THINK*, YOU STUPID NATIVE.
M-MR. PIANO RETREATED TO HIS PRIVATE OFFICE WITH MR. ANTONIO, SIR.

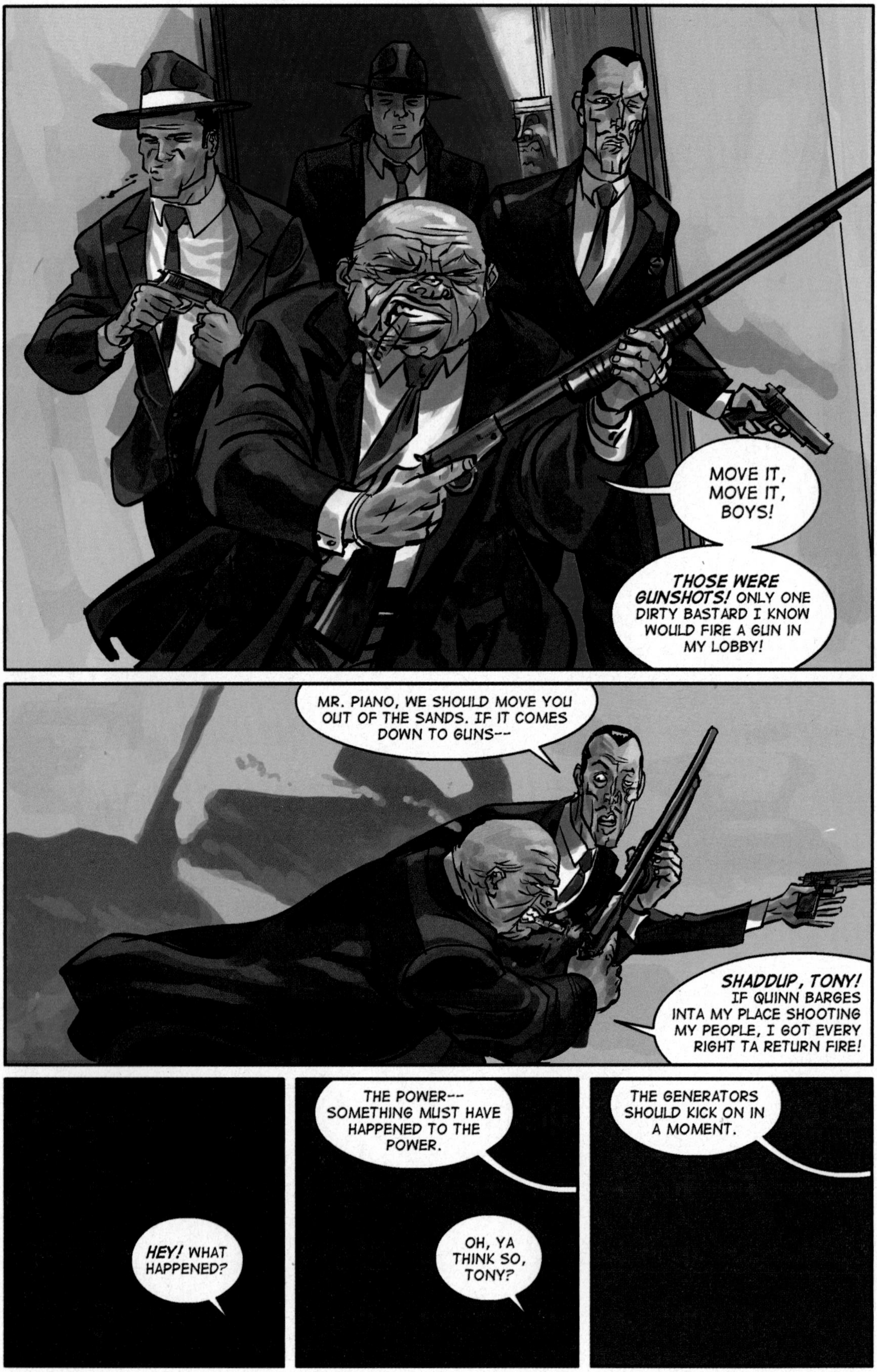
MOVE IT, MOVE IT, BOYS!
THOSE WERE GUNSHOTS! ONLY ONE DIRTY BASTARD I KNOW WOULD FIRE A GUN IN MY LOBBY!
MR. PIANO, WE SHOULD MOVE YOU OUT OF THE SANDS. IF IT COMES DOWN TO GUNS--
SHADDUP, TONY! IF QUINN BARGES INTA MY PLACE SHOOTING MY PEOPLE, I GOT EVERY RIGHT TA RETURN FIRE!
HEY! WHAT HAPPENED?
THE POWER-- SOMETHING MUST HAVE HAPPENED TO THE POWER.
OH, YA THINK SO, TONY?
THE GENERATORS SHOULD KICK ON IN A MOMENT.

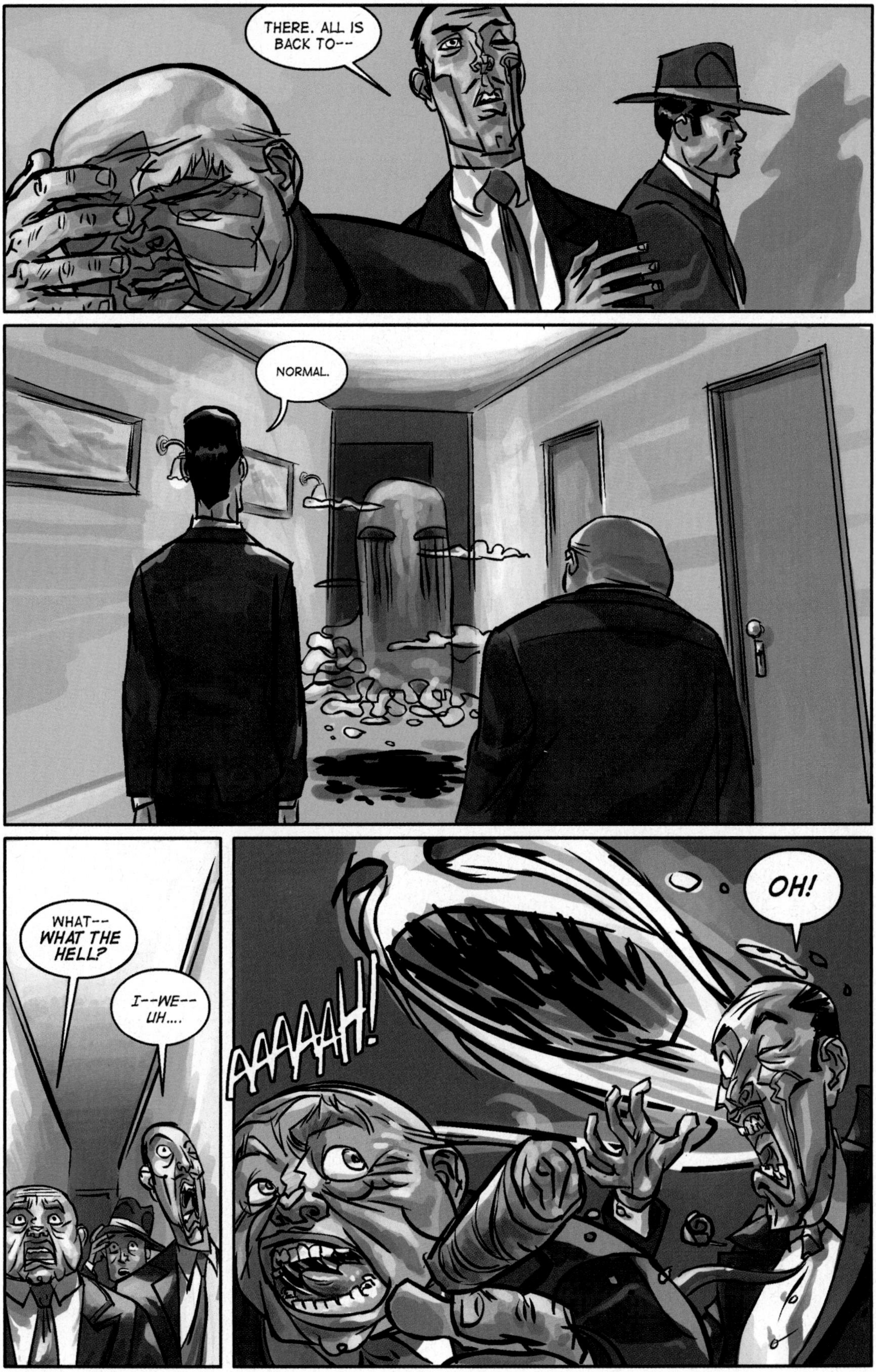
THERE. ALL IS BACK TO--
NORMAL.
WHAT-- WHAT THE HELL?
I--WE-- UH....
AAAAAH!
OH!

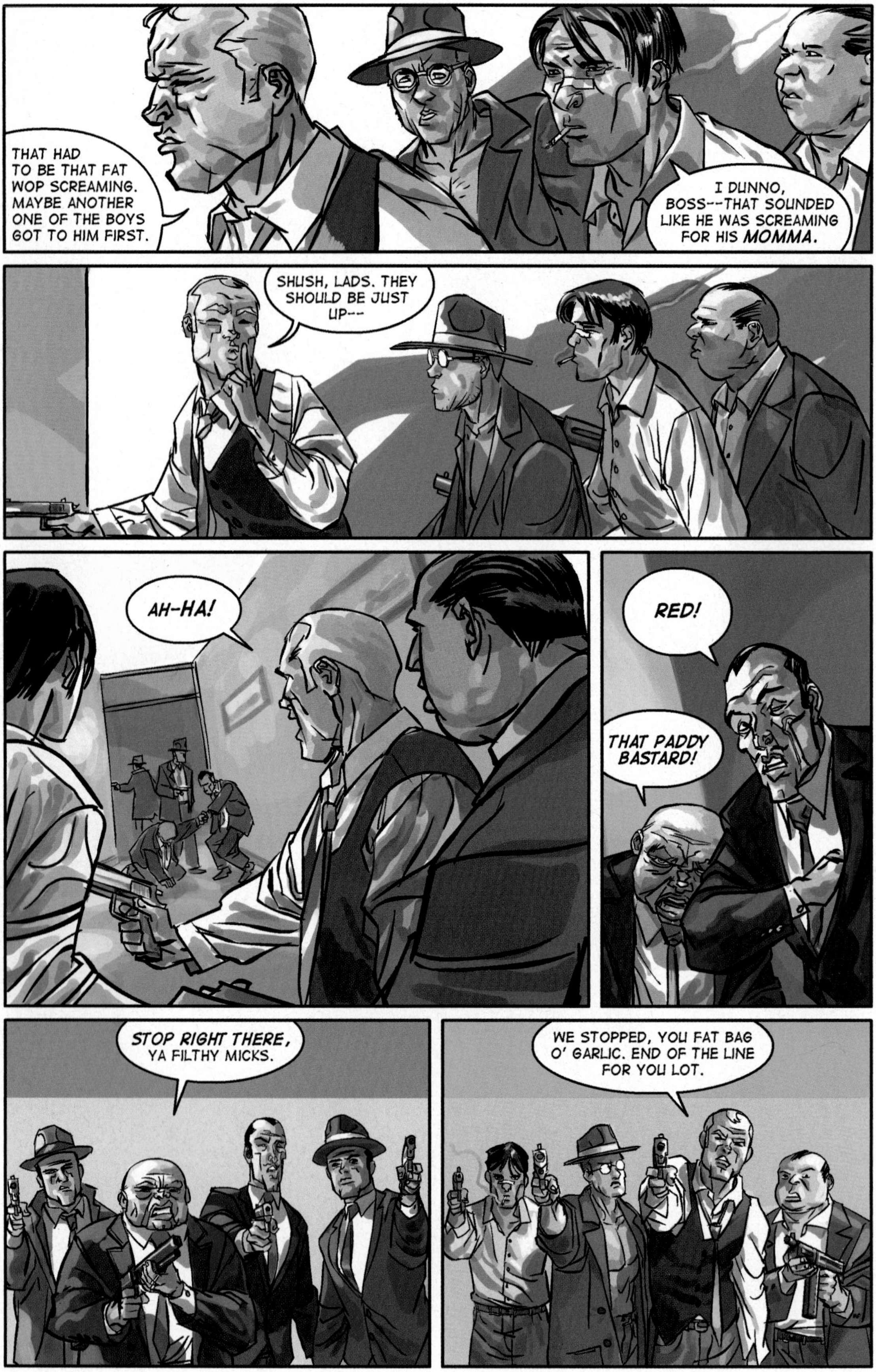
THAT HAD TO BE THAT FAT WOP SCREAMING. MAYBE ANOTHER ONE OF THE BOYS GOT TO HIM FIRST.
I DUNNO, BOSS--THAT SOUNDED LIKE HE WAS SCREAMING FOR HIS MOMMA.
SHUSH, LADS. THEY SHOULD BE JUST UP--
AH-HA!
RED!
THAT PADDY BASTARD!
STOP RIGHT THERE, YA FILTHY MICKS.
WE STOPPED, YOU FAT BAG O' GARLIC. END OF THE LINE FOR YOU LOT.

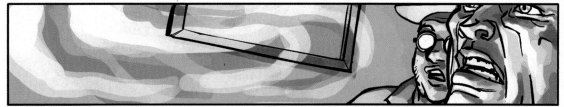

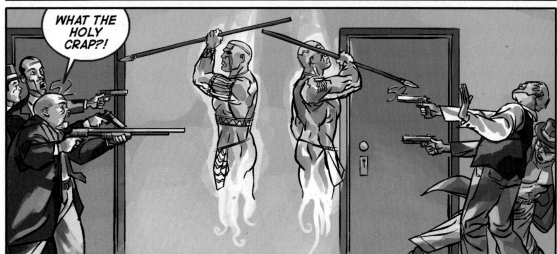

WHAT THE HOLY CRAP?!

DANNY! WHAT'S THAT?

MOTHER MARY!

SHOOT IT!

BANG! BANG!

KRAK! POW!

KRAK! BOOM! BOOM!

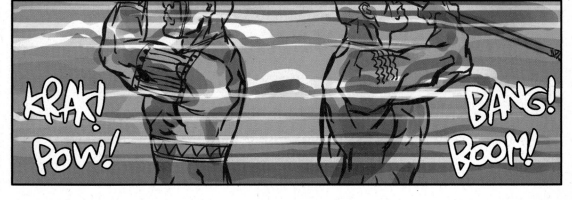

KRAK! POW!

BANG! BOOM!

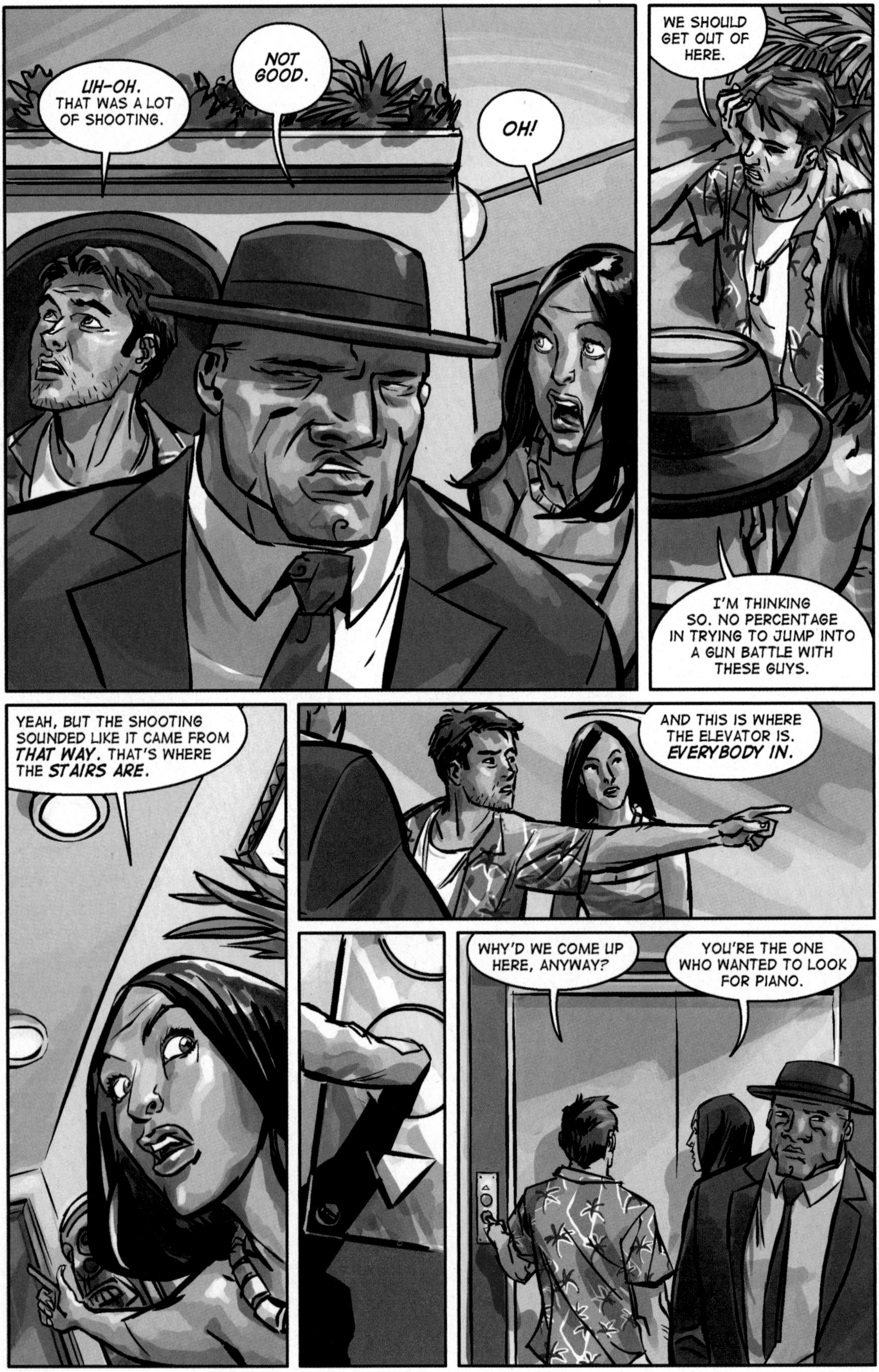
UH-OH. THAT WAS A LOT OF SHOOTING.
NOT GOOD.
OH!
WE SHOULD GET OUT OF HERE.
I'M THINKING SO. NO PERCENTAGE IN TRYING TO JUMP INTO A GUN BATTLE WITH THESE GUYS.
YEAH, BUT THE SHOOTING SOUNDED LIKE IT CAME FROM THAT WAY. THAT'S WHERE THE STAIRS ARE.
AND THIS IS WHERE THE ELEVATOR IS. EVERYBODY IN.
WHY'D WE COME UP HERE, ANYWAY?
YOU'RE THE ONE WHO WANTED TO LOOK FOR PIANO.

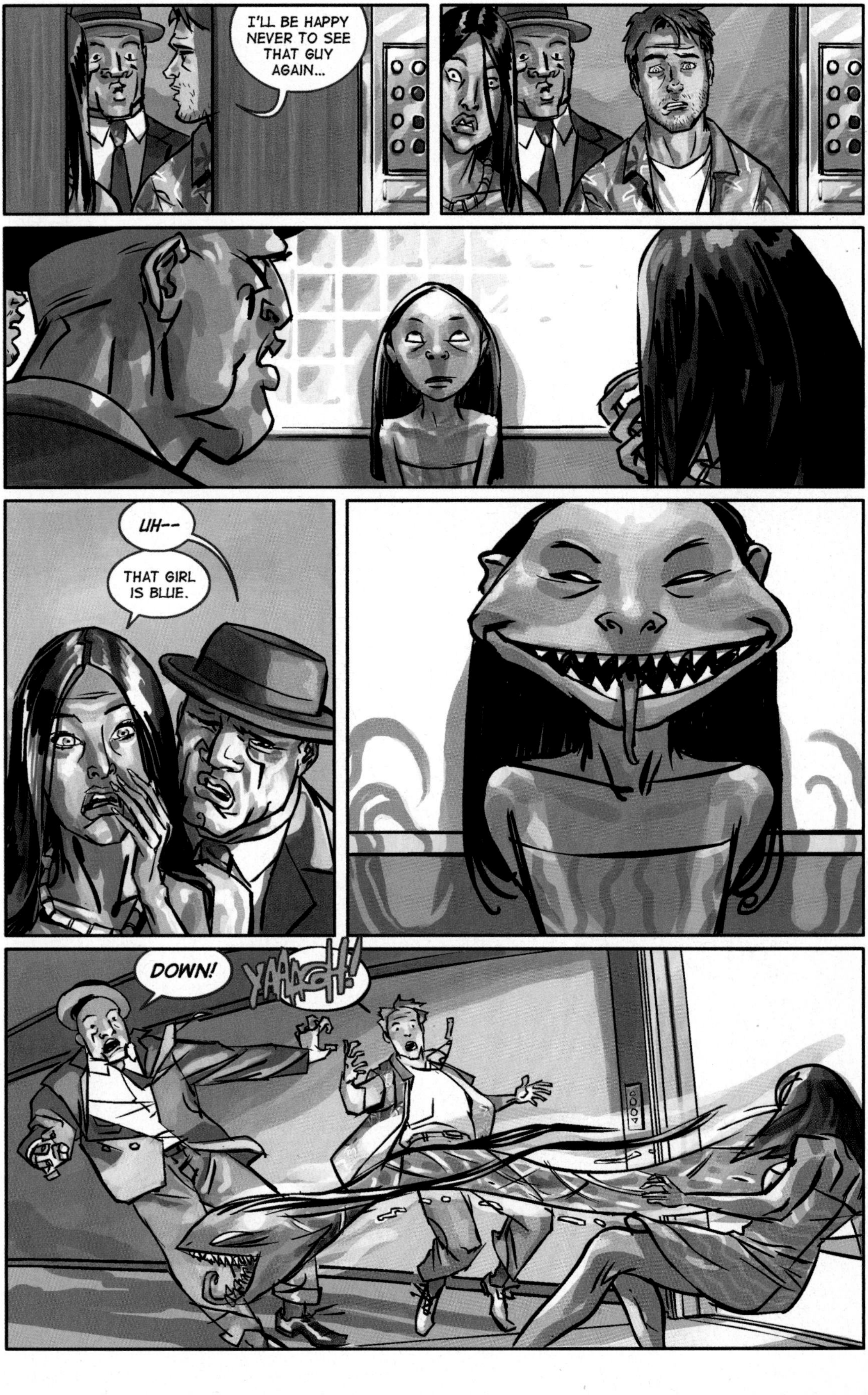
I'LL BE HAPPY NEVER TO SEE THAT GUY AGAIN...
UH--
THAT GIRL IS BLUE.
DOWN!
YAAAGH!!

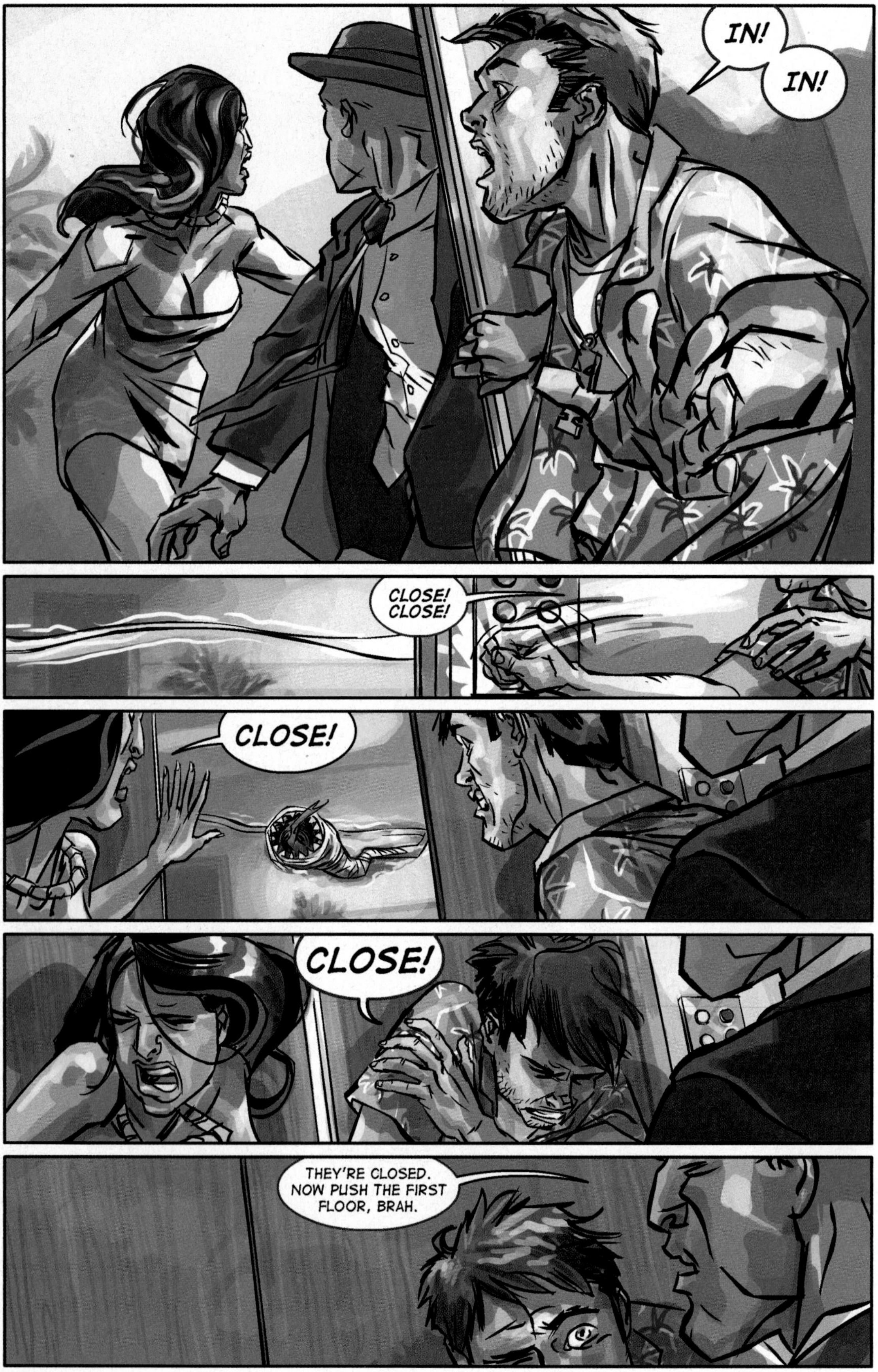
IN!
IN!
CLOSE!
CLOSE!
CLOSE!
CLOSE!
THEY'RE CLOSED.
NOW PUSH THE FIRST
FLOOR, BRAH.

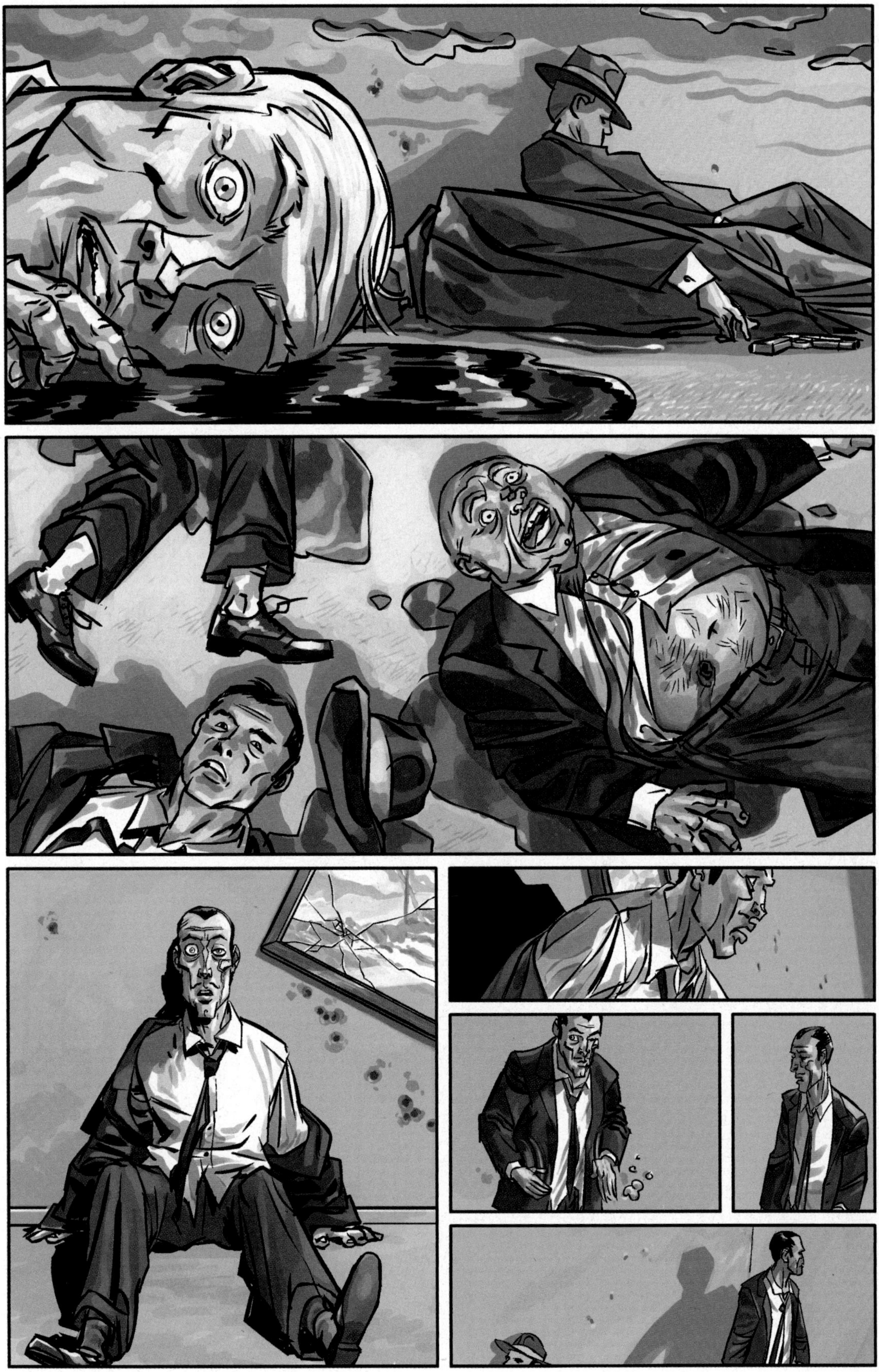

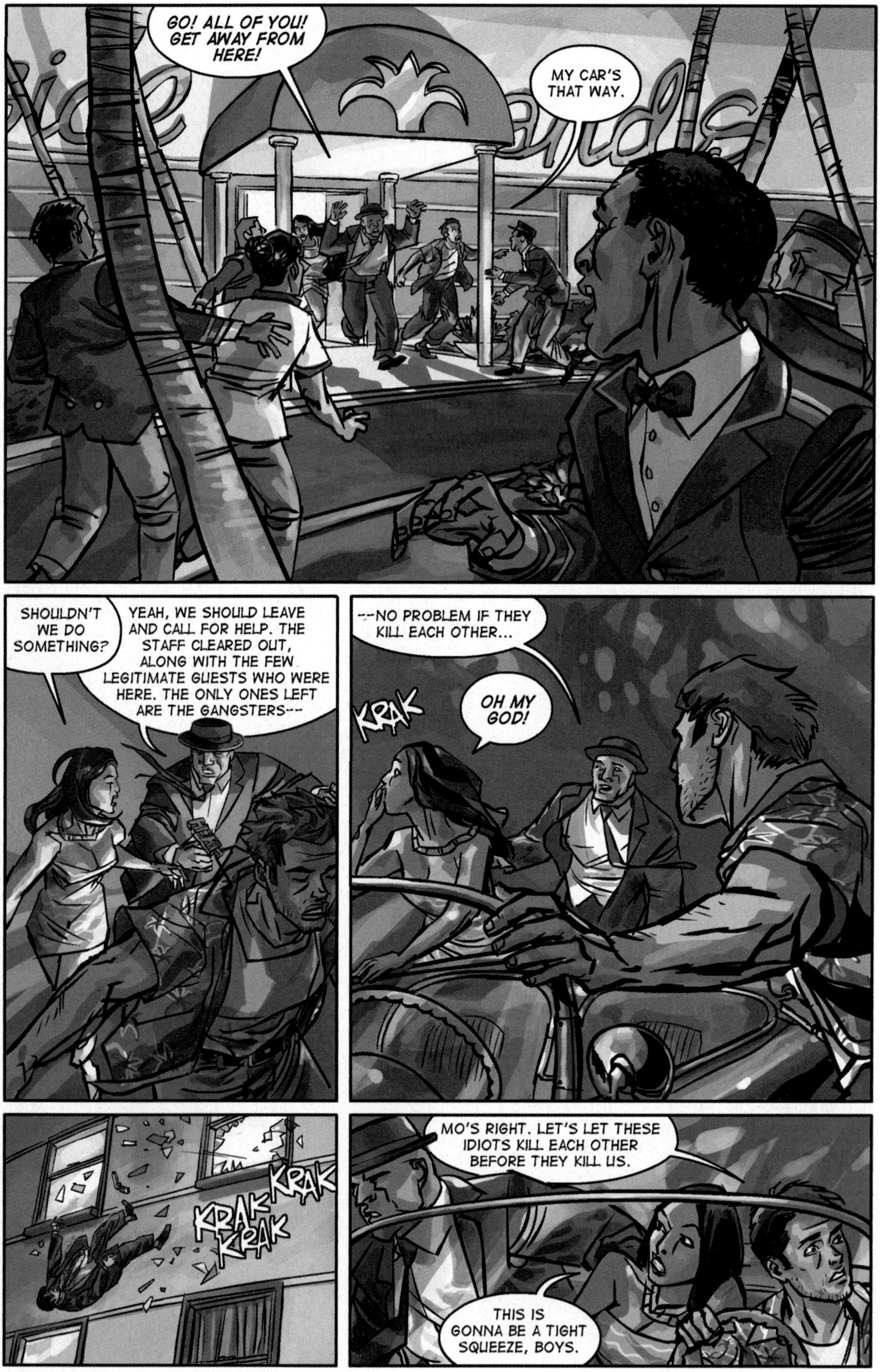
GO! ALL OF YOU! GET AWAY FROM HERE!
MY CAR'S THAT WAY.
SHOULDN'T WE DO SOMETHING?
YEAH, WE SHOULD LEAVE AND CALL FOR HELP. THE STAFF CLEARED OUT, ALONG WITH THE FEW LEGITIMATE GUESTS WHO WERE HERE. THE ONLY ONES LEFT ARE THE GANGSTERS--
KRAK
--NO PROBLEM IF THEY KILL EACH OTHER...
OH MY GOD!
KRAK
KRAK
KRAK
MO'S RIGHT. LET'S LET THESE IDIOTS KILL EACH OTHER BEFORE THEY KILL US.
THIS IS GONNA BE A TIGHT SQUEEZE, BOYS.

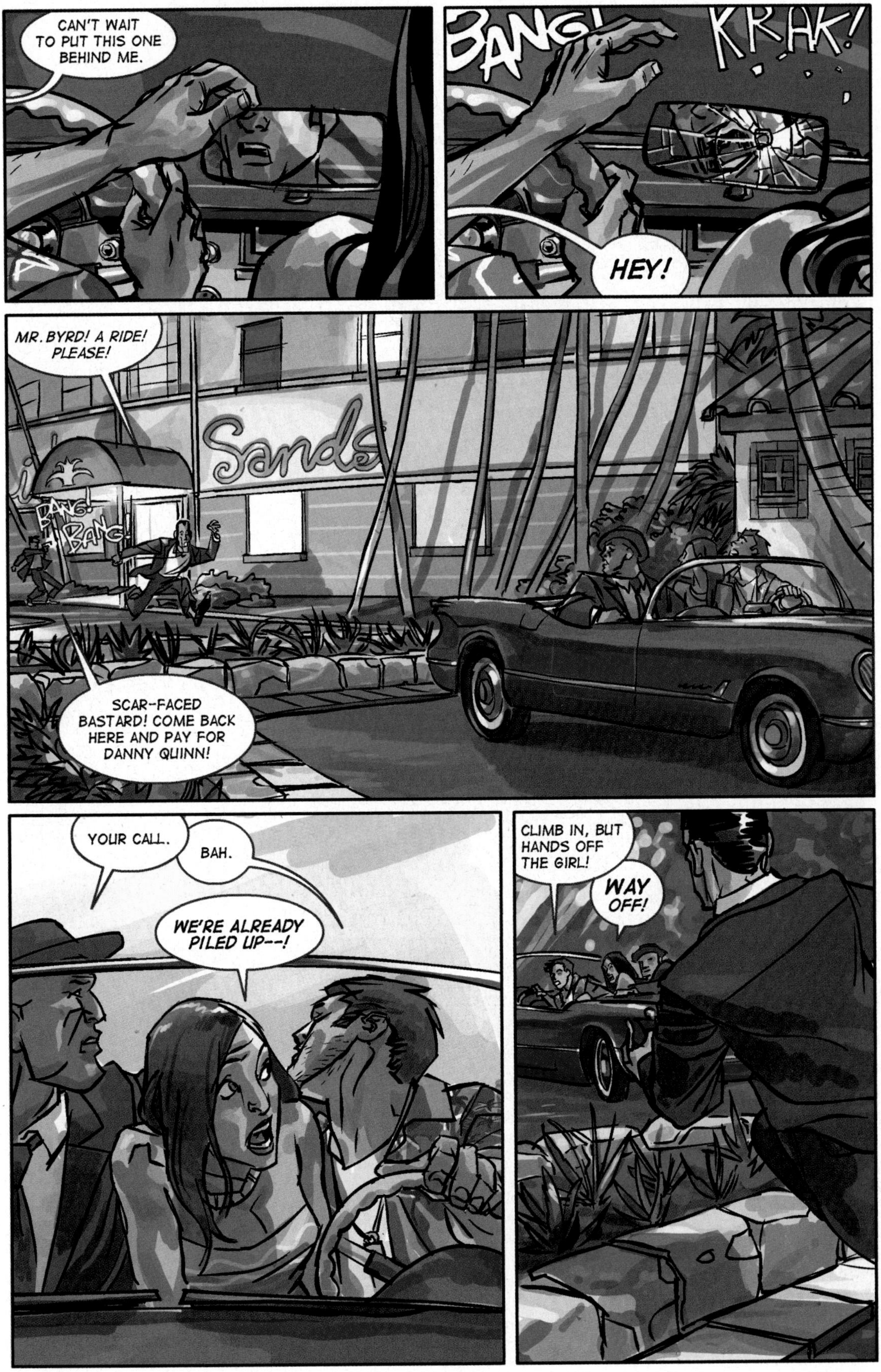
CAN'T WAIT TO PUT THIS ONE BEHIND ME.
BANG!
KRAK!
HEY!
MR. BYRD! A RIDE! PLEASE!
Sands
BANG! BANG!
SCAR-FACED BASTARD! COME BACK HERE AND PAY FOR DANNY QUINN!
YOUR CALL.
BAH.
WE'RE ALREADY PILED UP--!
CLIMB IN, BUT HANDS OFF THE GIRL!
WAY OFF!

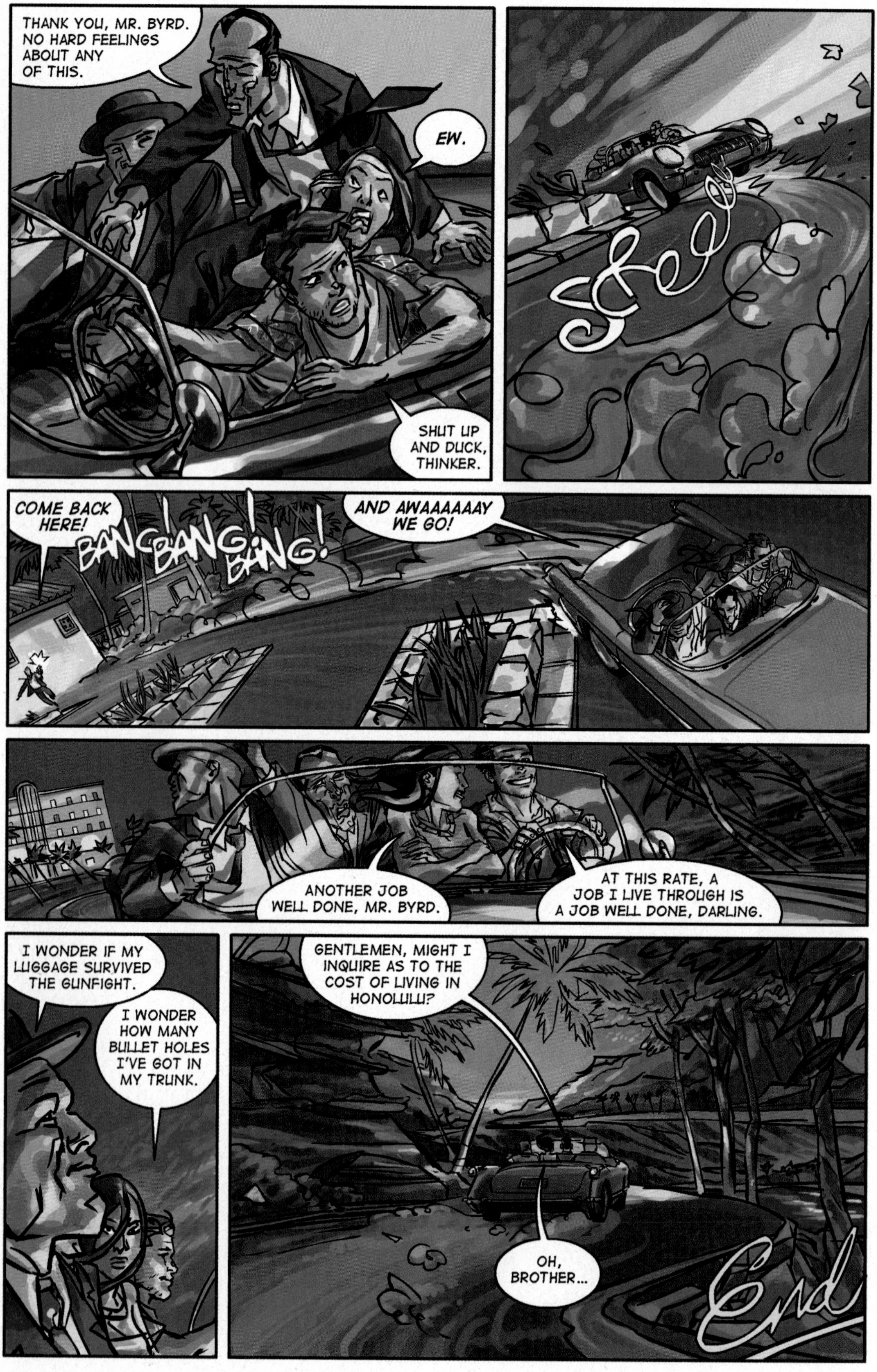
THANK YOU, MR. BYRD. NO HARD FEELINGS ABOUT ANY OF THIS.
EW.
SHUT UP AND DUCK, THINKER.
Screee
COME BACK HERE!
BANG BANG BANG BANG!
AND AWAAAAAAY WE GO!
ANOTHER JOB WELL DONE, MR. BYRD.
AT THIS RATE, A JOB I LIVE THROUGH IS A JOB WELL DONE, DARLING.
I WONDER IF MY LUGGAGE SURVIVED THE GUNFIGHT.
I WONDER HOW MANY BULLET HOLES I'VE GOT IN MY TRUNK.
GENTLEMEN, MIGHT I INQUIRE AS TO THE COST OF LIVING IN HONOLULU?
OH, BROTHER...
End

BONUS
SECTION

Rather than being told that we're insane, as expected, we actually received a lot of positive response to the **HUGE** Dick bonus section in the first trade collection. So here we are with the second book, and this foolish (and possibly dangerous) encouragement from readers has convinced us to once again swamp you with stuff you may or may not wish to see. Cool!

So what do we have? Well, this first part of the bonus section contains various extras that were printed in the back of the regular issues. And following this part are, well, other parts...containing other stuff. Never before has it been more obvious why I don't write this book.

On that subject - if the spelling of some words seem funny to you, it's not that I can't write but that I'm Australian...and can't write. Enjoy!

- Steven

A BRIEF GUIDE TO
BYRD'S HAWAII

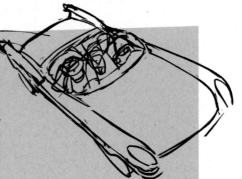

The 1954 Corvette

Byrd's ride in this series is a 1954 Corvette. Most models were Polo White, but there were models available in "Sportsman Red" (the color of Byrd's car), as well as "Pennant Blue," and a very few in black. There were around 3600 new Corvettes on the road in 1954, and the base price for the roadsters was $2,774.00.

Gambling

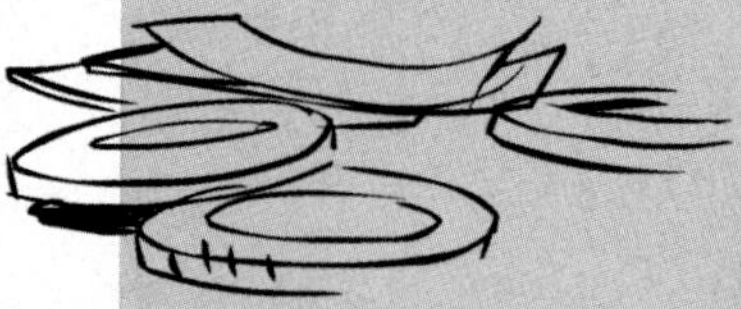

Gambling is illegal in Hawaii, and it's doubtful that will ever change. However, over the decades, gambling dens have flourished, often with the cooperation of local authorities. In Byrd's day it wouldn't have been unusual for a gambling operation to exist, with off duty police officers watching the door for undesirables. Currently, Hawaii is one of six states that also outlaws online gambling, although not much is done to police the crime.

Organized Crime

In reality, most organized crime in Hawaii was controlled by local syndicates. But our story takes place at a time when American mobsters were making a mint with gambling dens in places like Havana (before Castro seized power and "nationalized" the mob businesses, thereby depriving them of millions in profits), and this story assumes that the competing gangs would be striking out in search of similar pastures of green.

BACK COVERS

As with the first series, each issue of The Last Resort featured a character drawing on the back cover, mini versions of which we've reproduced here. Collect them all!

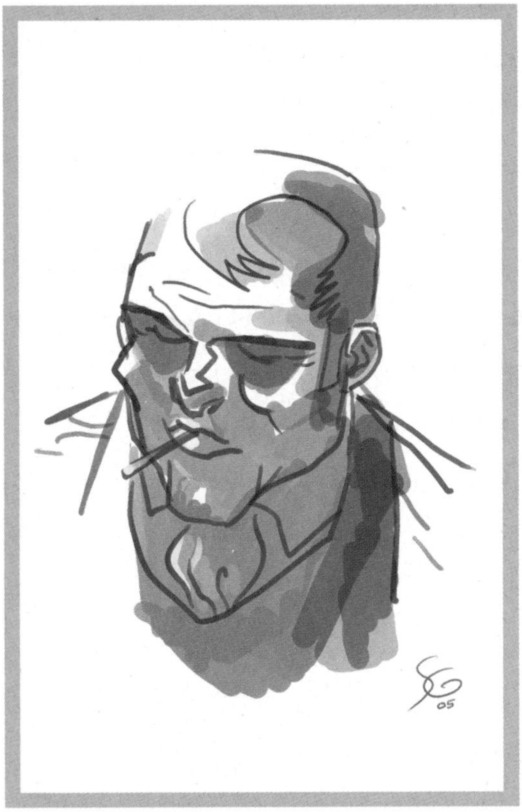

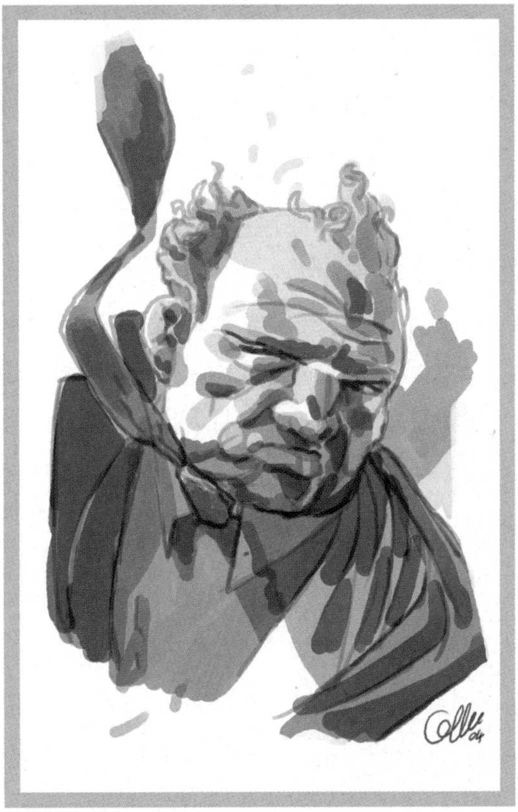

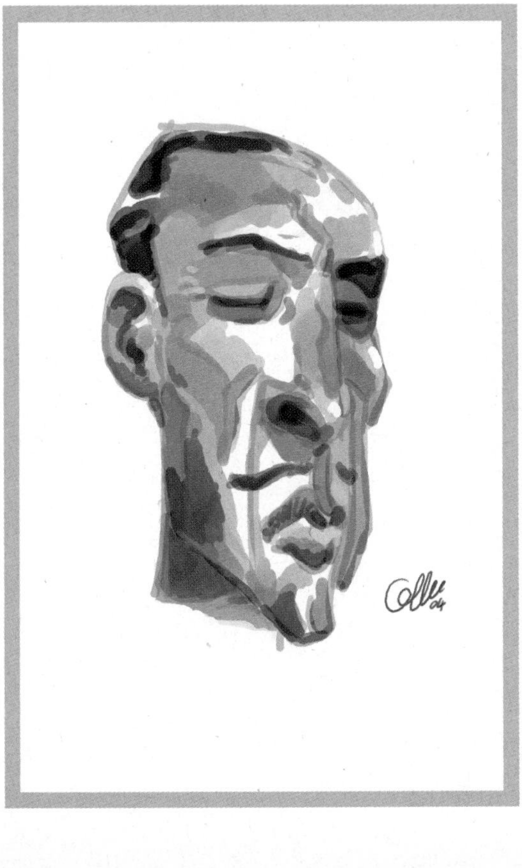

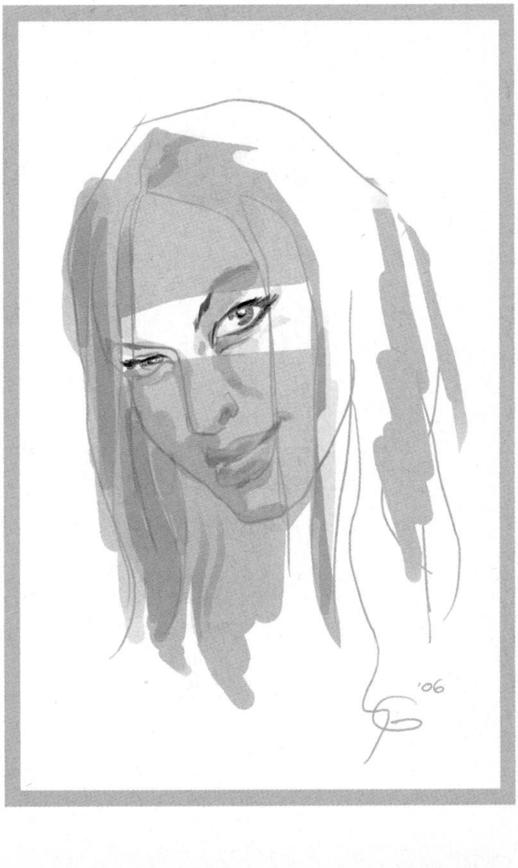

SICK of that
good-for-nothing

artist of your **favourite** comic book series taking forever to get the latest issue onto the shelves and into your waiting arms? **Well wait no longer** thanks to the brand-new limited edition **Hawaiian Dick Finger Puppets!** YES, that's right -- gone are the days of asking your friendly comic shop assistant the dreaded words, "Is it in yet?", because now, thanks to Hawaiian Dick Finger Puppets, Dick is **always in** and YOU, Dear Reader, can enjoy a fresh serving whenever you want!

Remember, with Hawaiian Dick Finger Puppets, Byrd, Mo and the gang are just a raised finger away.

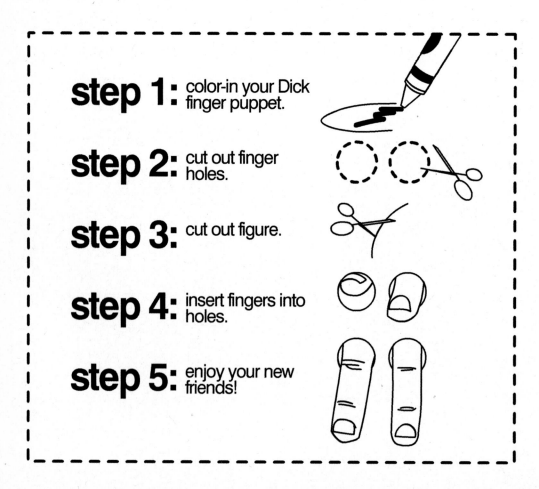

step 1: color-in your Dick finger puppet.

step 2: cut out finger holes.

step 3: cut out figure.

step 4: insert fingers into holes.

step 5: enjoy your new friends!

byrd

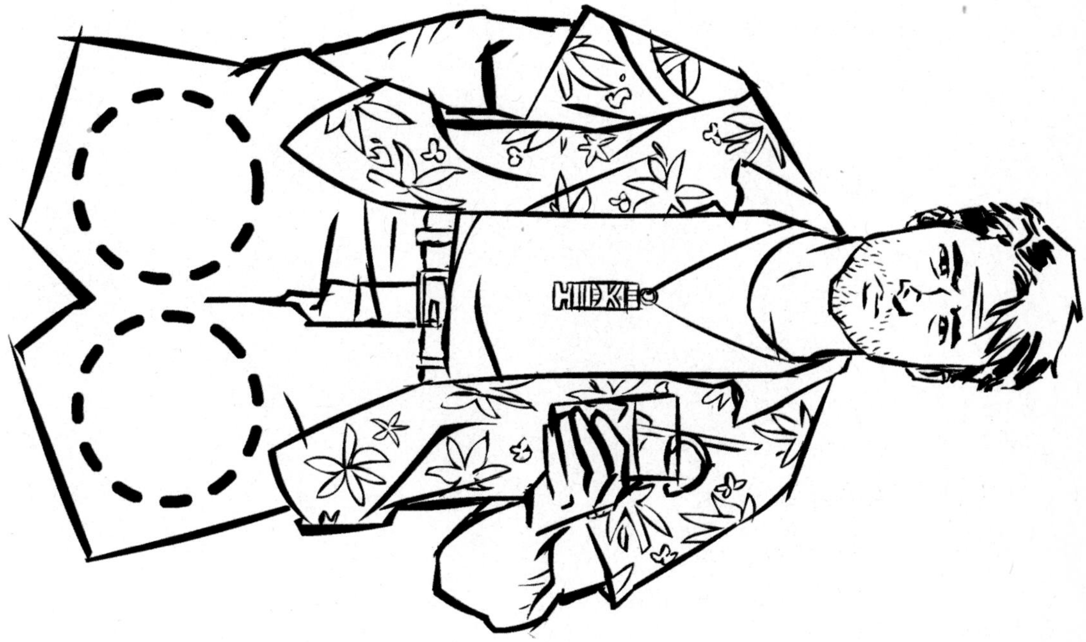

kahami

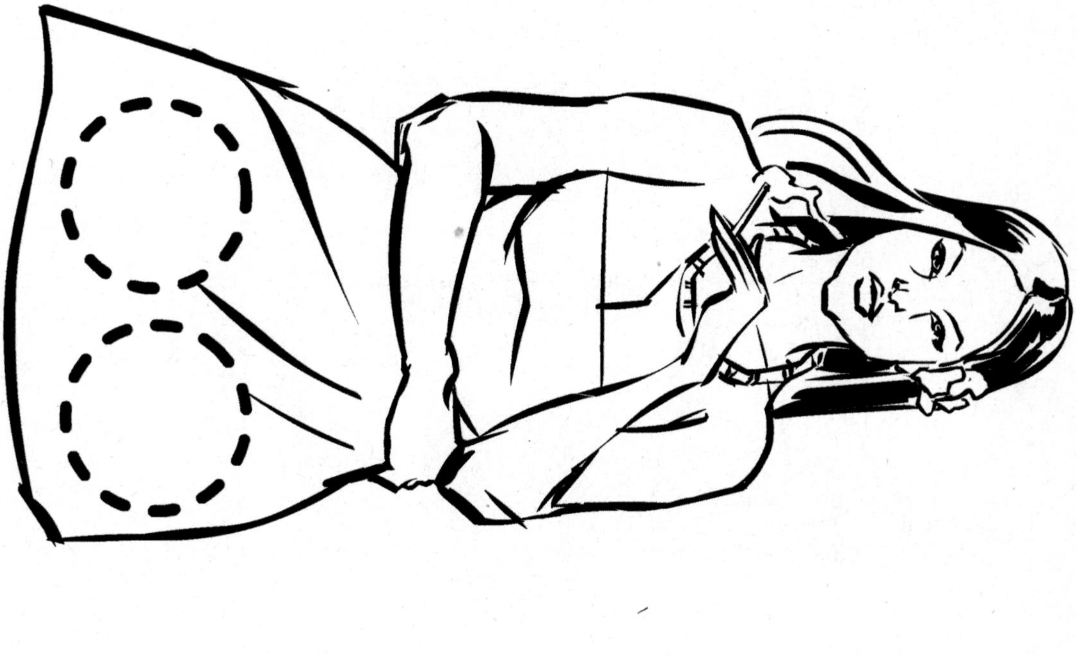

"dandy"
danny quinn

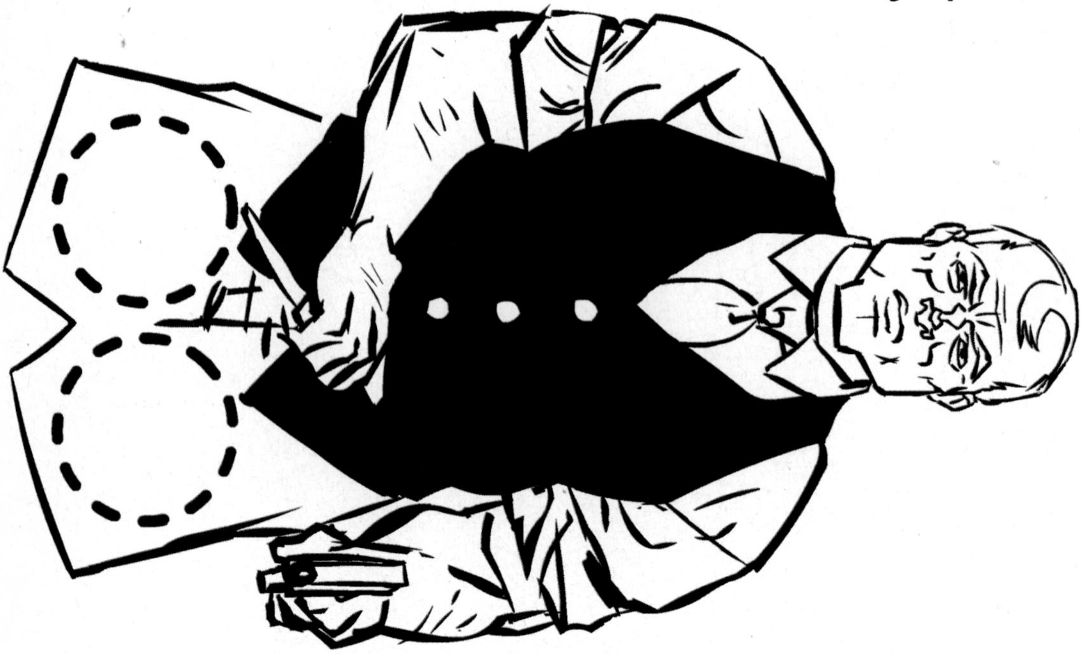

red piano

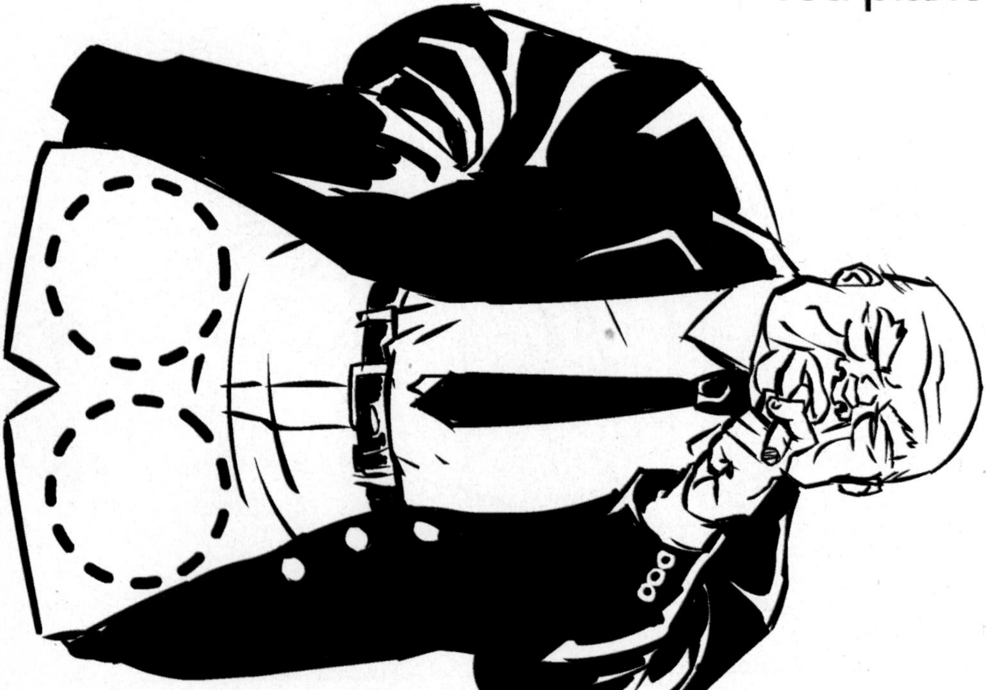

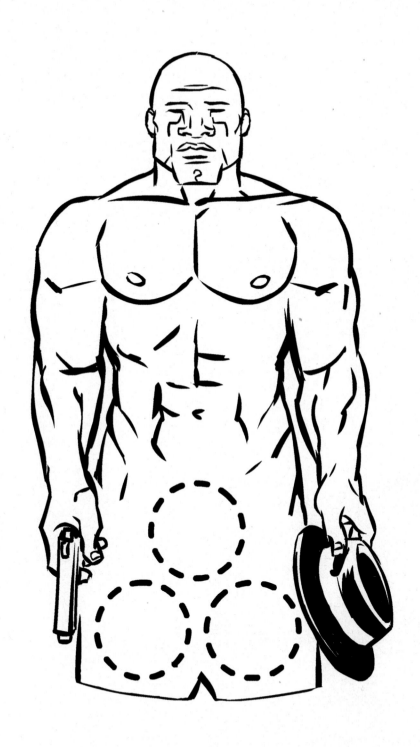

mo kalama

POSTERS

These are small versions of posters/pinups printed in the The Last Resort **#4**, and, seeing as they weren't part of the story at all, they allowed me to try something a little different stylistically.

I always enjoy developing different styles and experimenting with new ways of drawing (well, new ways to me at least). I do this partly because I like the challenge, and partly because you never know when people are going to be finally sick of the style you're using, or realise you suck.

Which would be shocking I know, because, I mean, my grandmother says I draw real pretty, and after all, she got me hooked on coffee when I was about five, without which my young mind wouldn't have been hyper-active or overstimulated enough to draw relentlessly for about 20 hours a day, and therefore not have led me to the curs--I mean, blessed situation I'm in now. So this proves her to be of a mythical-like wisdom above the rest of us...doesn't it? Or is that just me? My priorities may differ.

Anyway, the pinups....Well, being something new, they took a while and a lot of effort but looked nifty enough in the end, so it was all worthwhile. Expect more.

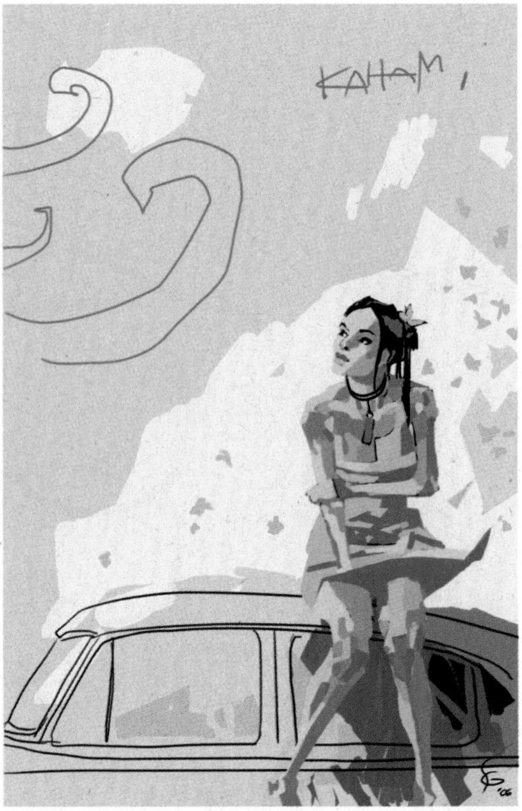

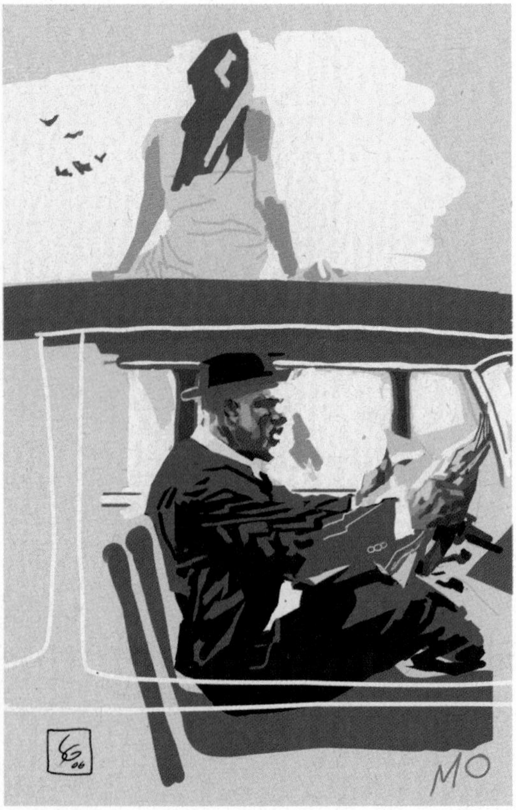

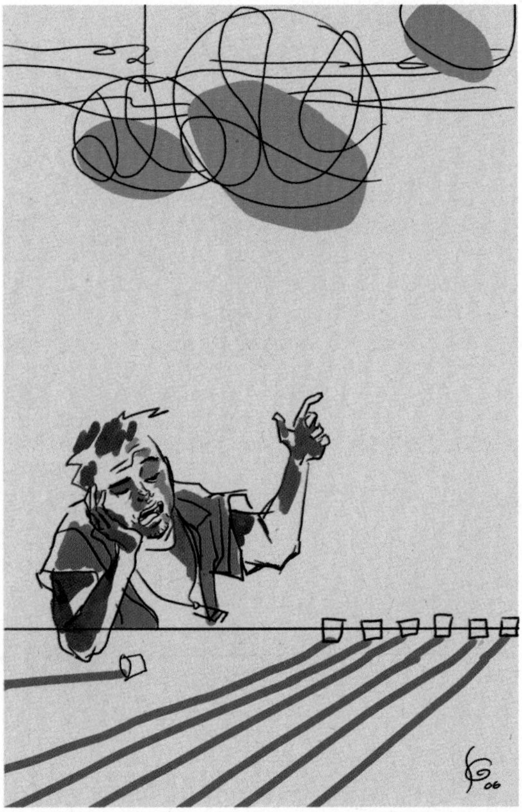

BEHIND THE SCENES

Or, as I call it:
Ruining The Magic

How did Quinn look before becoming the dashing gent we see in the book? How much (or little) preparation does Steven do when drawing a page? And how did he get that scribbly thing to look so...scribbly?! All is revealed in the section that will give much-needed insight into the inner workings of what some may refer to, loosely, as an artist...of sorts.

- Steven

RED PIANO

As you can probably tell, I originally planned Red Piano's appearance to have a red theme. Yeah...I know...how totally original and brilliant. But, while I did at least keep up this colour theme for Piano's office, I drifted off-track with the character itself. In fact, as the series progressed, Danny Quinn's Irish blood boils over more often than Piano's, giving Danny (if anything) more of that reddish glow.

But I was pretty happy with Piano in the end. After all, do you see DANNY QUINN on the cover of the trade paperback? No. You see Red Piano in all his not-quite-red-at-all glory. Now, behold my original child-like scratchings:

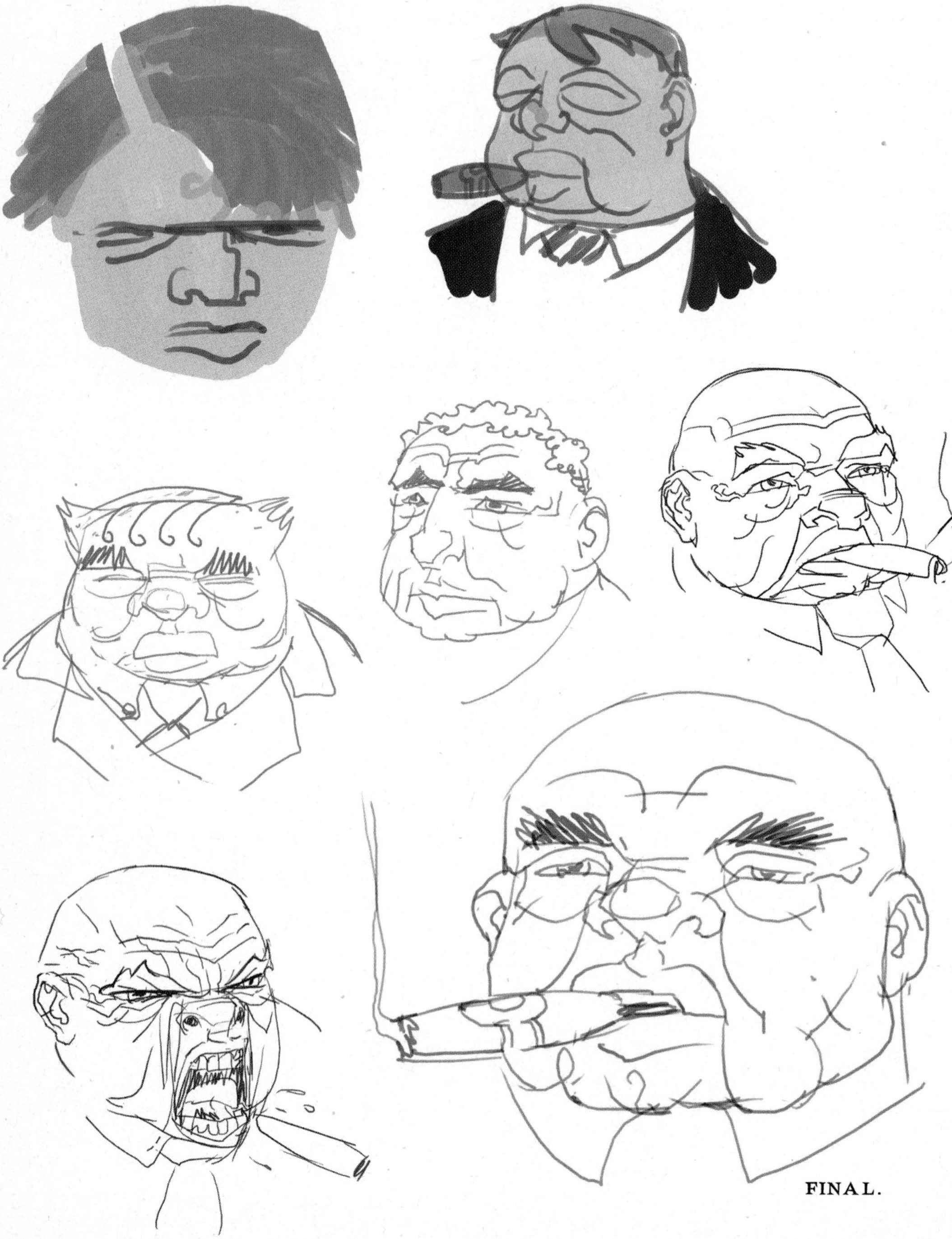

FINAL.

'DANDY' DANNY QUINN

Probably my favourite character of the series, our Danny is.

I knew the sort of look I wanted for Mr. Quinn, a driven man of high aspirations mixed with a touch of desperation, but getting it just right took a bit of time. Here's a few attempts and the final design I was happy with.

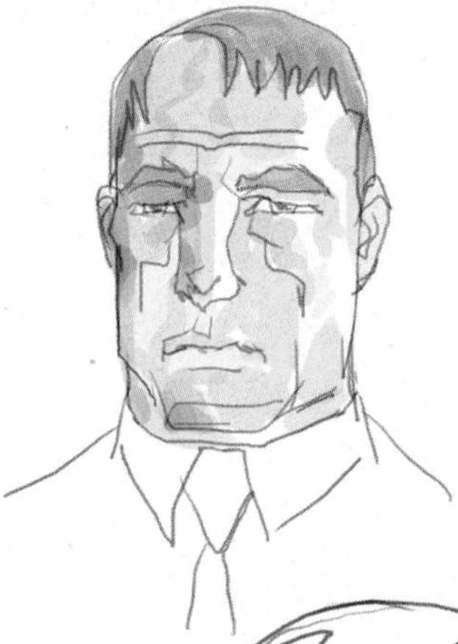

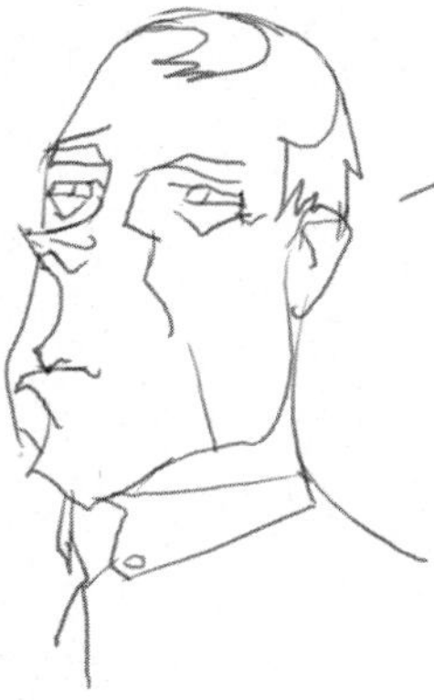

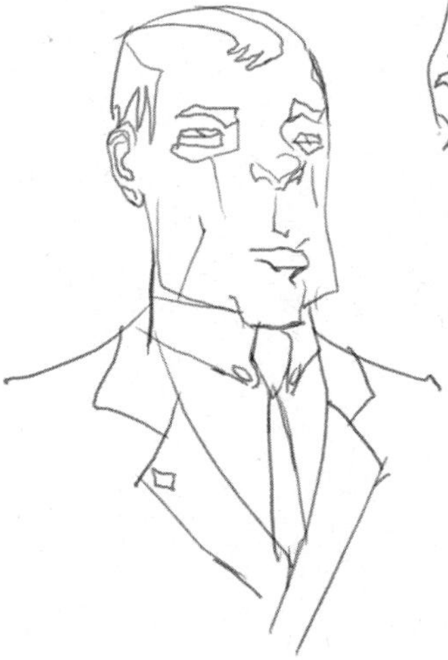

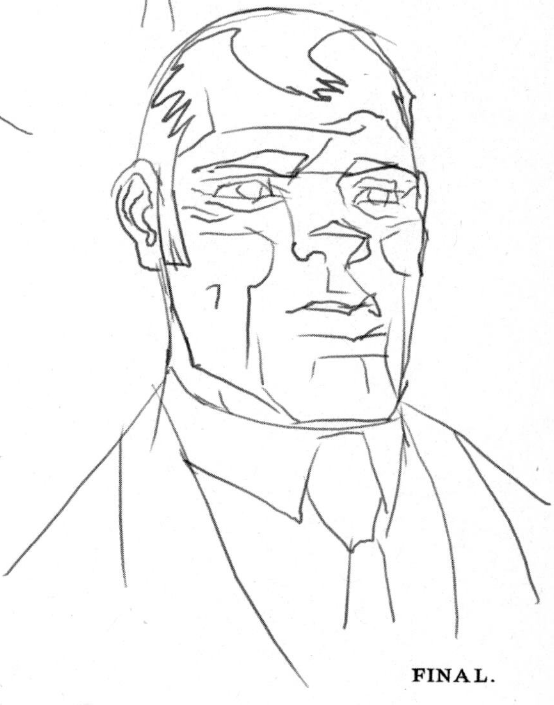

FINAL.

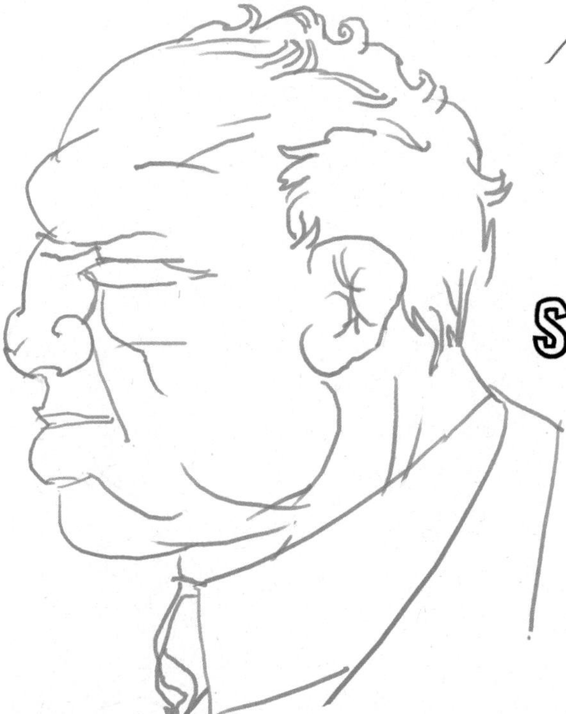

STEW MULLIGAN

This one came to me right away; a retired, heavy-drinking Irish boxer pretty much drawing itself. Just add a cheap, old, slightly-worn suit and there you go.

THE THINKER ANTONIO ANTHONY

This one didn't change a whole lot from its initial conception. Most of the work involved playing around with slight changes until Antonio had the right kind of overcompensating-ugly-with-forced-sophistication look that we felt would suit his personality. You'll notice that in the final sketch I forgot his moustache. In fact, for a while after the final sketch I forgot his moustache. All the way until about half way through the first issue in fact, at which point I had to go back and draw it into all his panels. I'm clever like that.

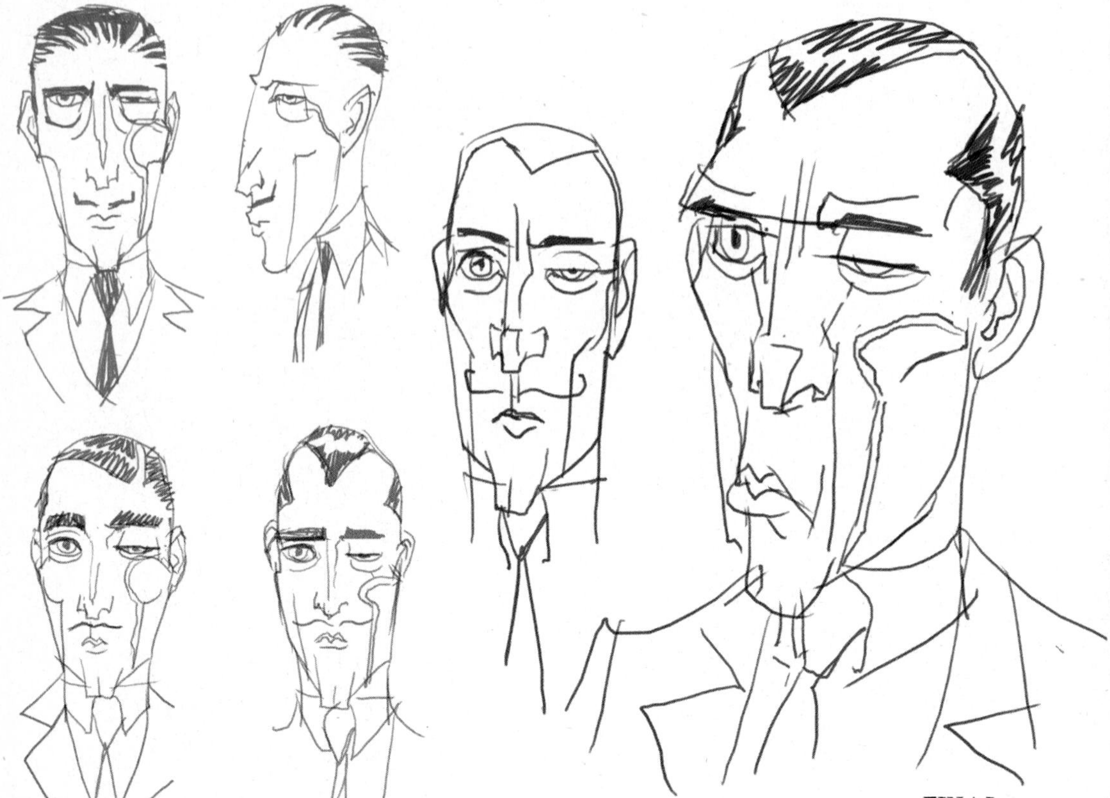

FINAL.

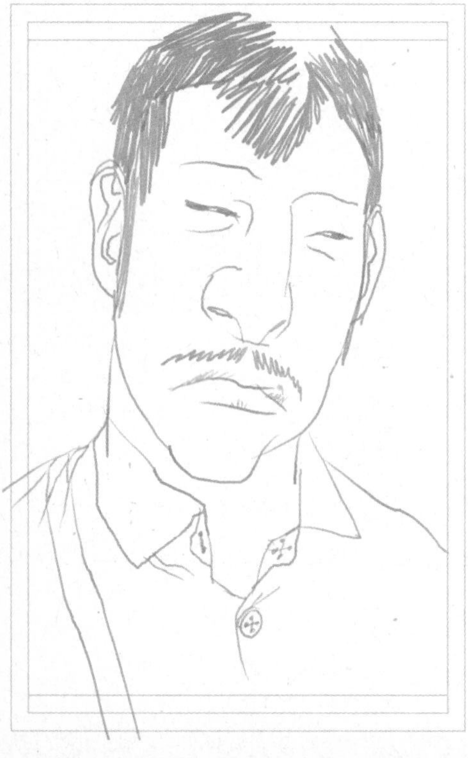

AGENT CHRIS DUQUE

Another easy one, my first sketch being the design I'd use.

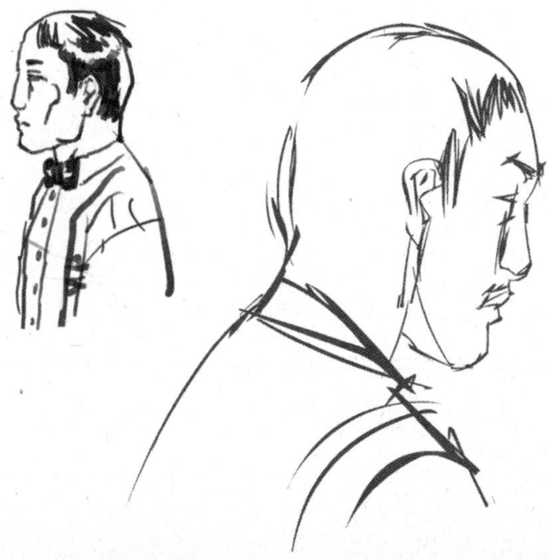

KAHAMI

A sketch to practice both the new art style I was using for issue one, and new ways to draw old characters.

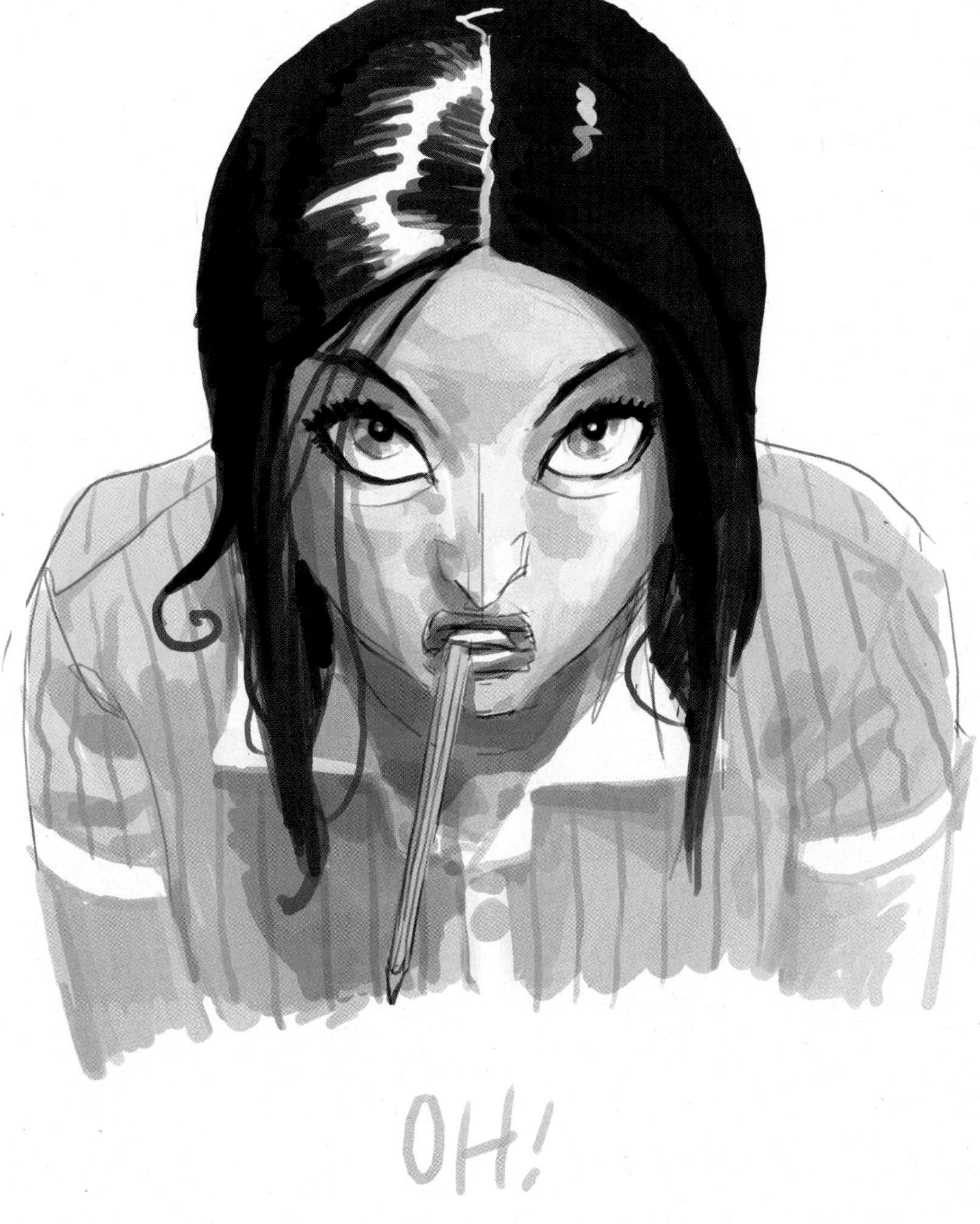
OH!

ISSUE 1

After giving the first two series' covers a "pencilly" look, people suggested I draw a whole ISSUE in this new style. So I attempted to do just that, which...turned out to not be such a good idea, as the book's late schedule partially proves. In fact, you could say that this issue was drawn kinda backwards, ie: The layout stage for each page actually looked inked, and the "final inks" stage looked pencilled. So yeah, backwards.

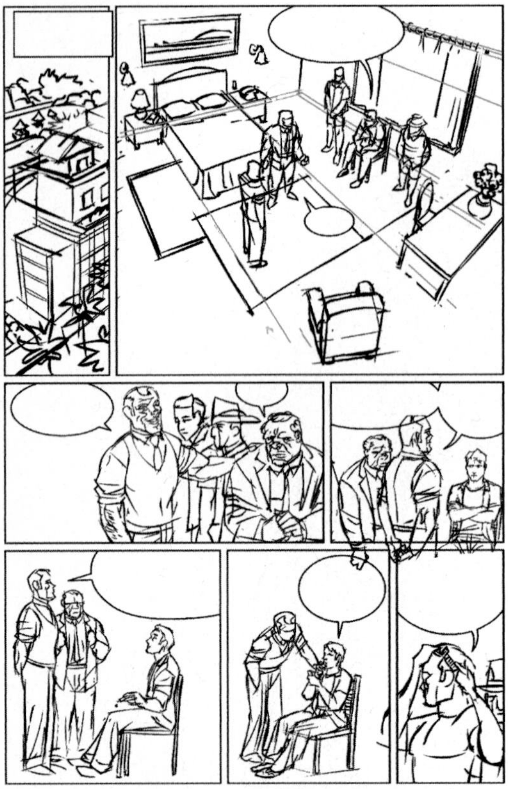

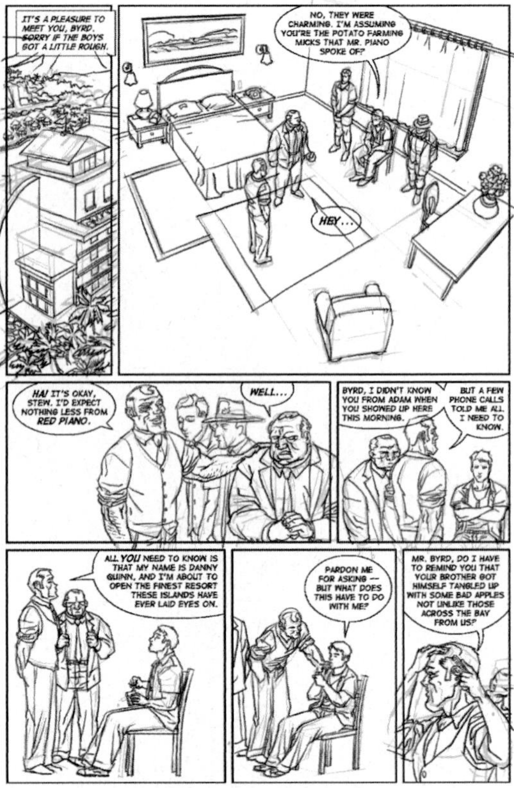

IT'S A PLEASURE TO MEET YOU, BYRD. SORRY IF THE BOYS GOT A LITTLE ROUGH.
NO, THEY WERE CHARMING. I'M ASSUMING YOU'RE THE POTATO FARMING MICKS THAT MR. PIANO SPOKE OF?
HEY...
HA! IT'S OKAY, STEW. I'D EXPECT NOTHING LESS FROM RED PIANO.
WELL...
BYRD, I DIDN'T KNOW YOU FROM ADAM WHEN YOU SHOWED UP HERE THIS MORNING.
BUT A FEW PHONE CALLS TOLD ME ALL I NEED TO KNOW.
ALL YOU NEED TO KNOW IS THAT MY NAME IS DANNY QUINN, AND I'M ABOUT TO OPEN THE FINEST RESORT THESE ISLANDS HAVE EVER LAID EYES ON.
PARDON ME FOR ASKING -- BUT WHAT DOES THIS HAVE TO DO WITH ME?
MR. BYRD, DO I HAVE TO REMIND YOU THAT YOUR BROTHER GOT HIMSELF TANGLED UP WITH SOME BAD APPLES NOT UNLIKE THOSE ACROSS THE BAY FROM US?

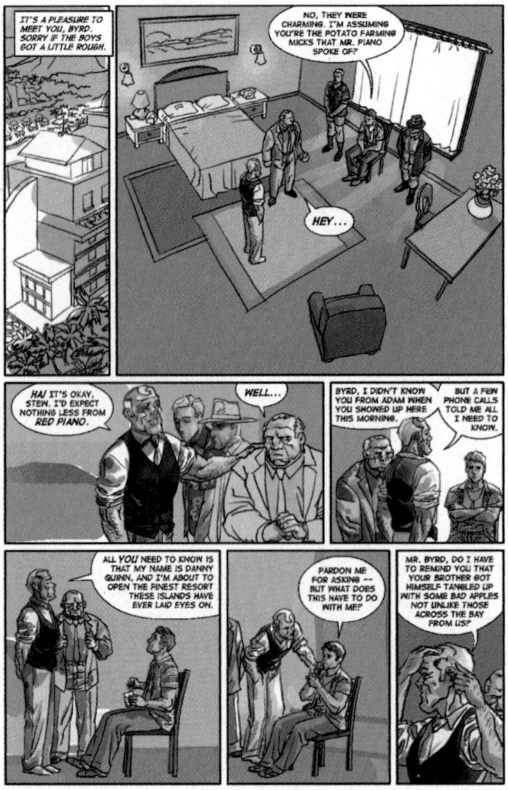

IT'S A PLEASURE TO MEET YOU, BYRD. SORRY IF THE BOYS GOT A LITTLE ROUGH.
NO, THEY WERE CHARMING. I'M ASSUMING YOU'RE THE POTATO FARMING MICKS THAT MR. PIANO SPOKE OF?
HEY...
HA! IT'S OKAY, STEW. I'D EXPECT NOTHING LESS FROM RED PIANO.
WELL...
BYRD, I DIDN'T KNOW YOU FROM ADAM WHEN YOU SHOWED UP HERE THIS MORNING.
BUT A FEW PHONE CALLS TOLD ME ALL I NEED TO KNOW.
ALL YOU NEED TO KNOW IS THAT MY NAME IS DANNY QUINN, AND I'M ABOUT TO OPEN THE FINEST RESORT THESE ISLANDS HAVE EVER LAID EYES ON.
PARDON ME FOR ASKING -- BUT WHAT DOES THIS HAVE TO DO WITH ME?
MR. BYRD, DO I HAVE TO REMIND YOU THAT YOUR BROTHER GOT HIMSELF TANGLED UP WITH SOME BAD APPLES NOT UNLIKE THOSE ACROSS THE BAY FROM US?

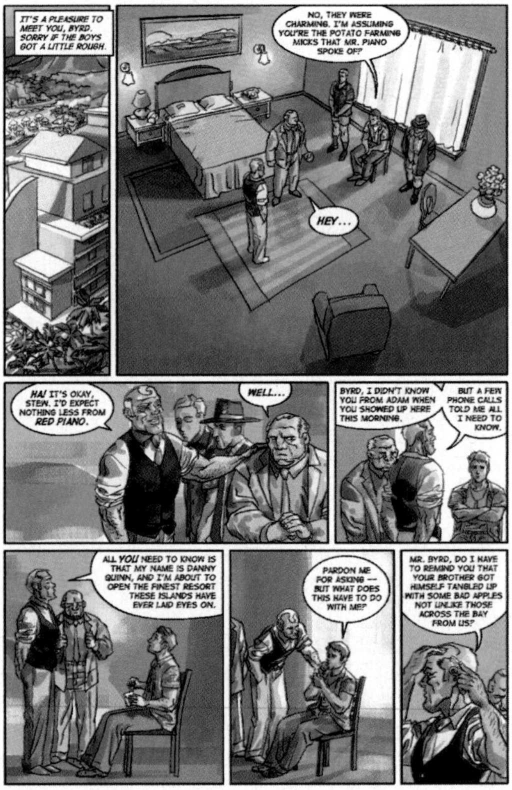

IT'S A PLEASURE TO MEET YOU, BYRD. SORRY IF THE BOYS GOT A LITTLE ROUGH.
NO, THEY WERE CHARMING. I'M ASSUMING YOU'RE THE POTATO FARMING MICKS THAT MR. PIANO SPOKE OF?
HEY...
HA! IT'S OKAY, STEW. I'D EXPECT NOTHING LESS FROM RED PIANO.
WELL...
BYRD, I DIDN'T KNOW YOU FROM ADAM WHEN YOU SHOWED UP HERE THIS MORNING.
BUT A FEW PHONE CALLS TOLD ME ALL I NEED TO KNOW.
ALL YOU NEED TO KNOW IS THAT MY NAME IS DANNY QUINN, AND I'M ABOUT TO OPEN THE FINEST RESORT THESE ISLANDS HAVE EVER LAID EYES ON.
PARDON ME FOR ASKING -- BUT WHAT DOES THIS HAVE TO DO WITH ME?
MR. BYRD, DO I HAVE TO REMIND YOU THAT YOUR BROTHER GOT HIMSELF TANGLED UP WITH SOME BAD APPLES NOT UNLIKE THOSE ACROSS THE BAY FROM US?

ISSUE 1 / UNUSED LAYOUTS

A selection of sketches for panels that were dumped or redrawn because they didn't work or were simply, well, not good.

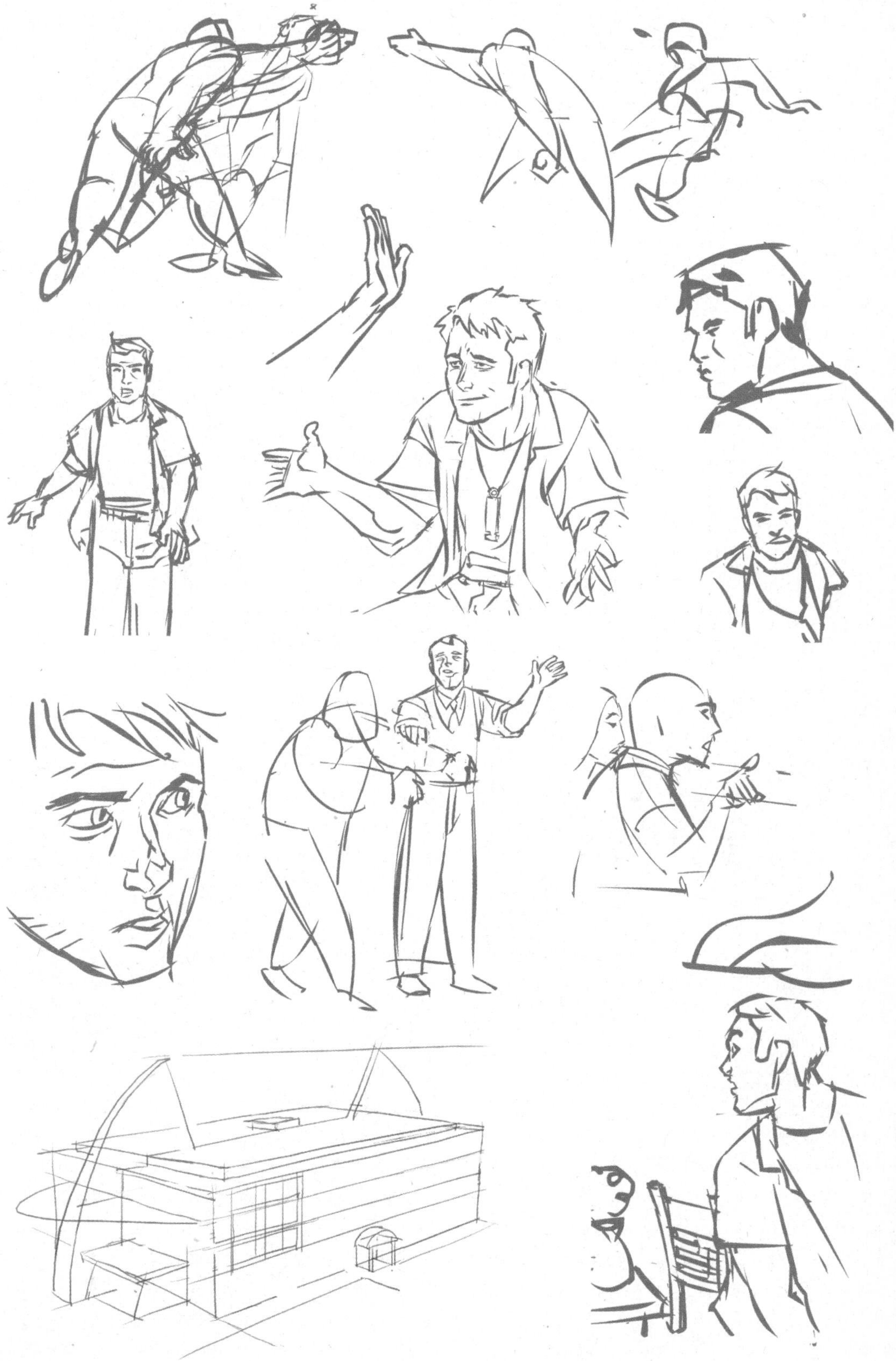

ISSUE 1 / INKY LAYOUTS

Here are a few pages from issue 1 in their layout/pencil stage - Layouts which (as mentioned earlier) you could say have more of an ink/finish look than the actual finished artwork does for this issue. So a little different. But hey, you have to try these things.

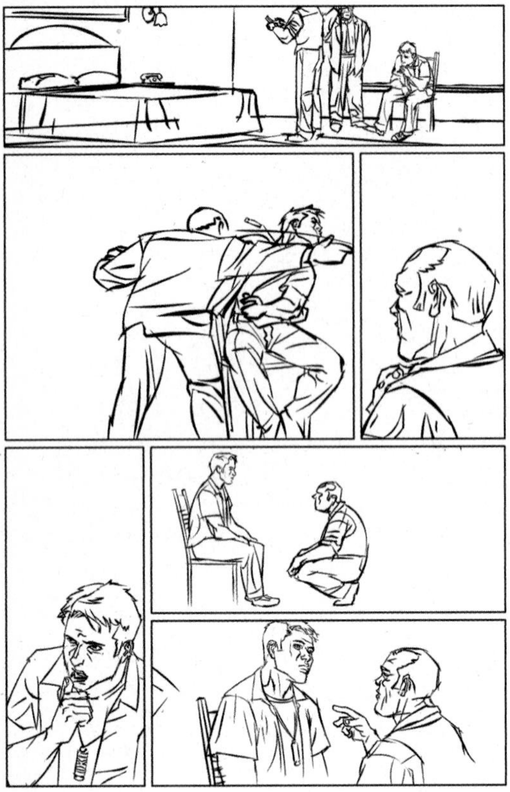

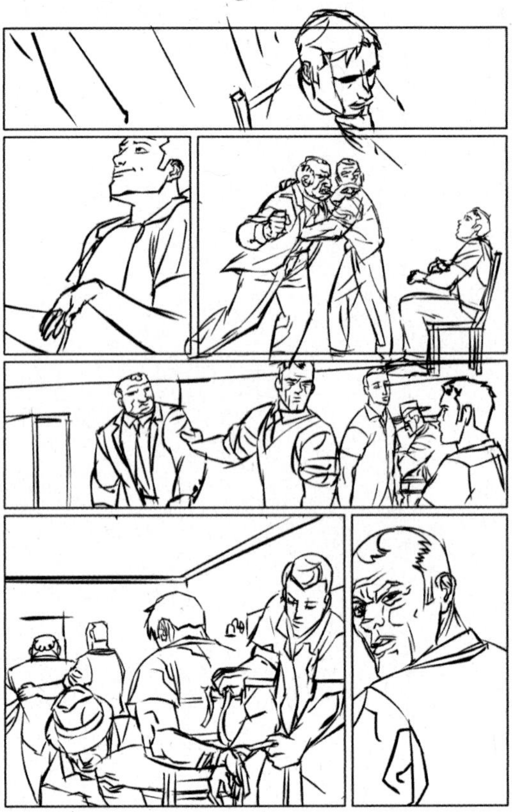

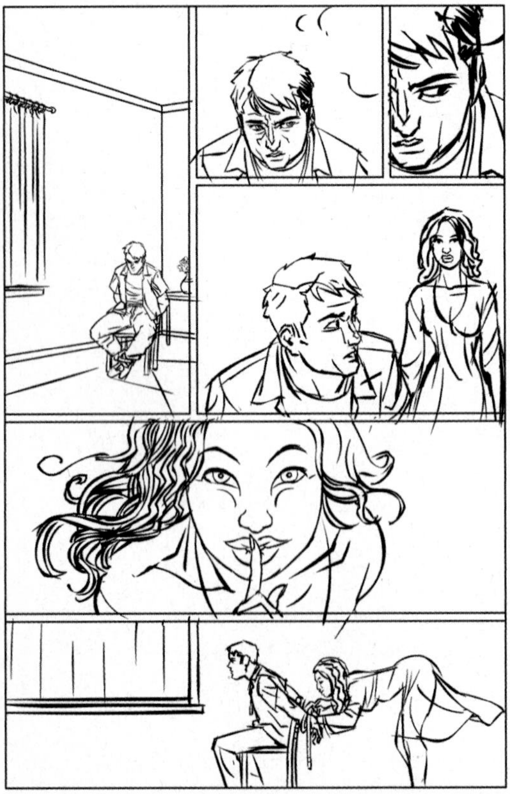

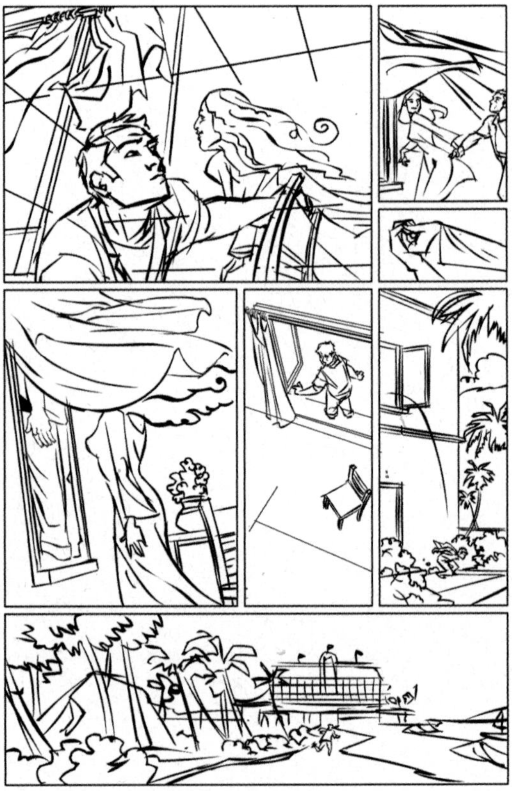

ISSUE 3 / PAPER! PENCILS!

I began issue 3 with some *very* rare pencil sketches. Drawn drunk as a result of testing cocktail recipes from the first Dick trade paperback of course....at least, that's my excuse for how dodgy they look and I'm sticking to it. "Bruised Kidney For A Hawaiian Dick" is very tasty by the way. You should try it. And, just like whiskey, the more you drink the better the book looks. So again, I recommend it.

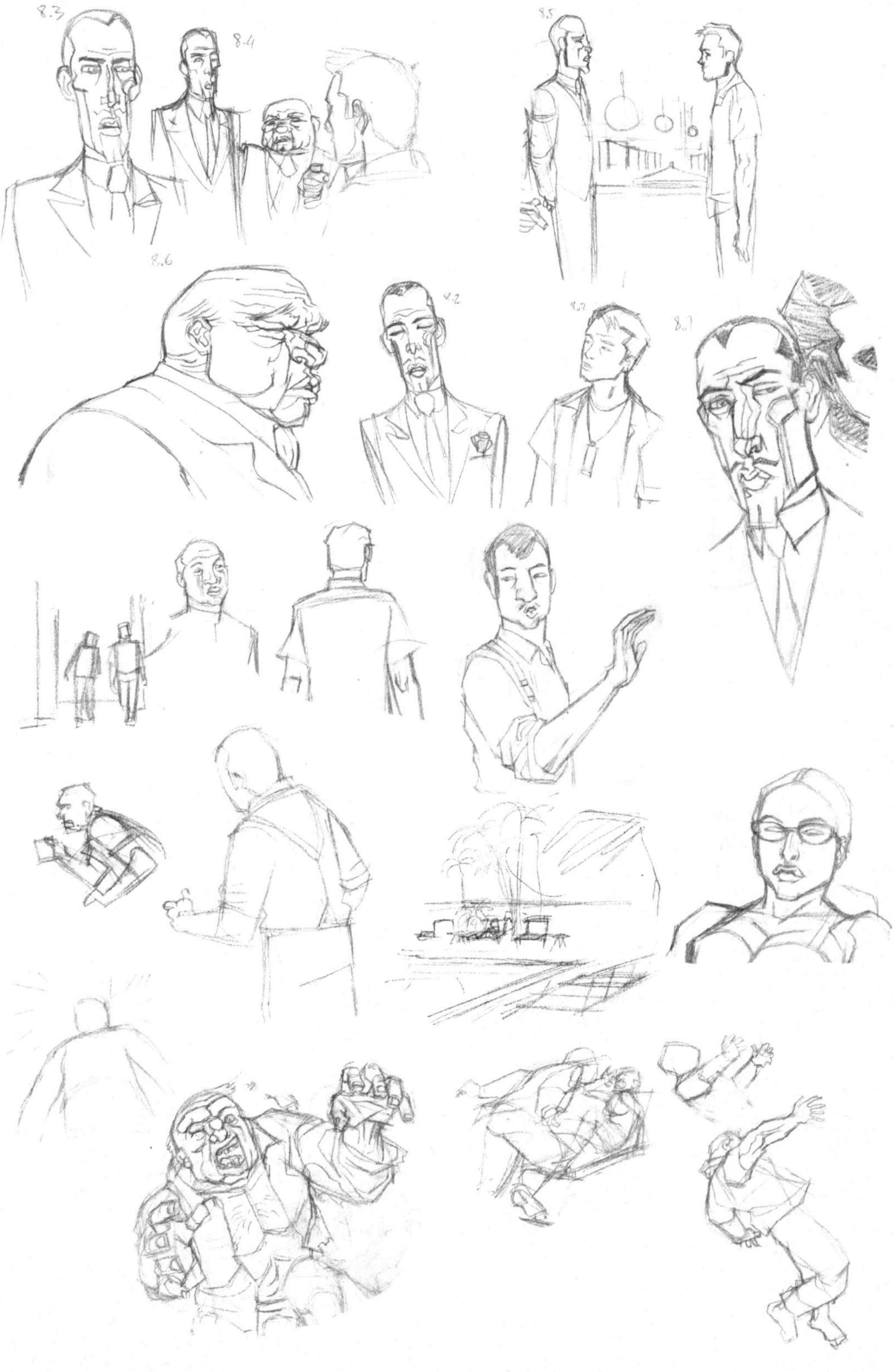

ISSUE 3 / GOOD SKETCHES

A selection of panel sketches that landed on the page looking pretty much how I wanted (which is rare) and therefore remained fairly unchanged through to final inks.

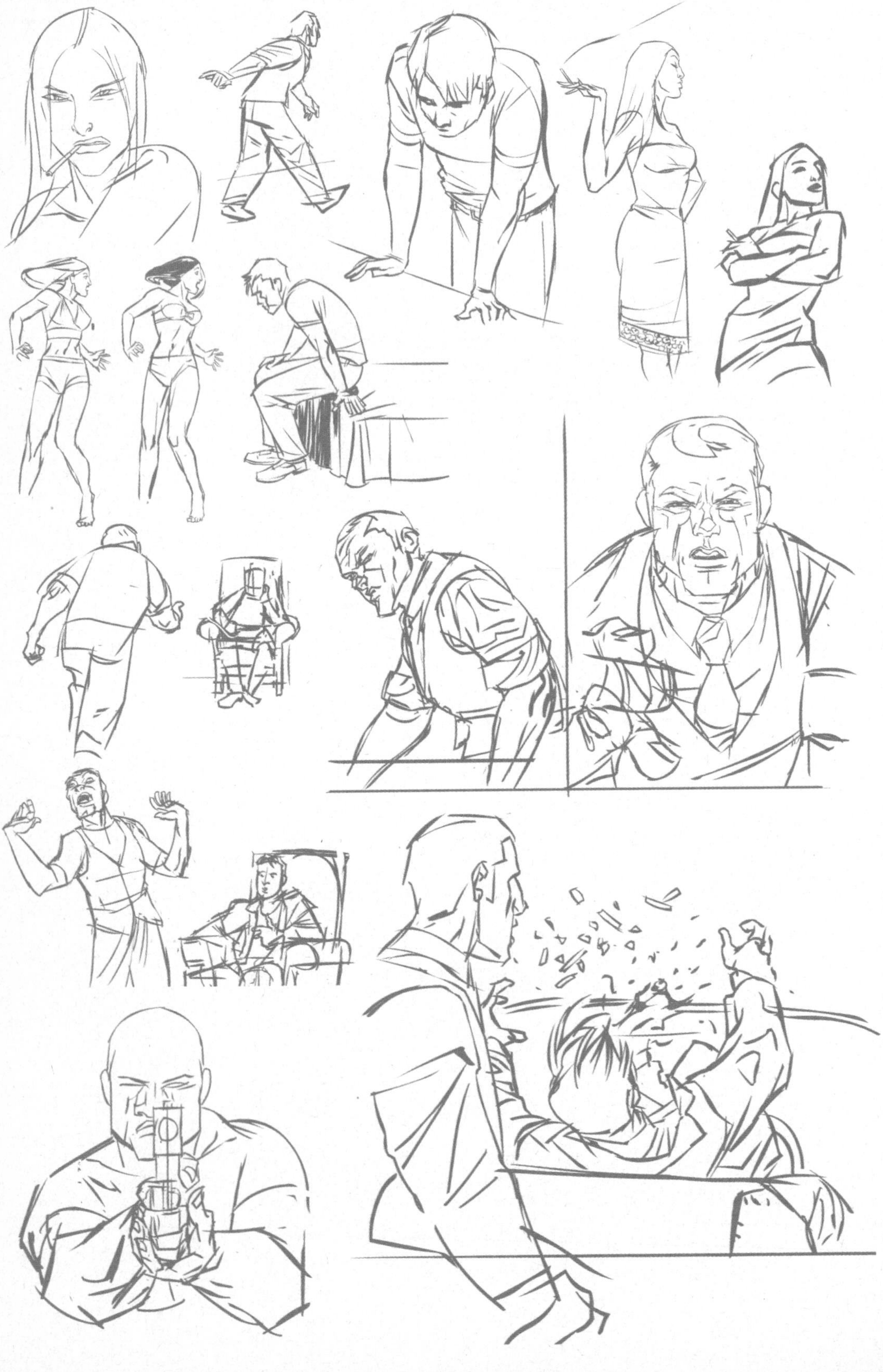

ISSUE 3 / NOT-SO-GOOD SKETCHES

A selection of sketches for panels that were either dumped or redrawn because they didn't work, or were simply below my *ahem* usual high standards.

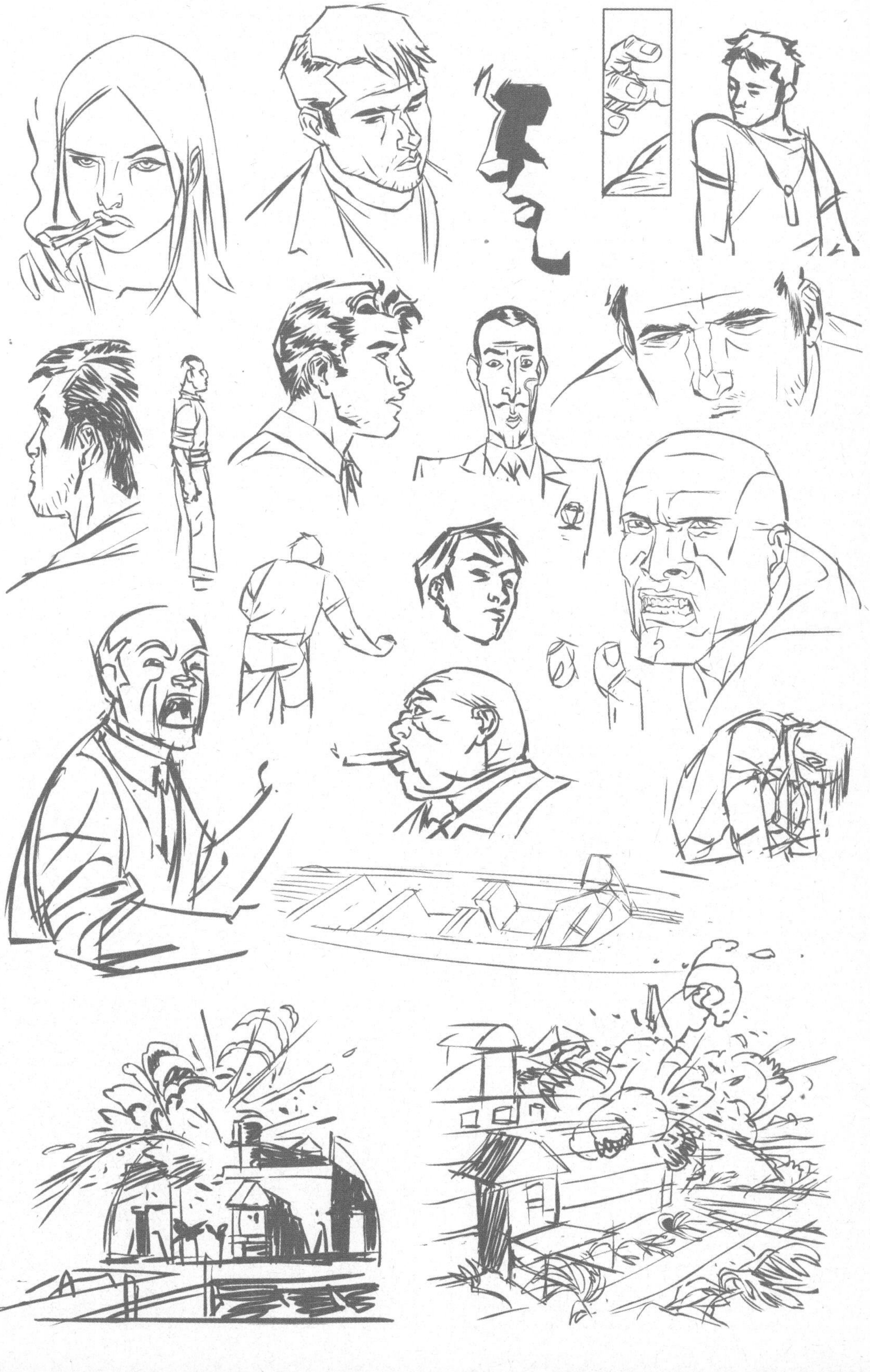

ISSUE 3 / ALL IN PERSPECTIVE

Some panels take longer than others. Some panels take a LOT longer than others. And this would be one of them. It can happen for any number of reasons. Here it was due to a lot of lines and a lot of attempts at getting the right frame and then "lens" perspective I wanted.

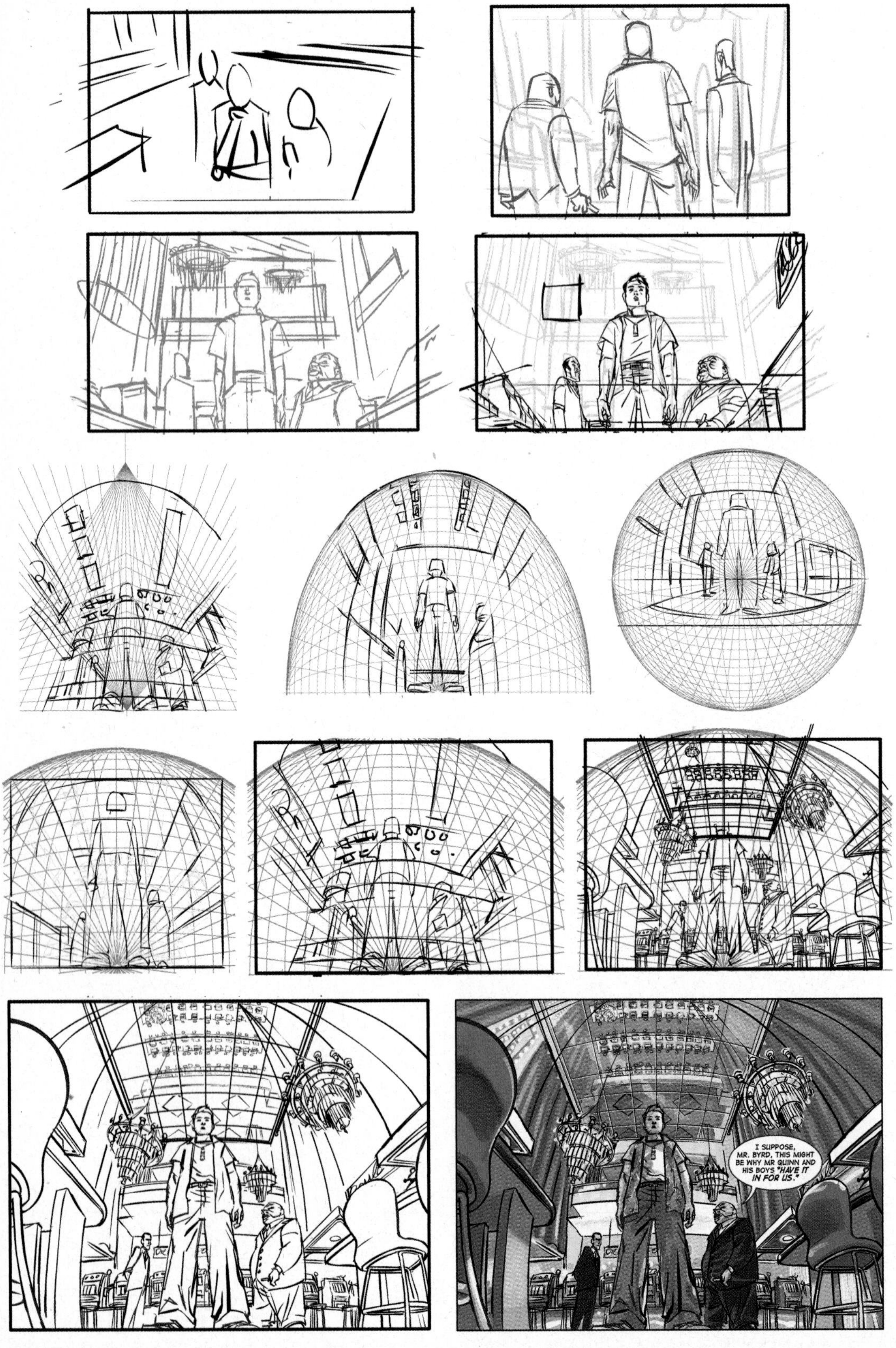

I SUPPOSE, MR. BYRD, THIS MIGHT BE WHY MR QUINN AND HIS BOYS "HAVE IT IN FOR US."

ISSUE 4 / GRAPHICAL NOTES

When Clay sends over a new script and I'm reading it for the first time, I'll pause to scribble down very quick graphical "notes" on how I'd like to draw a page or character based on images his words put in my head. I also hear his voice in my head, but that's for another book. Anyway, often some of my better ideas come from these first script reads - and seeing as I have the World's Worst Memory, it's always good to get these ideas down before I'm distracted five seconds later by the complexities of remembering to eat, breathe, etc. and forget them for all of time. Which is a bad thing. I think. Anyway, here are the issue 4 notes, in roughly page order (continued on next page).

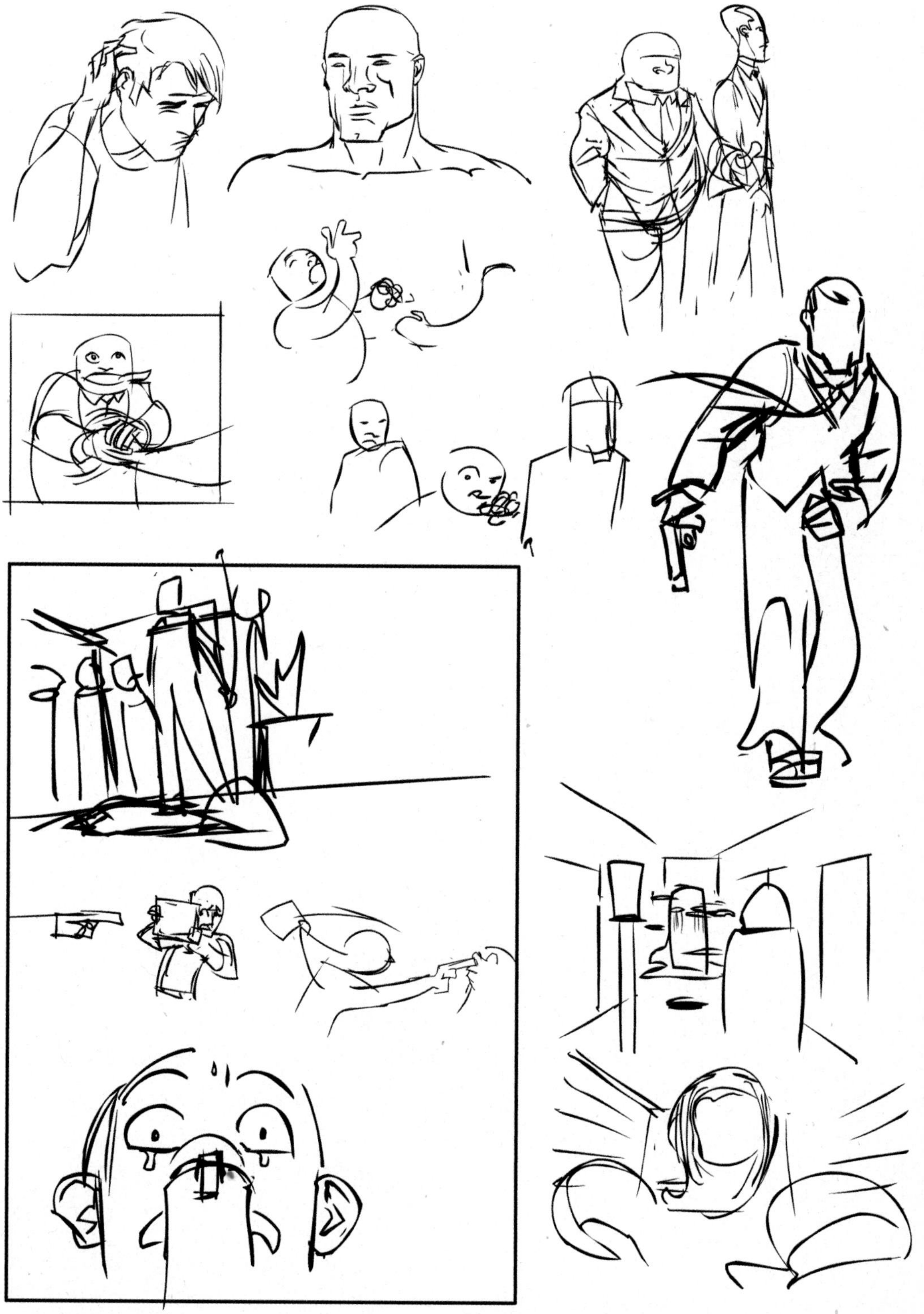

GRAPHICAL NOTES CONT.

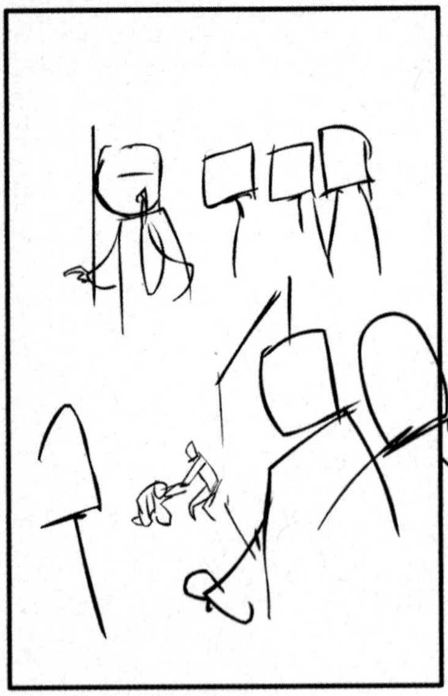

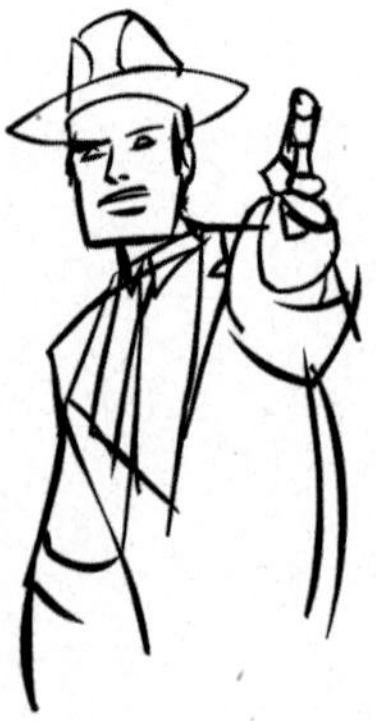

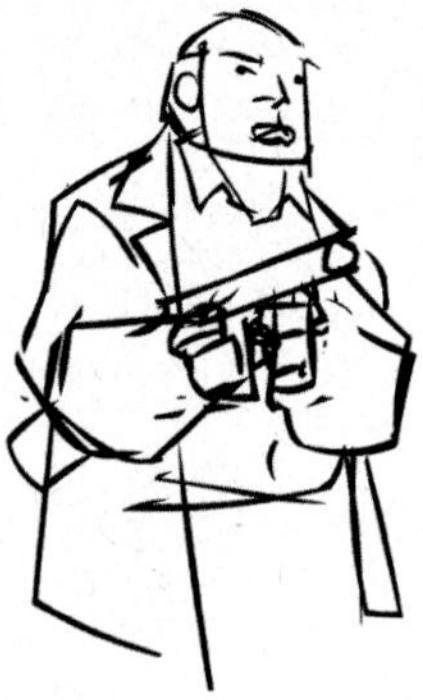

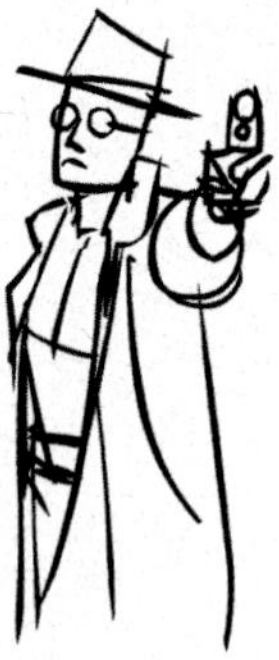

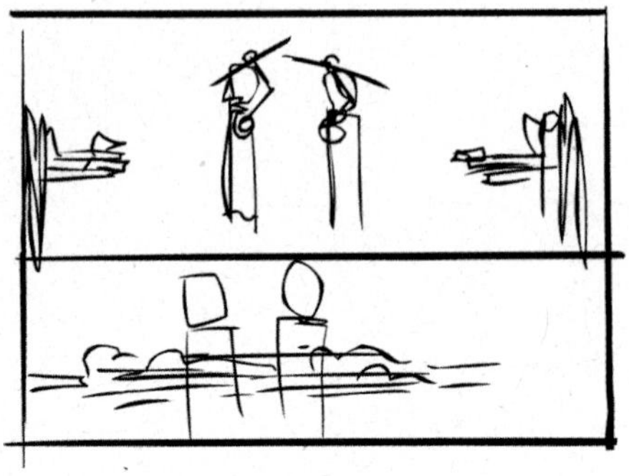

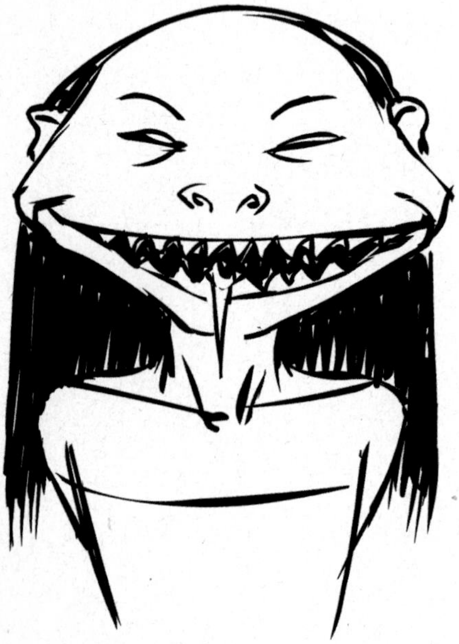

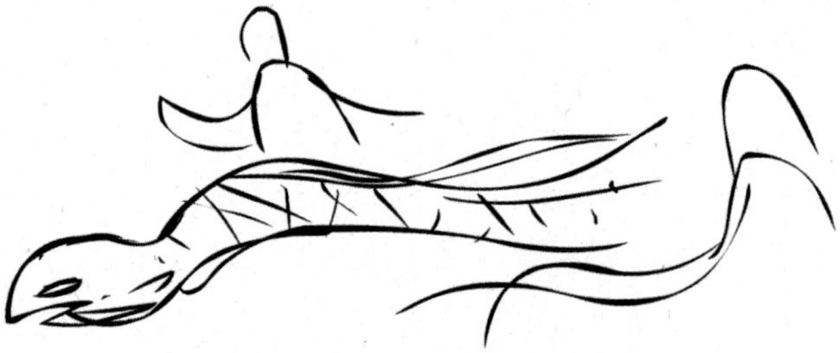

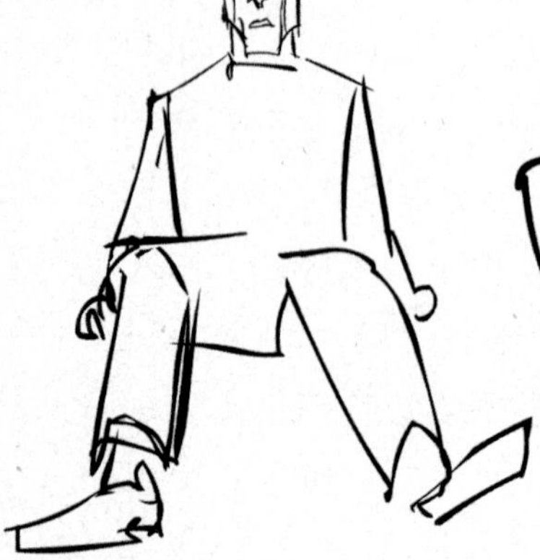

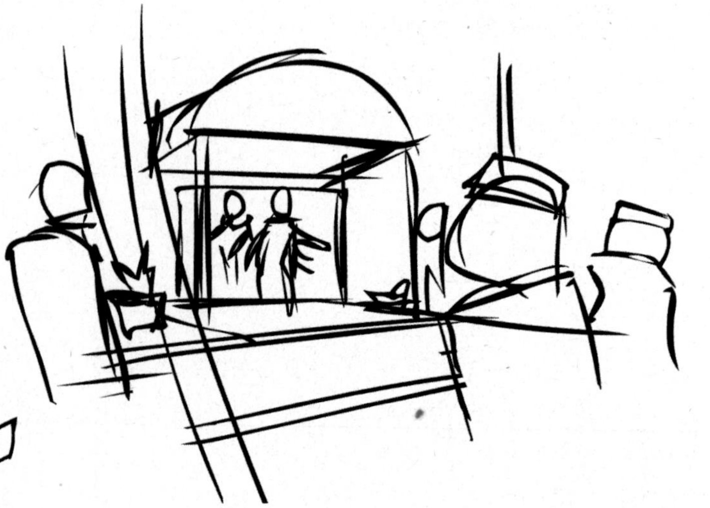

ISSUE 4 / GOOD SKETCHES

When a sketch **DOESN'T** make me scream and cry about why I didn't just choose something sensible for a career like engineering or doughnut maker, then it's a good sketch. These would be some lucky few good sketches, remaining fairly unchanged through to finished inks.

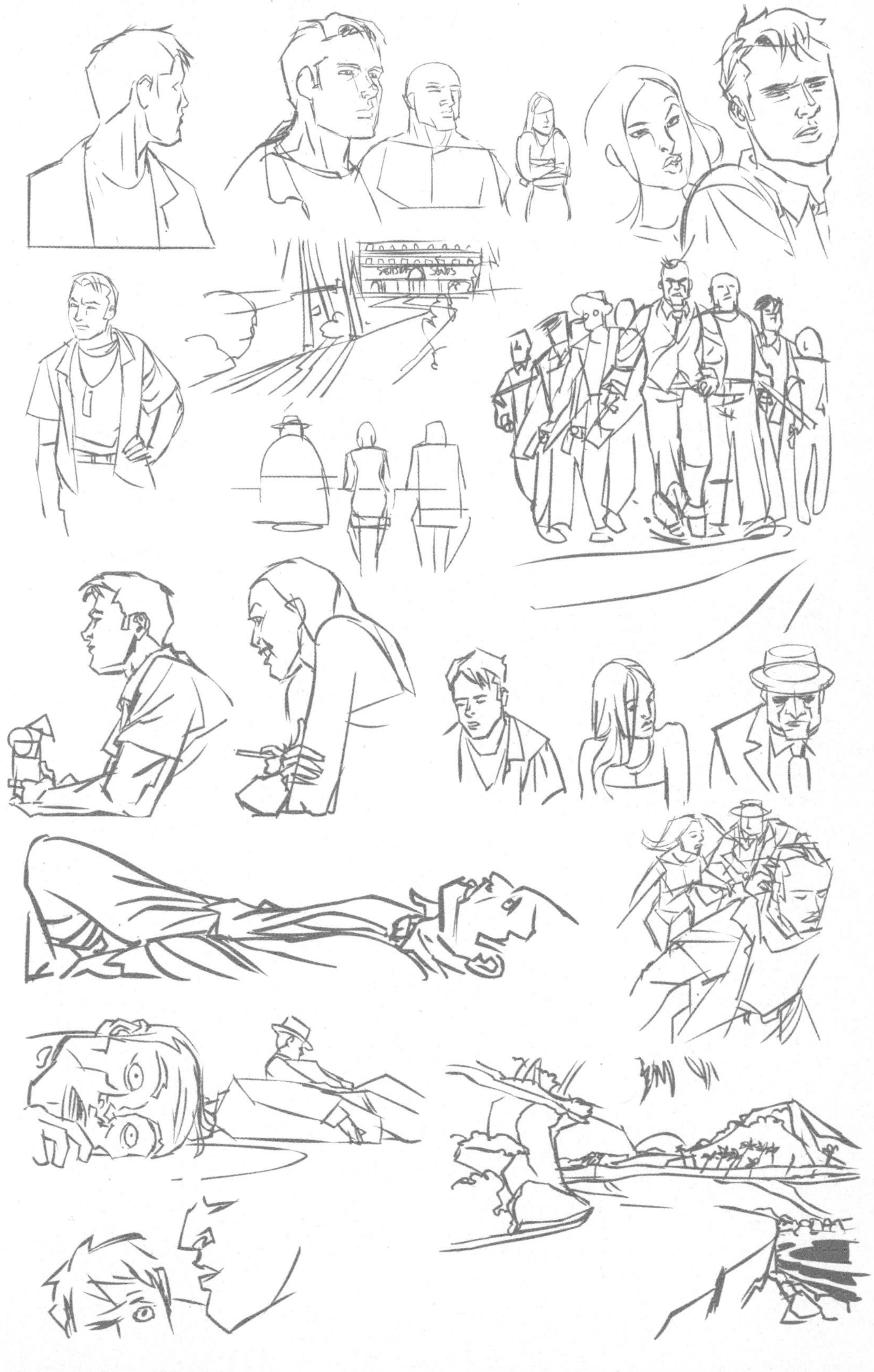

ISSUE 4 / NOT-SO-GOOD SKETCHES

...and now some not as successful sketches. A selection of roughs for panels that were either dumped or redrawn. Either because they didn't work, or were good in my little head but looked horribly mutilated once getting onto the page, the poor things. You feel sad now, no?

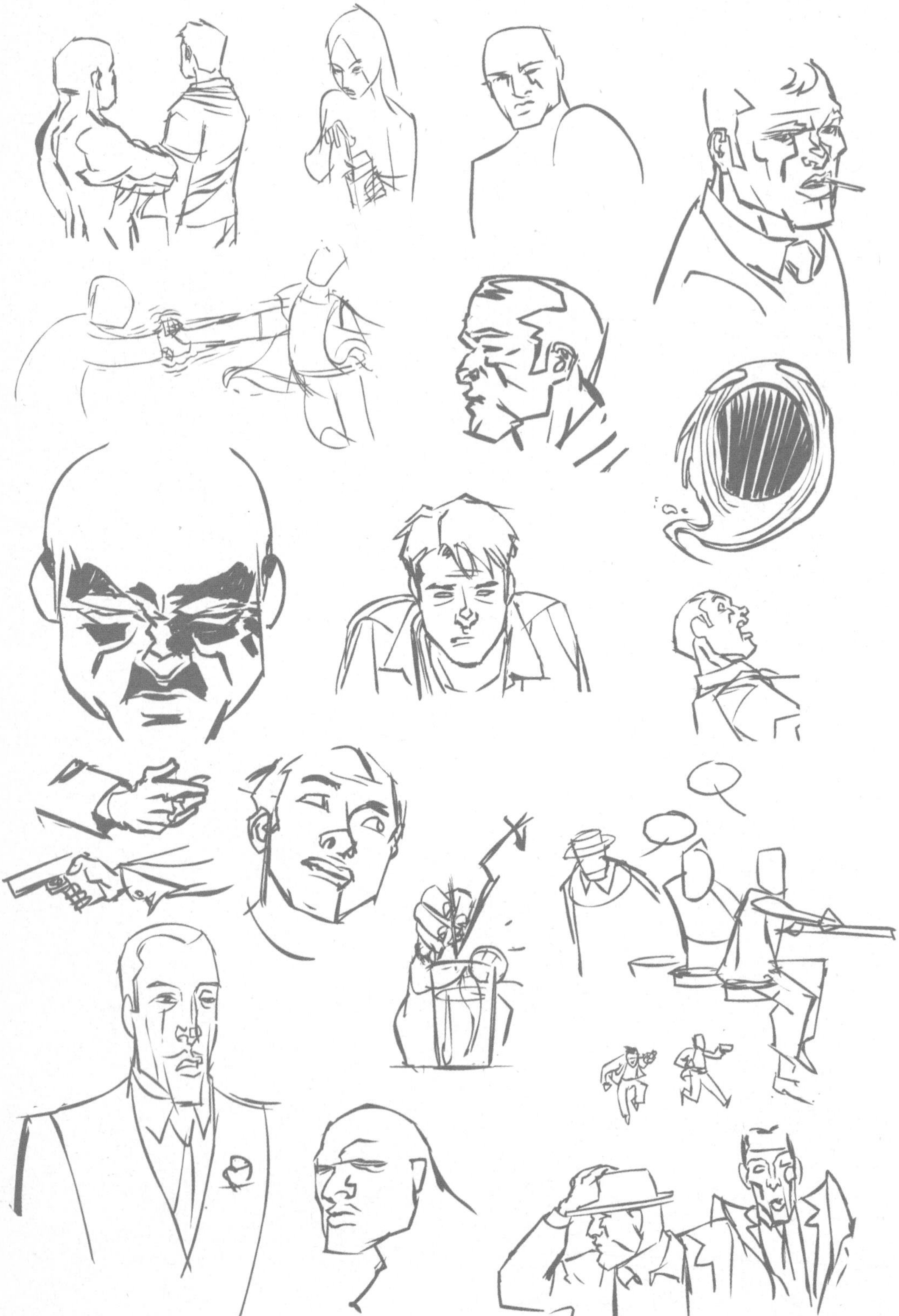

COVERS UNUSED AND SKETCHED

The large-mouthed spirit cover shown below was the original (advertised) cover for issue **4**, but, by the time I'd finally drawn that issue I decided it needed a better one, so that was the end of that. The other three pieces are various cover roughs I dumped before taking further.

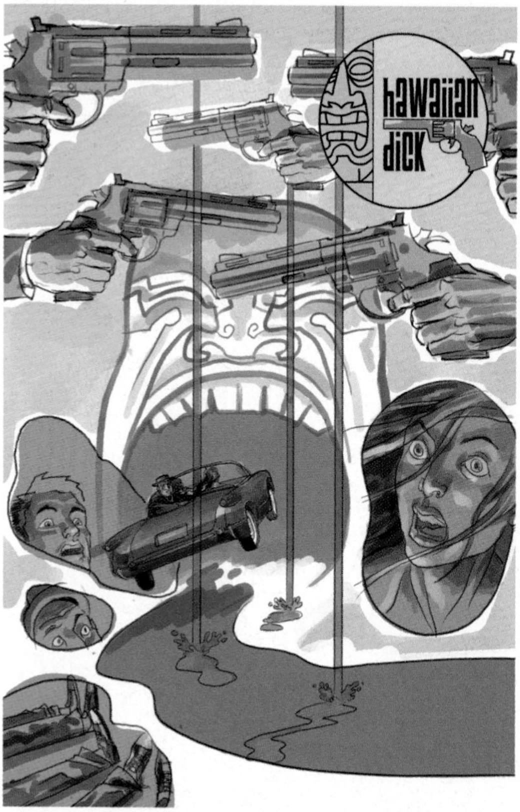
hawaiian dick

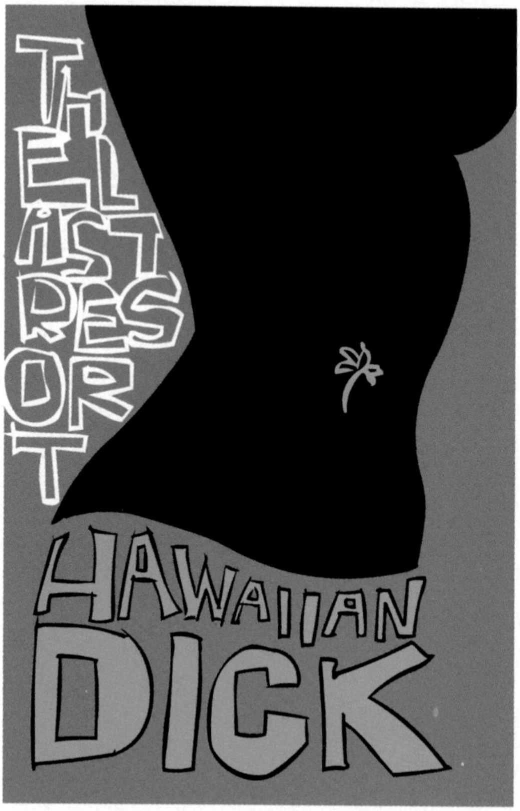
TH
EL
AST
RES
OR
T
HAWAIIAN
DICK

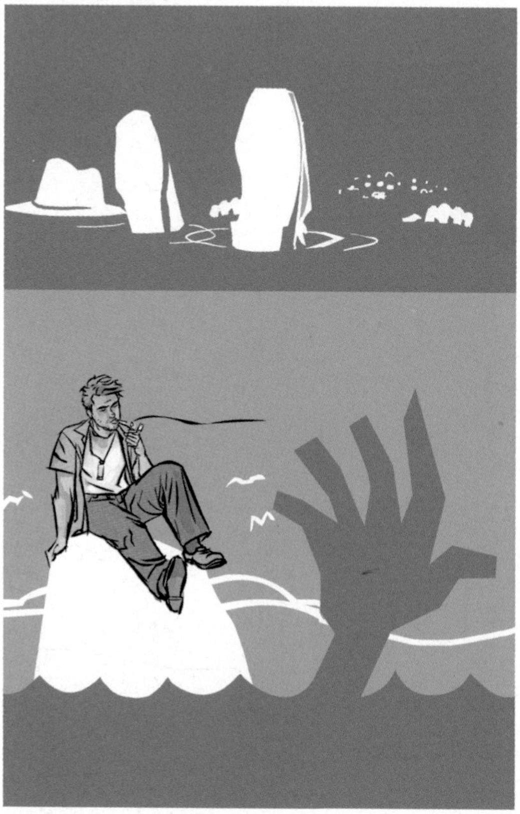

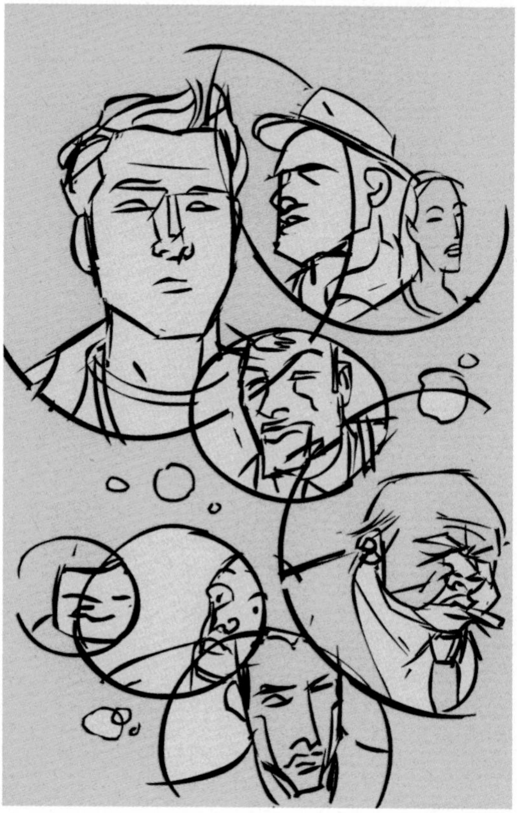

CLOTHING PATTERNS

A selection of print patterns I designed and used for Byrd and Kahami's clothing throughout the book (though not shown to scale). When it came to Byrd's shirts, balancing "loud and tacky" with "not completely clashing with the entire rest of the book and all artwork contained within" was always a bit of a challenge. So I tried to keep the designs fairly simple.

Another fun fact: Byrd's shirts move towards reddish hues by the end of each series as the stories reach their volcanic-like climax! Yep.

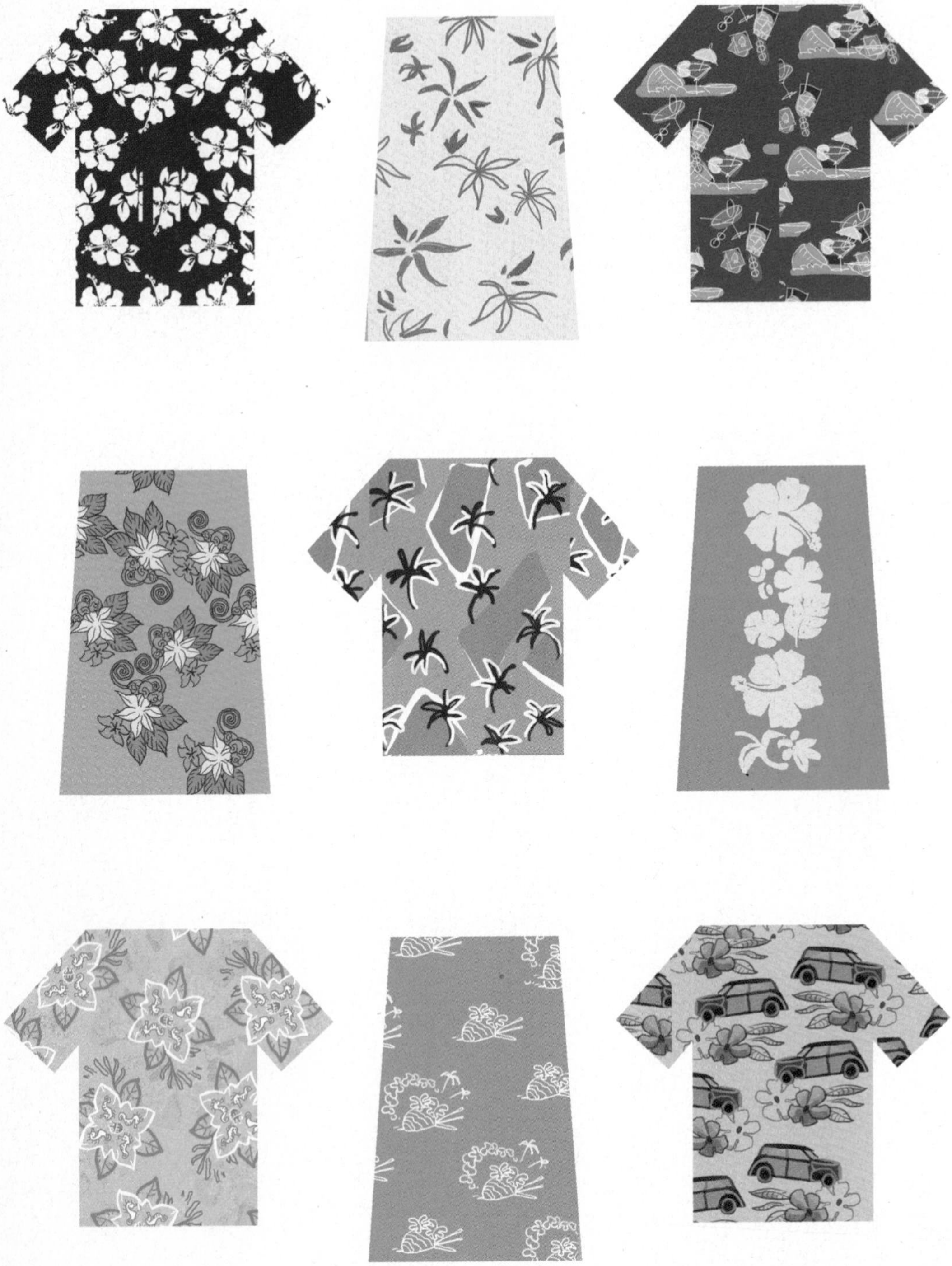

PROMOTING DICK

A collection of promotional and solicitation ads for the series, used and unused. Mostly unused, actually, so seen here first, you lucky little devils.

- Steven

SOLICITATION ADS

PREVIEW
8 Eisner nominated FULL COLOR PAGES AT
HAWAIIANDICK.COM
hawaiian dick

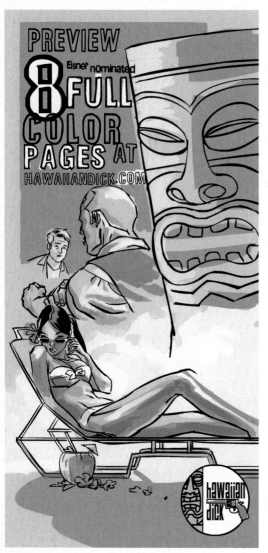

These are the solicitation ads used for issues 3 and 4 respectively. Actually, these are RE-solicitation ads, due to the series being so incredibly late. But I took that as an opportunity to create some poster-like art for the new ads, rather than just using conventional cover art, which is the norm, and I find boring (even though it perhaps makes more sense sales-wise).

My favourite element of the ads, and the part I felt turned out best, is the simple drawing of Mo with the gun. Which is why I later took that piece and used it for the re-worked issue 3 cover.

THE LAST RESORT
checking out
4
hawaiian dick
byrd of paradise
Also available - HAWAIIAN DICK: BYRD OF PARADISE series 1 TPB!

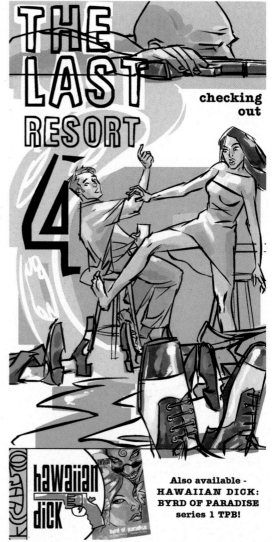

UNUSED ART

Some more unused concept artwork, plus, playing around with colour schemes for the issue 3 solicitation ad.

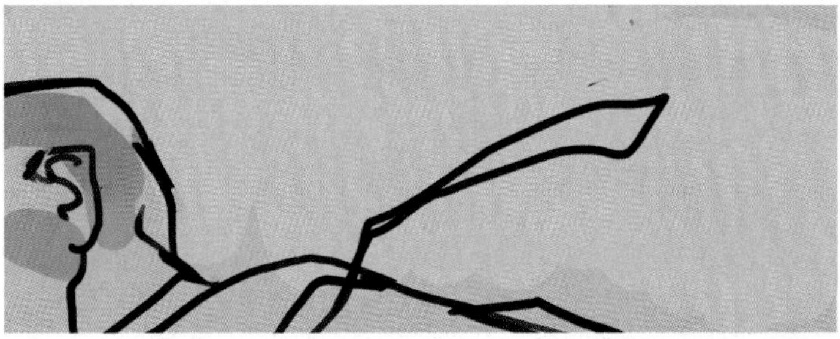

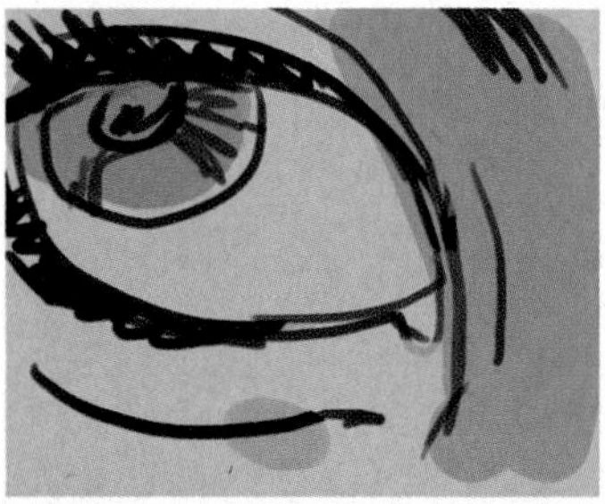

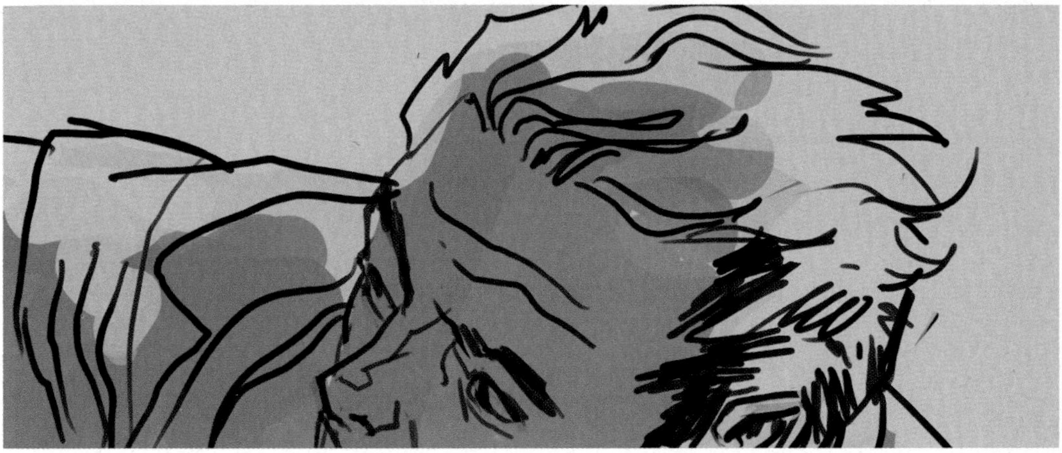

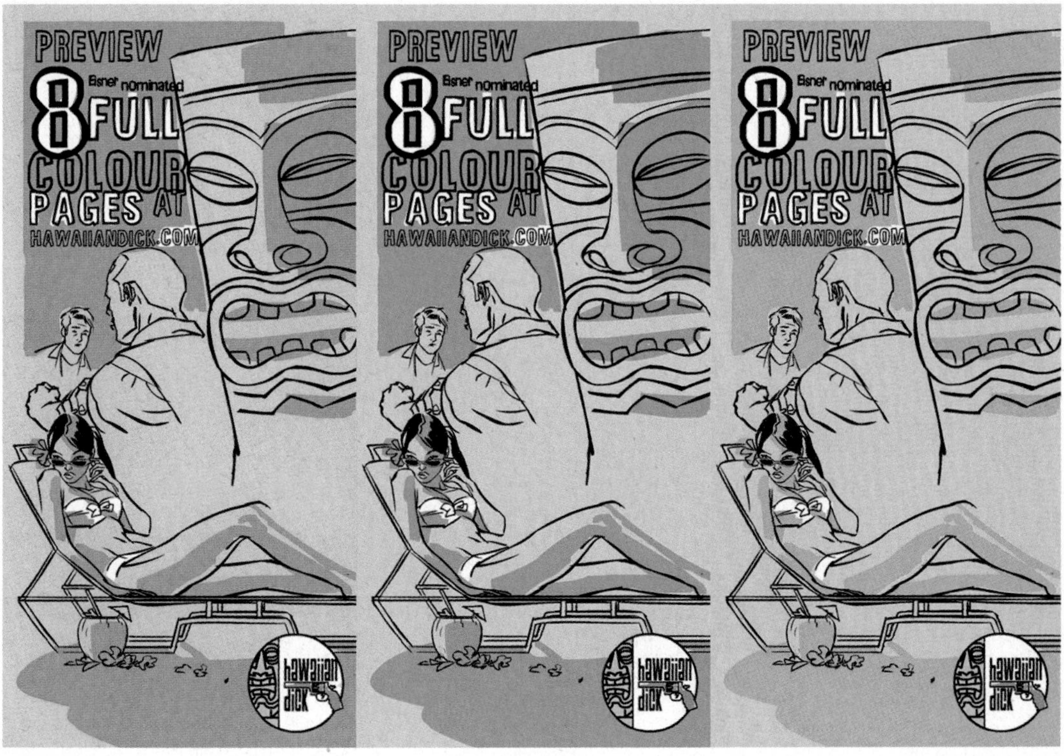
PREVIEW
8 Eisner nominated FULL COLOUR PAGES AT
HAWAIIANDICK.COM
hawaiian dick

UNUSED PROMO DESIGNS

These last pages contain concept ad artwork created early on and never used. However, you may see some of these designs in the future, as I quite like some, even if they are a little...different.

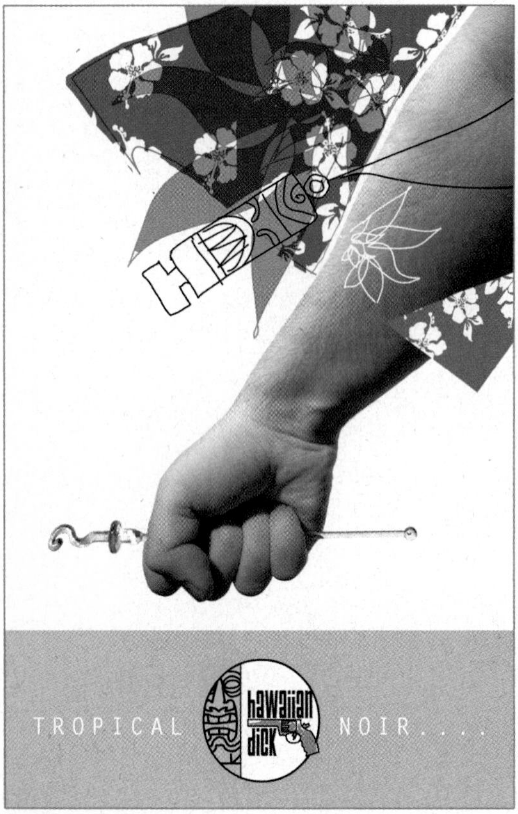

TROPICAL
hawaiian dick
NOIR....

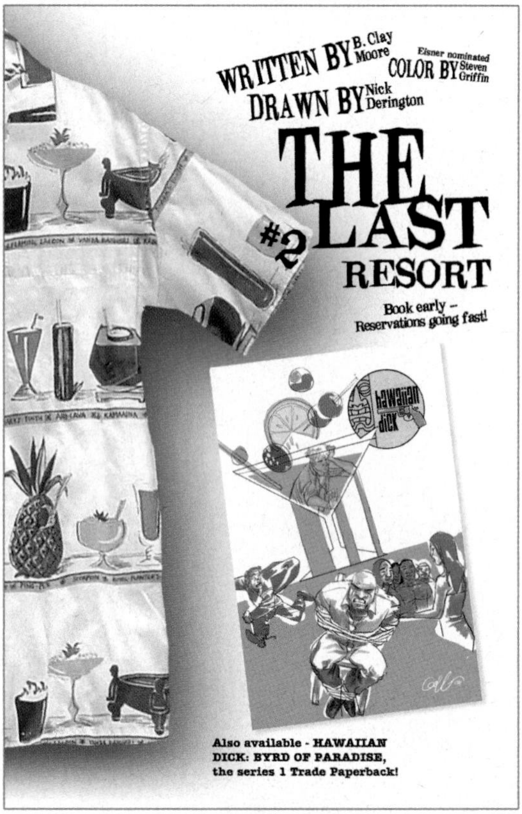

WRITTEN BY B. Clay Moore
Eisner nominated COLOR BY Steven Griffin
DRAWN BY Nick Derington
THE #2 LAST RESORT
Book early – Reservations going fast!
hawaiian dick
Also available - HAWAIIAN DICK: BYRD OF PARADISE, the series 1 Trade Paperback!

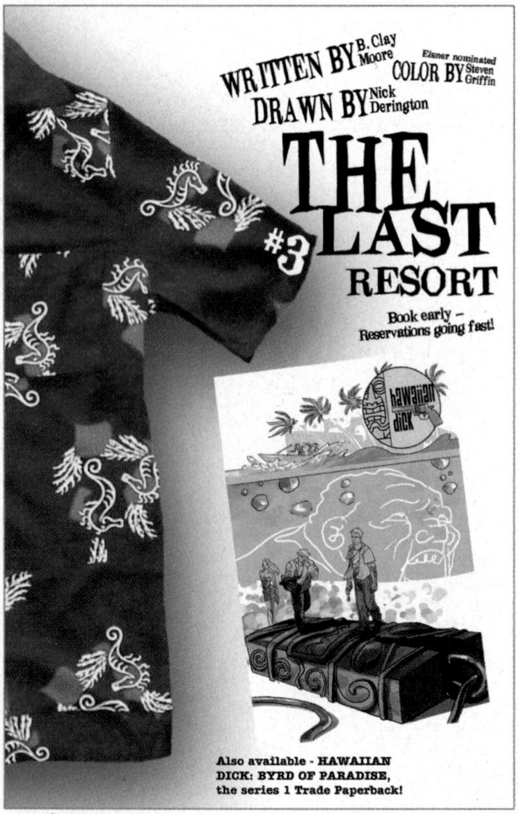

WRITTEN BY B. Clay Moore
Eisner nominated COLOR BY Steven Griffin
DRAWN BY Nick Derington
THE #3 LAST RESORT
Book early – Reservations going fast!
hawaiian dick
Also available - HAWAIIAN DICK: BYRD OF PARADISE, the series 1 Trade Paperback!

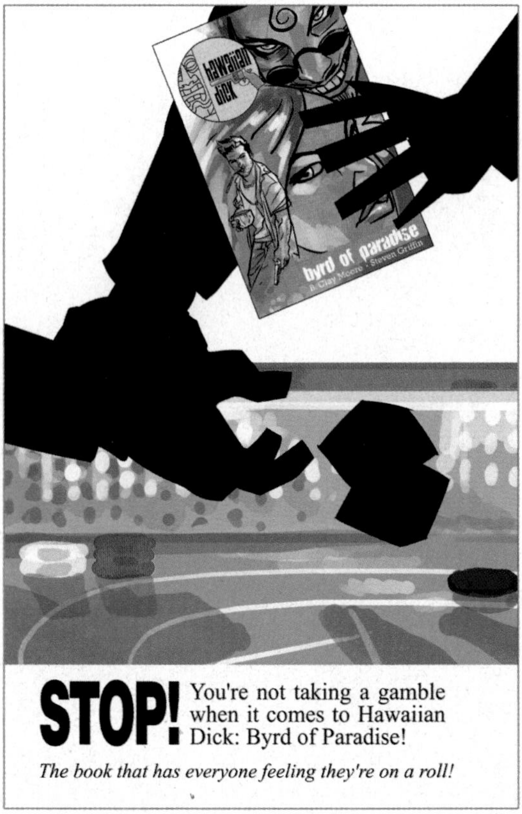

hawaiian dick
byrd of paradise
STOP! You're not taking a gamble when it comes to Hawaiian Dick: Byrd of Paradise!
The book that has everyone feeling they're on a roll!

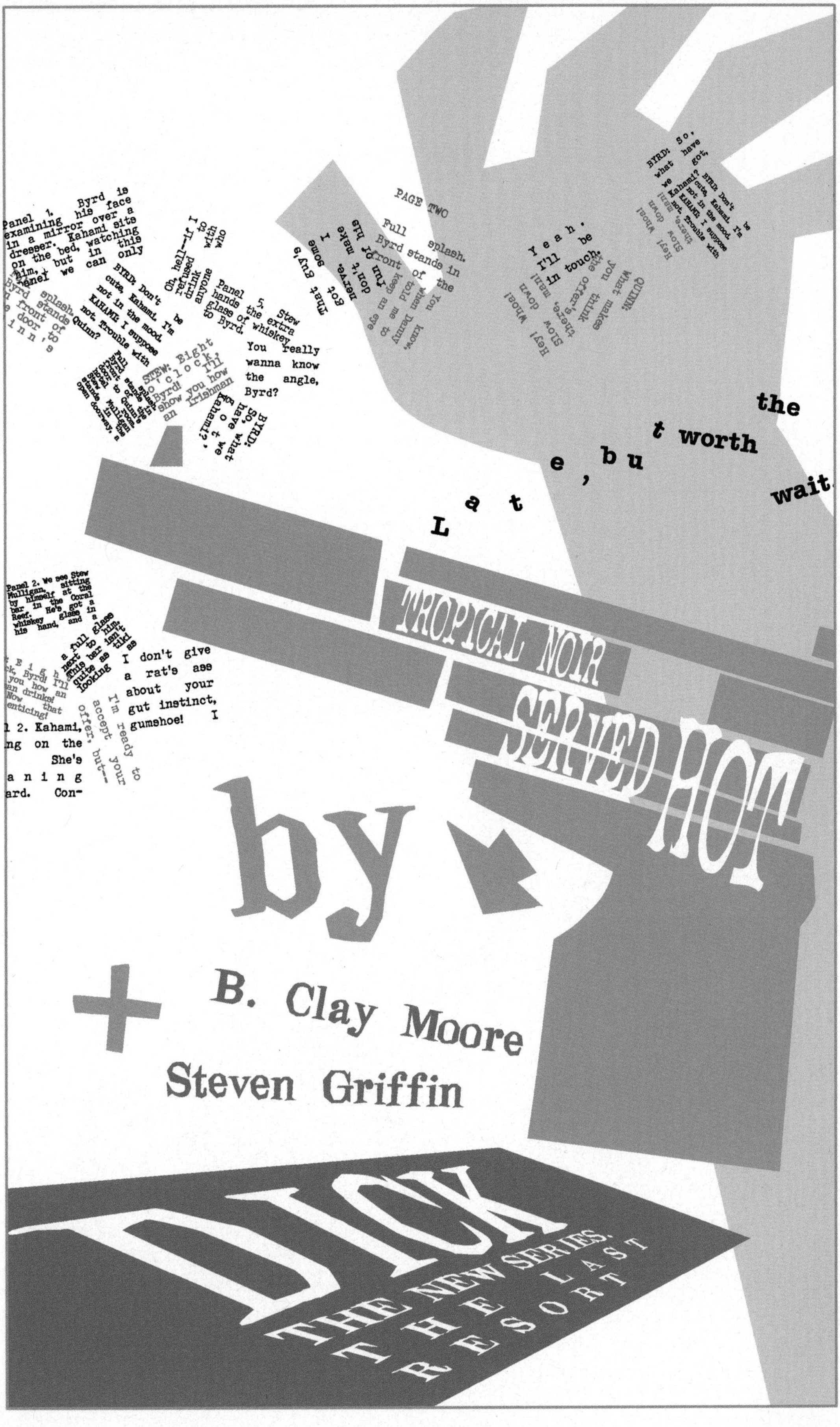
Late, but worth the wait.
TROPICAL NOIR SERVED HOT
by
B. Clay Moore
Steven Griffin
DICK
THE NEW SERIES:
THE LAST RESORT

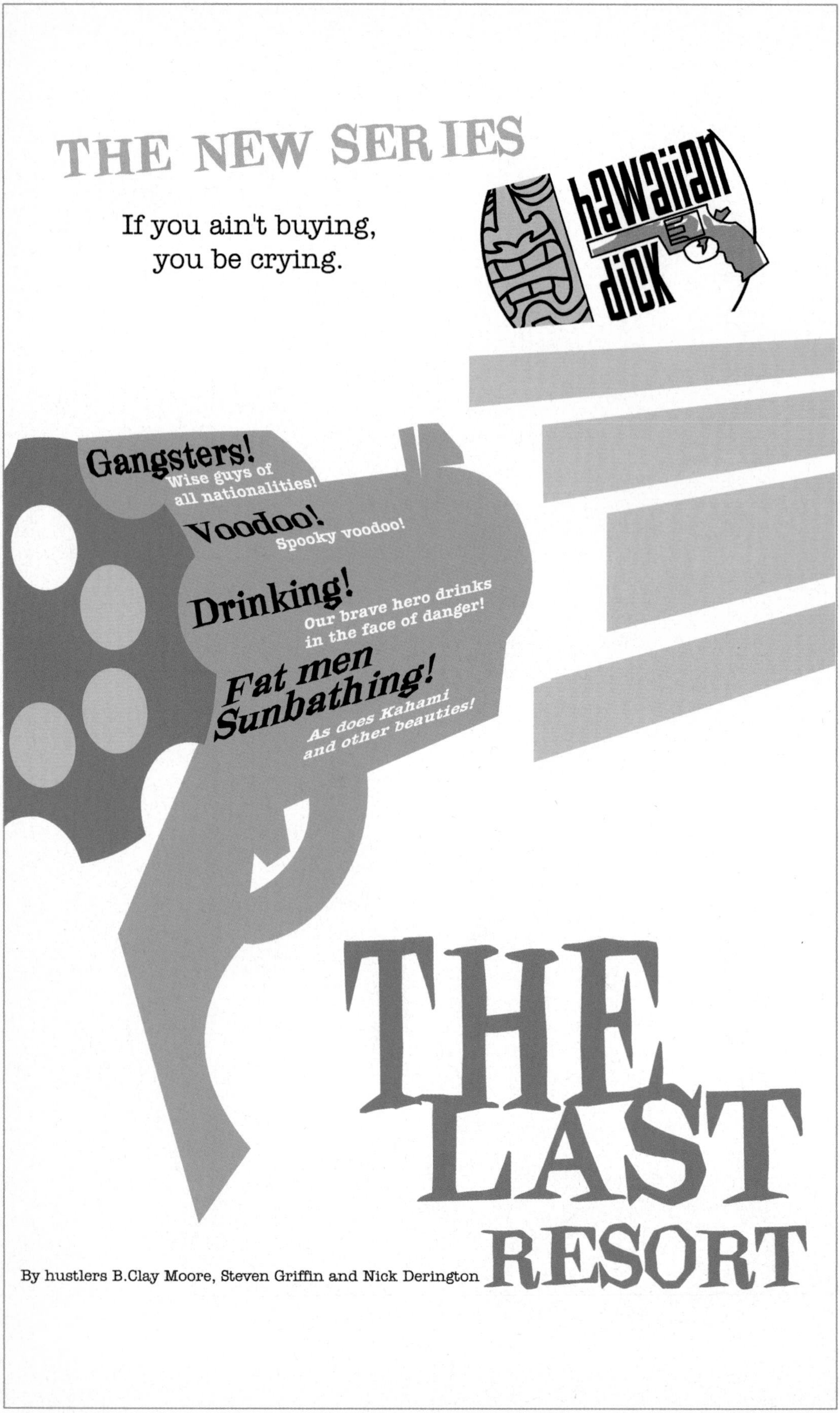
THE NEW SERIES
If you ain't buying,
you be crying.
hawaiian dick
Gangsters!
Wise guys of all nationalities!
Voodoo!
Spooky voodoo!
Drinking!
Our brave hero drinks in the face of danger!
Fat men Sunbathing!
As does Kahami and other beauties!
THE LAST RESORT
By hustlers B.Clay Moore, Steven Griffin and Nick Derington

LITTLE PAINTINGS

As my colouring is sometimes more like little paintings...not necessarily **GOOD** paintings, but paintings nonetheless, I thought I'd do something a little different for this part of the Bonus Section - and that is show a selection of panels from the series minus their inks and lettering. ie. nothing but the colouring underneath.

Of course, removing the inks also means that a lot of the drawing is gone - Characters are without real facial features or hair-lines, etc; and I don't colour properly behind solid black ink fills or word balloons, so those chunks are lacking too. But still, it gives you an idea.

And remember, good art should be able to tell the story without the dialogue, and good colouring should be able to tell the story without the rest of the art...or something.

- Steven

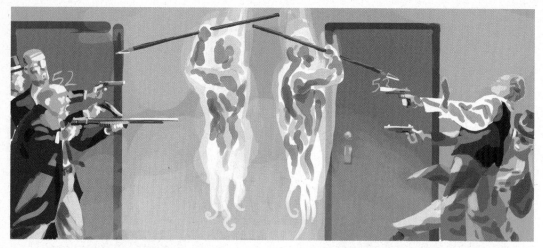

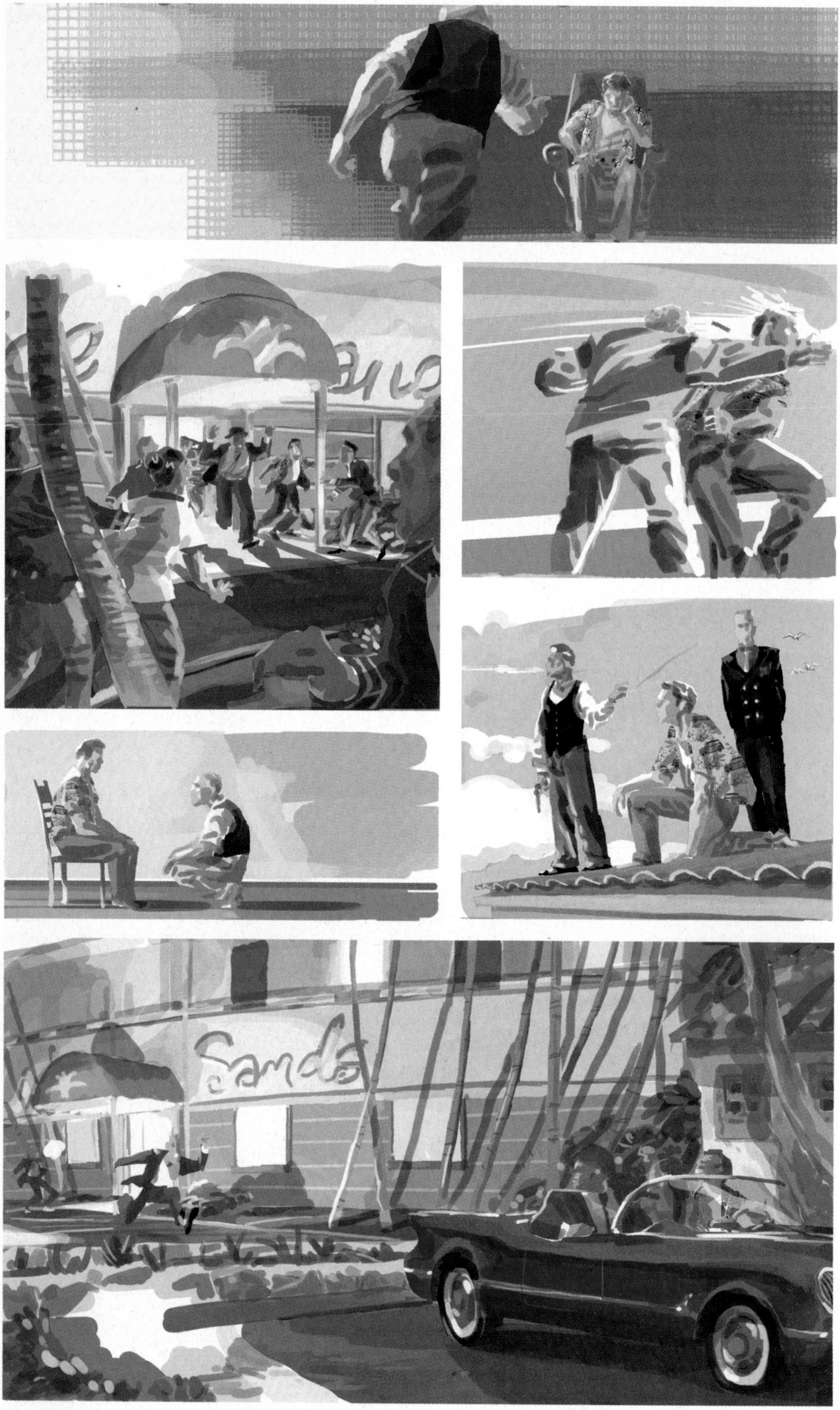
Sands

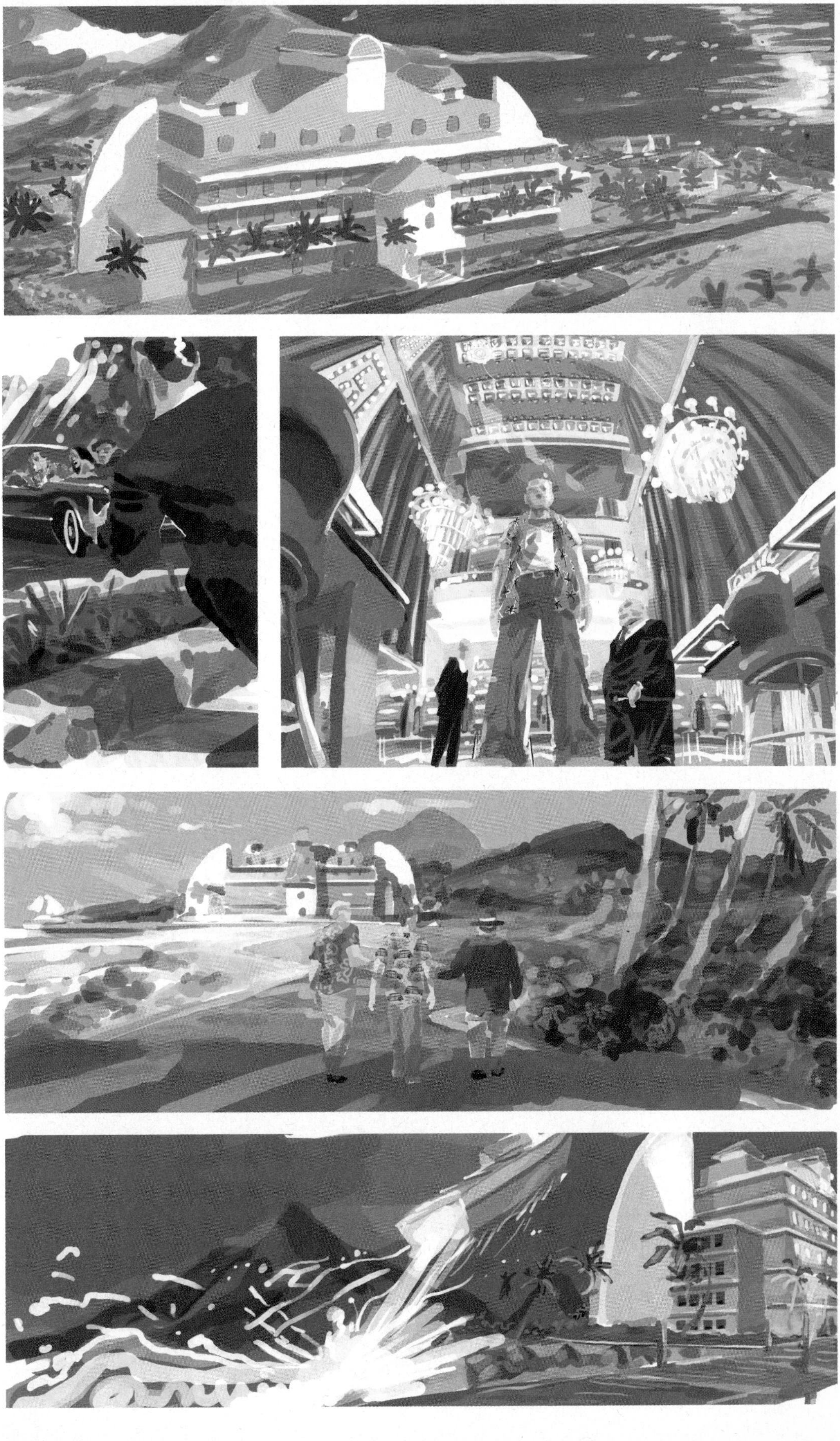

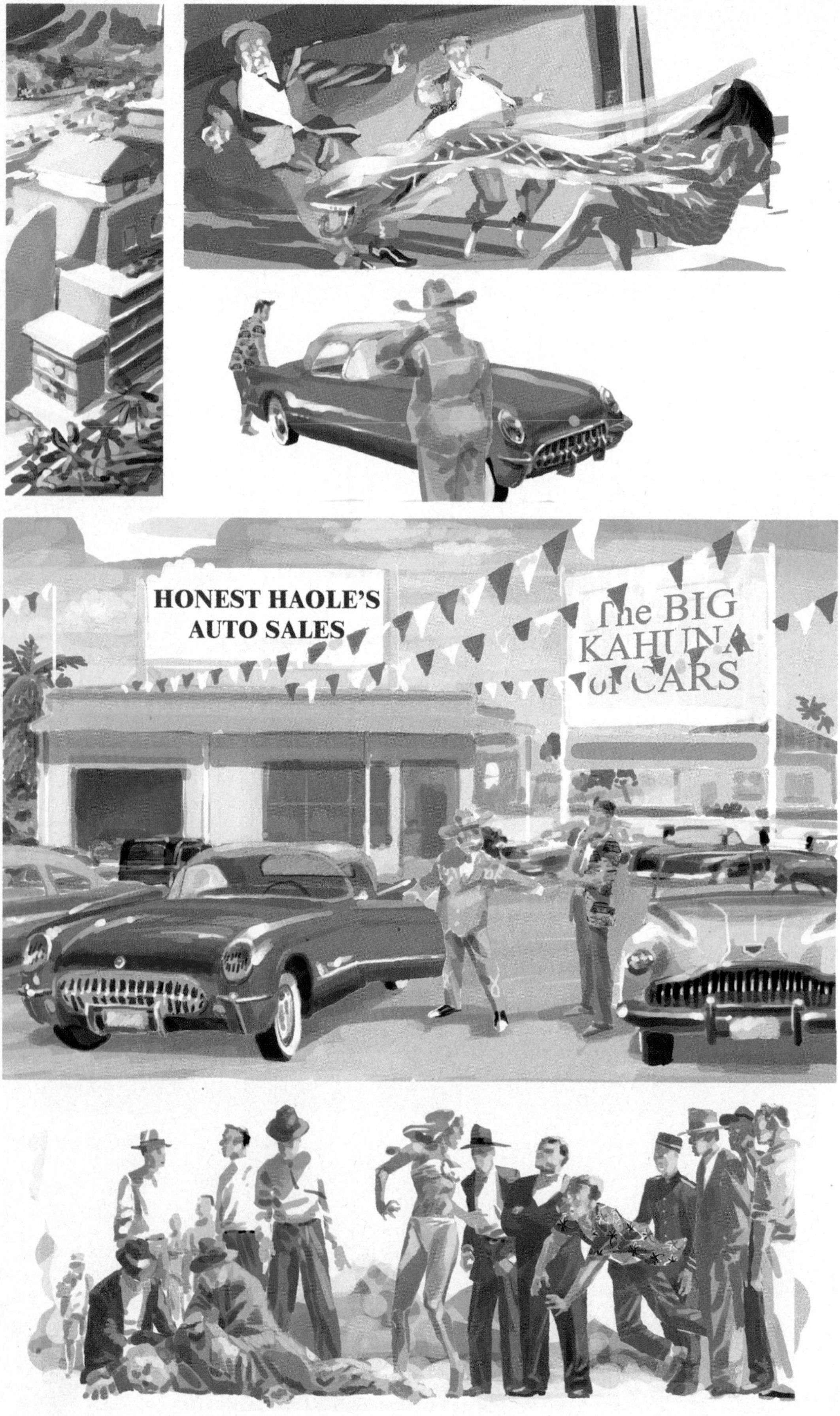
HONEST HAOLE'S
AUTO SALES
The BIG
KAHUNA
of CARS

ORIGINAL PITCH

NOTE: This next section details the plot of the first series - Hawaiian Dick: Byrd of Paradise - so if you've yet to read it, you should do so first, lest the story be ruined.

To end the trade, we're printing the original Hawaiian Dick pitch as sent to Image Comics. The pitch included story and character summaries; four story art pages; and character art sheets (not included here). The first two art pages were reused in the actual series, and the last two pages, from later on in the story, were redrawn as the script was revised.

At this point we intended the book to be black and white, for that authentic noir look, but when Image gave us the option of doing it in colour, we went for it. It was a LOT more work than the 4-tone greyscale I'd planned for the series, but I'm a sucker for punishment. And Hawaii doesn't look quite right in grey.

- Steven

HAWAIIAN DICK
(Byrd of Paradise)
by B. Clay Moore and Steven Griffin

The Concept

The *X-Files* meets the *Rockford Files* in a film *noir* version of 1950s Hawaii.

Byrd, a former big city detective, is recruited to track down a stolen car. In the process of investigation, Byrd and his sidekick, detective Mo Kalama, stumble upon a complicated kidnapping plot. Before the case is solved, the two will cross paths with an eccentric drug lord and his scheming henchmen, the psychic aunt of two island beauties, the vengeful Night Marchers of the Pali Highway, and the murdered kidnapping victim, returned from the dead.

The Setting

Hawaii, 1953. While Hawaii was a tourist hotspot in the fifties, Honolulu had yet to undergo the massive expansion it would see in the sixties. Byrd's world is one of well-worn Honolulu streets, haunted tropical highways, and tiki-themed lounges just off the beaten tourist path.

Key Elements

Hawaiian Dick will utilize its setting and timeframe to the fullest. Byrd's cases invariably involve Hawaiian mythology and folklore, and the stories borrow their "feel" from fifties film noir. The action is sudden and slightly over-the-top, reflecting the nature of its cinematic inspiration, and the supernatural lurks around every corner.

Format

A three-issue limited series.

The Characters

Byrd: A WW II vet in his early thirties, Byrd was thrown off his stateside police force after an "incident" with a suspect. With nowhere else to go, Byrd turned to his Army buddy, Mo Kalama, a detective in Hawaii. He now lives just off the beach in a small, run-down house, various remnants of his city apartment scattered about. He spends his days drinking tropical concoctions and his nights helping Mo with cases that fall just beyond the jurisdiction of the police. World-weary and slightly cynical, Byrd is nonetheless a fairly upbeat person. He looks upon his current situation with bemusement more than bitterness.

Mo Kalama: A hulking Hawaiian detective, Mo constantly sports a porkpie hat and tight-fitting blue suit. In general, Mo is more concerned with solving cases and getting the job done than following procedure. He keeps an eye on Byrd, to whom he owes a wartime debt of gratitude.

Kahami: Kahami is a local bar girl who assists Mo and Byrd in this initial case. Although she possesses considerable sex appeal, and a sly, knowing nature, she serves more as an assistant to Byrd and Mo than a romantic interest. As Byrd and Mo become embroiled in this case, Kahami's family ties provide the keys to solving the mystery.

Bishop Masaki: Masaki is the island's most notorious drug lord. Masaki's cool Japanese exterior conceals a vengeful streak that forces its way to the front when he feels he's been crossed. Generally flanked by his monosyllabic henchmen, Masaki favors flamboyant white suits and always carries a diamond-tipped cane.

Leila Rose (Kahami's sister): Although Leila Rose is perhaps the key character in bringing the story elements together, she never appears in the story alive. Masaki's favorite girl, her kidnapping and subsequent death draw the characters together. As a living, breathing girl, Leila Rose longed for more excitement than the island could provide, and she found that in Bishop Masaki. As a corpse, Leila Rose refuses to die, wandering the island in a mindless state, caught somewhere between life and death.

Auntie Chan: Auntie Chan is a wizened old woman, familiar with the spirit world. In fact, she makes her living as a psychic, maintaining a crumbling storefront in downtown Honolulu. When the mother of Kahami and Leila Rose was murdered, Auntie Chan took the girls in and raised them as her own. Madam Chan's smiling, gregarious facade belies a scheming, razor sharp mind, obsessed with maintaining (or restoring) the honor of her girls. As the story evolves, we discover that it was Auntie Chan who orchestrated Leila Rose's kidnapping.

The Night Marchers: The ghosts of ancient Hawaiian warriors, the Night Marchers prowl the Pali Highway at night, exacting revenge on those who fail to show the proper respect for their land.

The Story

Issue one: Byrd is called in to track down a stolen car. When he finds out the car's trunk stores items belonging to Bishop Masaki, he assumes the items to be drugs and begins the investigation. Mo Kalama joins Byrd in tracking down the car. The two stop into Mo's favorite lounge and meet Kahami, an attractive bargirl who will play a key role in the story.

After a high-speed chase and shootout along the Pali Highway, Byrd and Mo discover the dead body of a young woman in the bullet-riddled trunk of the stolen car. They learn she is Leila Rose, kidnapped from Bishop Masaki for ransom. The issue closes as Mo and Byrd come face-to-face with Night Marchers.

Issue two: Opens with the Night Marchers carrying Grimes off into the night. Byrd and Mo escape to Byrd's house, with the kidnapping victim's body in tow. As the detectives approach the house, they see lights, and an unfamiliar car parked out front. Byrd decided to go in, leaving Mo on the porch.

Inside the house, Byrd is confronted by Bishop Masaki (along with two of his thugs). Masaki wants his help in finding his missing girl, Leila Rose. Mo is dragged in from the porch by the thugs, and the detectives agree to look for the missing girl, despite their knowledge that she lies dead in the back of Mo's car.

When the two return to the car for the body after Masaki and his men depart, the body is gone, the back door of the car wide open.

The next day, Byrd meets Kahami at the Outrigger, and she takes him to meet Auntie Chan, who is something of an amateur witch doctor. Meanwhile, Mo, bleary-eyed from the night before, is called on to investigate a strange sighting near one of Bishop Masaki's warehouses.

After meeting Auntie Chan, Byrd learns that Leila Rose (Masaki's dead girl) is the sister of Kahami, and was raised by Auntie Chan.

Meanwhile, we see Graves (the man who hired Byrd) again, in a virtual repeat of the time Byrd accosted him outside his office. Only this time it's Masaki's henchmen who slam him against the wall. Under interrogation, he tells Masaki of Mo and Byrd's involvement in Leila Rose's disappearance.

In the closing scene, Mo stumbles across the zombified Leila Rose, lurking in one of Masaki's warehouses.

Issue three: In the opening, Mo is pushed aside by the zombie, and spends the rest of the issue trailing her. Byrd receives a phone call from Masaki, luring him to the docks with Kahami as bait. Byrd contacts Auntie Chan to verify that Kahami's missing. Mo then figures out that Leila Rose is shambling toward the docks.

It begins to rain.

Byrd makes it to the docks and encounters Masaki. The two scuffle. Byrd gets the upper and goes to Kahami's aid, but is flattened by Masaki's diamond-tipped cane. At this point Auntie Chan arrives, much to the amusement of Masaki. Chan attacks Masaki for his role in corrupting Leila Rose, and, we learn, for leading her late sister (Kahami and Leila Rose's mother) to her death. Masaki shoots Chan, wounding her.

Before he can take further action, another figure emerges from the rain. Masaki sees through the rain that it's Leila Rose and starts to go to her. But, in a flash of lightning, her zombie state is revealed, and, through the storm, she rushes to the horrified Masaki, taking him into the roiling water with a zombie kiss.

After the two are swept away, we learn from Auntie Chan that she resurrected Leila Rose as a vehicle of her vengeance. This horrifies Kahami, and Byrd deduces that Chan was also behind the initial kidnapping of Leila Rose. It turns out that Chan would rather see her girls dead than despoiled by Masaki. She holds Byrd and Kahami off with Masaki's gun and escapes into the rain. Mo finally shows up, too late.

Later, Auntie Chan is fleeing down the Pali Highway when her car stalls. As she curses her luck, she hears the sound of drumbeats. The car is surrounded by the shadowy figures of the Night Marchers.

In the epilogue, Kahami and Byrd collect Auntie Chan's things from her deserted storefront. Byrd decides then to make use of the space by setting up shop as a private investigator.

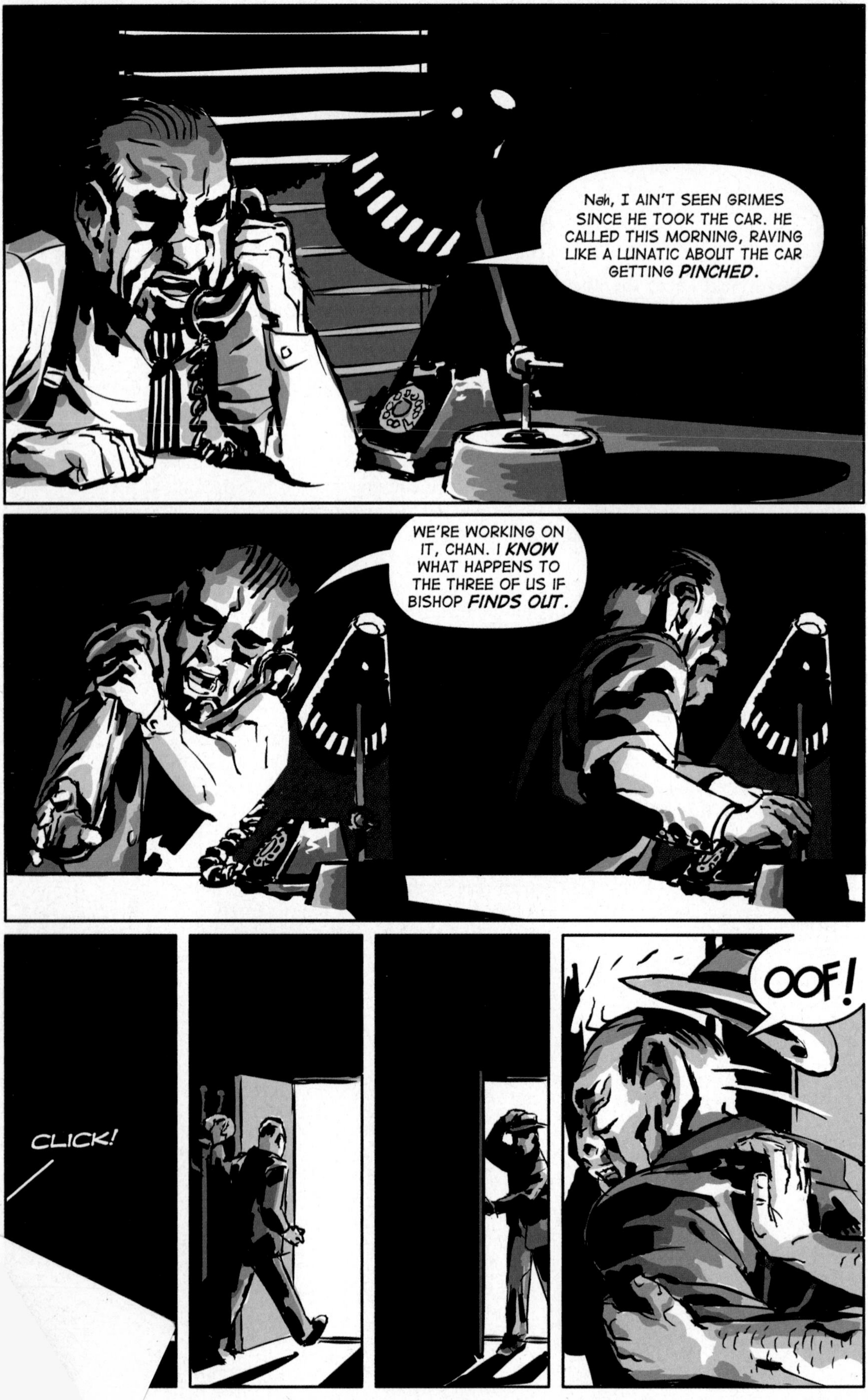
Nah, I AIN'T SEEN GRIMES SINCE HE TOOK THE CAR. HE CALLED THIS MORNING, RAVING LIKE A LUNATIC ABOUT THE CAR GETTING *PINCHED*.
WE'RE WORKING ON IT, CHAN. I *KNOW* WHAT HAPPENS TO THE THREE OF US IF BISHOP *FINDS OUT*.
CLICK!
OOF!

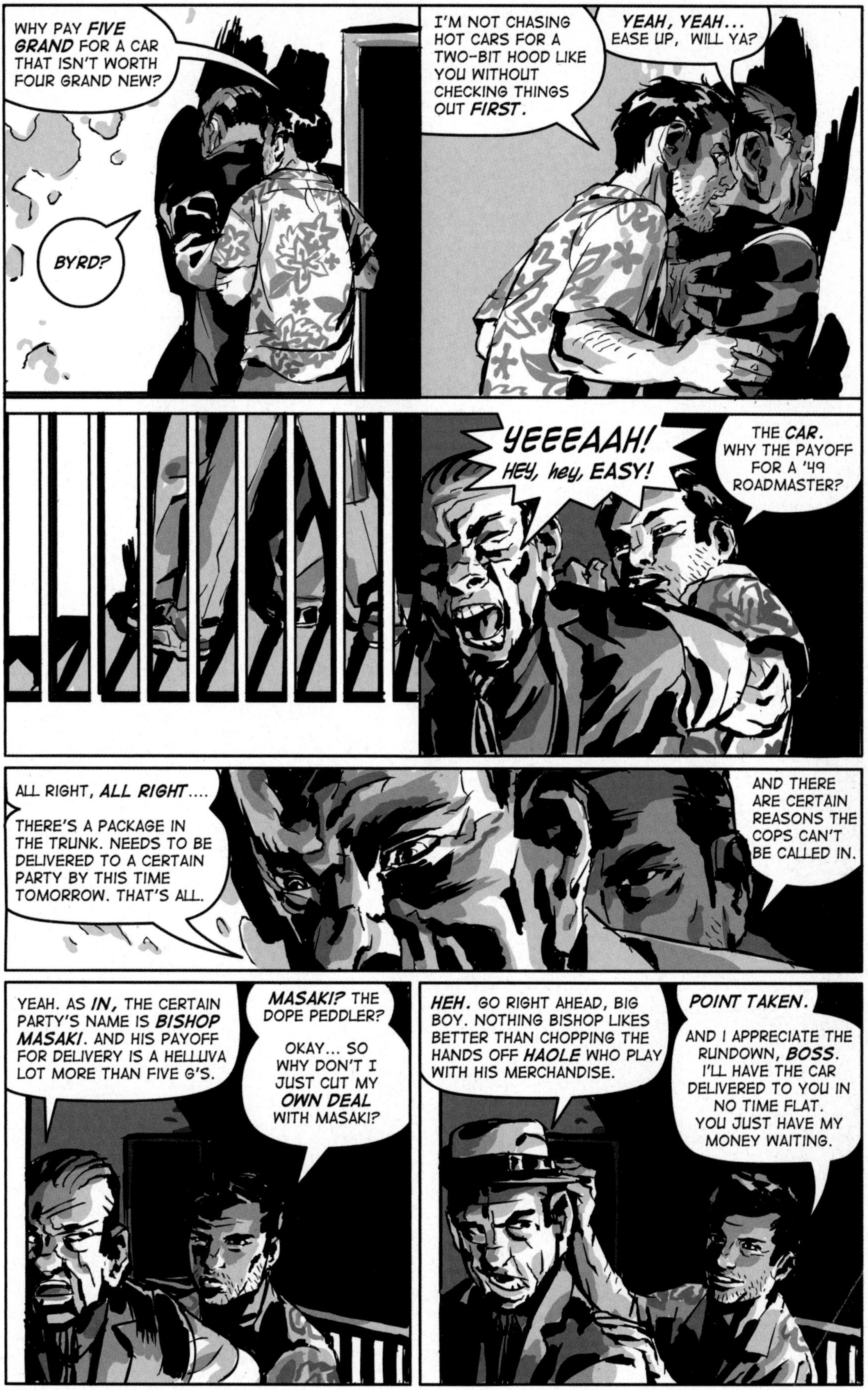
WHY PAY FIVE GRAND FOR A CAR THAT ISN'T WORTH FOUR GRAND NEW?
BYRD?
I'M NOT CHASING HOT CARS FOR A TWO-BIT HOOD LIKE YOU WITHOUT CHECKING THINGS OUT FIRST.
YEAH, YEAH... EASE UP, WILL YA?
YEEEAAH! HEY, hey, EASY!
THE CAR. WHY THE PAYOFF FOR A '49 ROADMASTER?
ALL RIGHT, ALL RIGHT....
THERE'S A PACKAGE IN THE TRUNK. NEEDS TO BE DELIVERED TO A CERTAIN PARTY BY THIS TIME TOMORROW. THAT'S ALL.
AND THERE ARE CERTAIN REASONS THE COPS CAN'T BE CALLED IN.
YEAH. AS IN, THE CERTAIN PARTY'S NAME IS BISHOP MASAKI. AND HIS PAYOFF FOR DELIVERY IS A HELLUVA LOT MORE THAN FIVE G'S.
MASAKI? THE DOPE PEDDLER?
OKAY... SO WHY DON'T I JUST CUT MY OWN DEAL WITH MASAKI?
HEH. GO RIGHT AHEAD, BIG BOY. NOTHING BISHOP LIKES BETTER THAN CHOPPING THE HANDS OFF HAOLE WHO PLAY WITH HIS MERCHANDISE.
POINT TAKEN.
AND I APPRECIATE THE RUNDOWN, BOSS. I'LL HAVE THE CAR DELIVERED TO YOU IN NO TIME FLAT. YOU JUST HAVE MY MONEY WAITING.

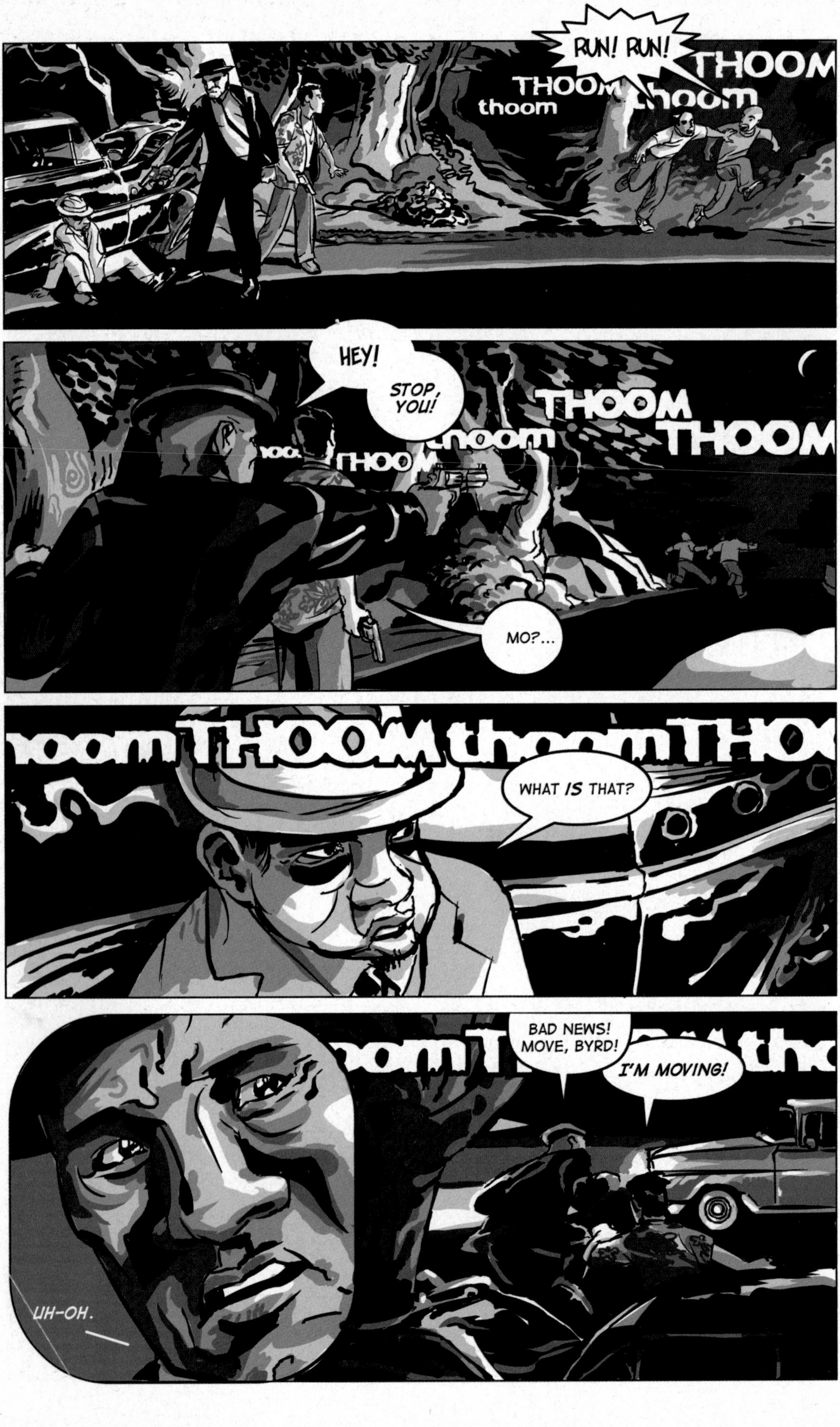
RUN! RUN!
THOOM
THOOM
thoom
thoom
HEY!
STOP, YOU!
THOOM
thoom
THOOM
MO?...
WHAT IS THAT?
BAD NEWS! MOVE, BYRD!
I'M MOVING!
UH-OH.

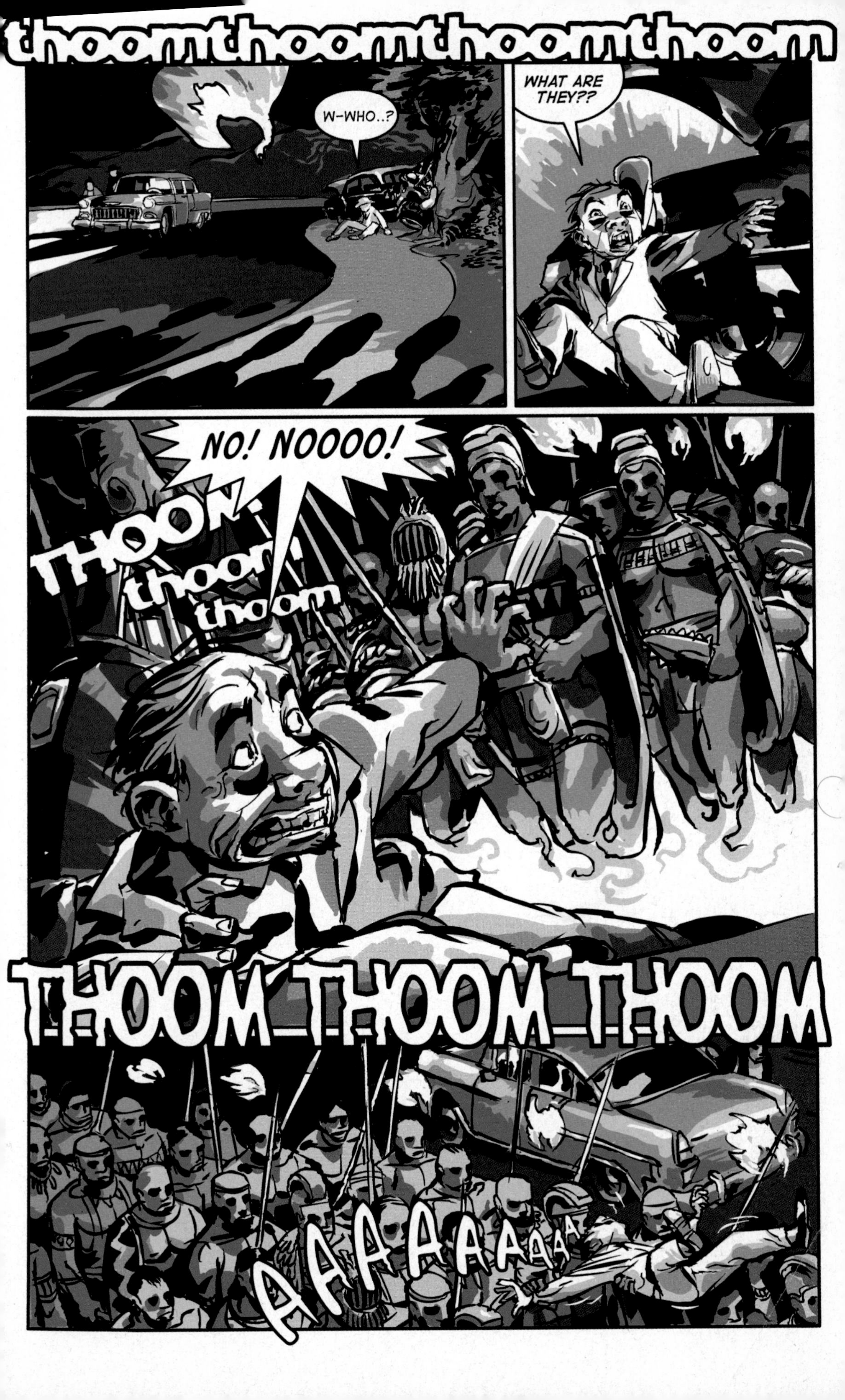
thoomthoomthoomthoom
W-WHO..?
WHAT ARE THEY??
NO! NOOOO!
THOOM! thoom! thoom
THOOM THOOM THOOM
AAAAAAAAA

THE
LAST
RESORT

ALOHA! Thanks for checking in with us this second time around. We hope you've enjoyed THE LAST RESORT, and if, for some reason, you haven't read its predecessor, HAWAIIAN DICK: BYRD OF PARADISE, we hope you grab that volume to complete your set.

And we sincerely hope you'll continue to follow the adventures of Byrd and crew as they navigate their way through our tropical noir take on fifties Hawaii.

MAHALO!

- Clay